NETWORK SYSTEMS

MODELING, ANALYSIS AND DESIGN

NETWORK SYSTEMS

MODELING, ANALYSIS AND DESIGN

Roshan Lal Sharma
Paulo T. de Sousa
Ashok D. Inglé
COMMERCIAL ELECTRONICS OPERATIONS
ROCKWELL INTERNATIONAL

VAN NOSTRAND REINHOLD DATA PROCESSING SERIES

 VAN NOSTRAND REINHOLD COMPANY
NEW YORK   CINCINNATI   TORONTO   LONDON   MELBOURNE

Van Nostrand Reinhold Company Regional Offices:
New York   Cincinnati

Van Nostrand Reinhold Company International Offices:
London   Toronto   Melbourne

Copyright © 1982 by Van Nostrand Reinhold Company

Library of Congress Catalog Card Number: 81-10295
ISBN: 0-442-26104-7

Manufactured in the United States of America

Published by Van Nostrand Reinhold Company
135 West 50th Street, New York, N.Y. 10020

Published simultaneously in Canada by Van Nostrand Reinhold Ltd.

15 14 13 12 11 10 9 8 7 6 5 4 3 2 1

Library of Congress Cataloging in Publication Data

Sharma, Roshan Lal, 1927–
  Network systems.

  (Van Nostrand Reinhold data processing series)
  Includes bibliographies and index.
  1. Telecommunication systems.   2. Data trans-
mission systems.   3. Computer networks.
I. deSousa, Paulo T.,   II. Inglé, Ashok D.
III. Title.
TK5102.5.S449   621.3815'3   81-10295
ISBN 0-442-26104-7   AACR2

SERIES INTRODUCTION

This insightful book will prove helpful to people who need to analyze, design, or understand a communication network. It offers a clearly presented, thorough grounding in the fundamental concepts. Where a mathematical view is common, the book provides a helpful explanation and then the essential mathematics. Most of the book is free of mathematical symbolism and readily understood—if the reader pays attention to the definitions presented in the opening chapters.

This book is especially strong on modeling communication networks for the purpose of analyzing and evaluating them. This book also is strong in presenting clearly the factors affecting the design of communication networks. The book takes a broad view of networks. Though it does cover the usual telephone networks, its main attention is on communication networks that have the computer as an important element.

NED CHAPIN

THE VAN NOSTRAND REINHOLD DATA PROCESSING SERIES

Edited by Ned Chapin, Ph.D.

IMS Programming Techniques: A Guide to Using DL/1
  Dan Kapp and Joseph L. Leben

Reducing COBOL Complexity Through Structured Programming
  Carma McClure

Composite/Structured Design
  Glenford J. Myers

Reliable Software Through Composite Design
  Glenford J. Myers

Top-Down Structured Programming Techniques
  Clement L. McGowen and John R. Kelly

Operating Systems Principles
  Stanley Kurzban, T. S. Heines and A. P. Sayers

Microcomputer Handbook
  Charles J. Sippl

Strategic Planning of Management Information Systems
  Paul Siegel

Flowcharts
  Ned Chapin

Introduction to Artificial Intelligence
  Philip C. Jackson, Jr.

Computers and Management for Business
  Douglas A. Colbert

Preface

During the early fifties, it appeared that nuclear science was the upcoming revolution. But computers stole the thunder—so it appeared at first analysis. The dark horse turned out to be communication technology. Communication is as old as civilization. Computers are as old as yesterday. It is a merging of the two, namely, the desire of humans to communicate with one another and the availability of cheap computing elements, that is resulting in the sudden explosion of communication technology in every human activity.

It is not the first time communication technology has raised its head in human history. A long century ago, the postal service began enabling humans to communicate with one another through a vast network of sorting stations and transportation facilities employed for carrying letters from one place to another, irrespective of distance, culture, and national boundaries.

A little later, the railroads afforded humans another opportunity to (1) communicate with one another and (2) transport heavy goods and human beings through a vast network of switching stations and railroad tracks. Networks-based postal service and railroads served humans while the industrial revolution took its natural course.

Communication technology took other big steps through the inventions of the telephone, radio, and television. To illustrate, large networks of telephone switching plants and transmission facilities enable a person in one country to dial directly another person in another country. Similarly extensive networks of radio and television enable the broadcasting of vital information to large populations quickly and effectively.

One may ask "what's next?". With the availability of excellent networks of postal service, railroads, telephones, radio and television, Telex and airlines, why look for more progress in communication technology?

The answer to that question is provided by the new revolution occurring in the computer field, which in turn is causing another upheaval in communication technology—the likes of which are beyond human comprehension at present. A keen eye can discern some tips of the iceberg already. Stored program controlled (SPC) switching exchanges are replacing the old electromechanical telephone exchanges in every country. The new SPC exchanges, coupled with the emerging digital switching and transmission facilities, are providing better quality of service, a host of user services, faster network configurability, a tighter control of all network resources, and a powerful ability to capture all the traffic and operational data, when compared with the older exchanges.

Cheap computing elements are also permitting processing power to be dispersed, not only where it is needed, but also where it will do the most good at the least cost to the user. This trend will continue until everyone will have at hand the means to solve pressing problems quickly and cheaply—problems dealing with either processing vital information or transmitting one's information to another point where it is needed for immediate consumption or further processing and subsequent transmission to another point. Multitudes of examples—such as corporate voice and data networks based on digital switching and transmission; such packet switching networks as the ARPA and the Autodin II; reservation networks employing automatic call distribution (ACD) for airlines, car rental companies, and hotel chains; distributed processing (DP) resource sharing networks; local networks for computer processing and communication; private automatic branch exchanges (PABXs); automated electronic fund transfer (EFT) systems for the banking industry; and distributed-data-base-management (DDBM) systems—are changing the pattern of our daily life without much fanfare.

A closer examination of these systems results in a self-evident truth—all systems can be described and understood in terms of networks. This applies not only to the existing systems, but also to the future systems that are still evolving.

It is our purpose in this treatise to describe some of the well-known systems in a unified, network-oriented language. This book will attempt to model, analyze, and design network systems in an integrated manner. We will emphasize methodology and techniques in place of mathematical rigor.

The book has three sections. Sections I, II, and III deal with modeling, analysis, and design, respectively. Section I consists of seven chapters, the first six of which deal with modeling concepts, and the last describing models of most well-known network systems. Section II consists of four chapters dealing with analysis techniques for network systems. Section III has six chapters that describe proven techniques for traffic analysis, topological organization, and network synthesis.

Acknowledgments for creating this book are far too many to be mentioned individually. Nevertheless, we must mention the highly creative environments originally set up under the guidance of Mr. A. A. Collins, founder of Collins Radio Co., and later nourished by the electronics operations of Rockwell International—environments that provided a unique experience and inspiration clearly needed for this type of venture. Acknowledgments are also due Ms. Deepak Sharma for the illustrations and Mrs. Pam Schemagin for the use of the word processing tools required to keep the multitudes of revisions and additions from killing this arduous project.

Contents

Section I
Modeling

Chapter 1
Concepts of Networks and Their Attributes

1.1 INTRODUCTORY REMARKS

A network exists whenever two or more elements interact with one another. A network can also be defined as consisting of nodes and links. Figure 1.1 illustrates a simple network consisting of two nodes and a single link. It shows that the two nodes communicate with one another, or, alternatively, some information flows between the two nodes via the link. Figure 1.2 represents a more complex network consisting of eight nodes and seven links. This illustration shows that node A communicates with all other nodes, although it fails to show if there is any communication among nodes 1, 2, 3, 4, 5, 6, and 7. The answer to that question can be answered only by knowing the functions performed by node A.

Before delving in detail into the various functions that can be performed by network nodes, it is proper to classify the various types of networks.

1.2 CLASSIFICATION OF NETWORKS

Any useful network-based system can be broken down into (1) a set of users, or subscribers, and (2) a network that provides one or more useful services to subscribers. See Fig. 1.3.

Discrete networks allow the flow of only discrete units of information entities from one node to another. There are two types of discrete networks:

1. physical networks designed for the movement of discrete physical items, such as processed material through a factory
2. communication networks for the transfer and processing of discrete units of information within the network

Although the techniques for modeling, analysis, and design of both physical and communication networks are similar, vocabulary and nomenclature are quite different. To limit the size of this book, this study will discuss only those networks that employ telecommunications, which involves the transmission, emission, or reception of signs, signals, written images, sounds, or intelligence of any nature by wire, radio, optical, or other electromagnetic means. In all the

Fig. 1.1. A network consisting of two nodes and a link.

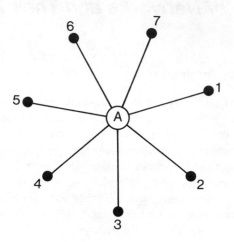

Fig. 1.2. A network consisting of eight nodes and seven links.

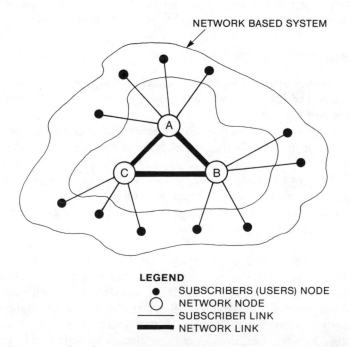

Fig. 1.3. A representation of a network system consisting of *N* users and a backbone network.

discussions that follow, the word *network* will mean only a communication network as defined above.

Networks can be classified according to the type of function or service they provide. Networks that provide communication among all subscribers are defined as *switched communication networks*. Telephone networks, Telex networks, airline message-exchange networks, and the famous ARPA network fall into the category of switched communication systems. The *nonswitched networks* provide communication between the subscriber and the network only. Timesharing networks and radio and television broadcasting networks are some well-known examples of this latter category.

Switched communication networks can be further divided into three types of networks:

1. circuit-switched (CS) networks that provide hardwire connection, through the networks, between two or more subscribers for the duration of the call. Once the connection is made, the user data is transparent to network nodes.
2. packet-switched (PS) networks that permit the transfer of information between two subscribers through the routing of addressed packets of information through the network. Both the links and network nodes are completely timeshared among all the users. Unlike the CS network, each PS node employs the store-and-forward technique for switching each packet. Only the primary storage, e.g., core storage, is generally involved to minimize delays. All packets are switched according to the first-in-first-out (FIFO) scheme, unless message priorities are employed.
3. message-switched (MS) networks. These receive the entire message, store it in secondary storage, and when the output link(s) is available, transmit it to the various subscribers. Although there may be several variations in the way a message is received and transmitted, for example, the message may or may not be received in the form of segments, most MS systems handle messages internally in the form of fixed-length segments, or cells, to maximize the utilization of expensive storage resources. An MS system usually provides long-term storage, on a secondary storage medium, to each message even after it has been delivered to all the destination subscribers. This capability allows quick retrieval of a message in case any questions arise regarding the validity of the message reception at a later time. Most MS systems also provide a permanent record of traffic handled in the form of a magnetic tape journal or log.

There are three types of nonswitched networks:

1. broadcast networks employed by radio, television, and satellite systems, in which one or more transmitting nodes broadcast information of interest

to a large number of subscribers situated within a certain geographical area.

2. single-node, data processing (DP) networks, in which several users obtain data processing service from the DP node within the network. The user generally sends a structured message to the network node and receives some output messages. DP service may be in the form of a batched DP, timesharing, remote-job-entry (RJE), remote-order-entry (ROE), or point-of-sale (POS) application. To receive DP service from two or more DP nodes in a network requires the superimposition of a switched network, resulting in a distributed computer network.

3. single-node, data-base-management (DBM) networks, in which several users obtain a data base type service from the DBM system. The user generally sends a structured message to the system node and receives the desired data element from the data base. When a data base is distributed

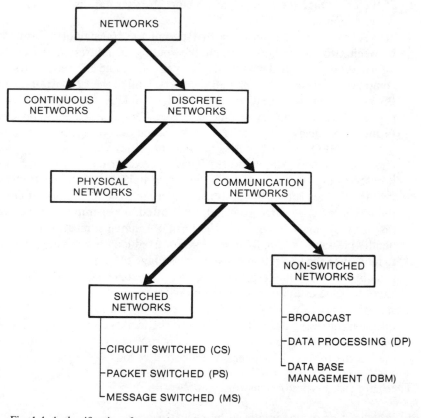

Fig. 1.4. A classification of networks and the types of networks included in this book.

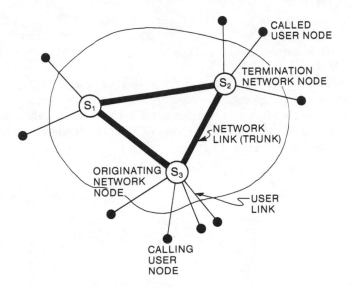

Fig. 1.5. A classification of nodes and links within a network system.

over two or more network nodes, the network is generally called a *distributed-data-base-management* (DDBM) *system.*

The above network classes are illustrated in Fig. 1.4.

Whereas the network provides a useful service to the users, or subscribers, nodes provide necessary functions required by the system, and links provide communication among all types of nodes. Links connecting network nodes are called *network links,* or simply *trunks,* and links connecting subscribers to network nodes are called *subscriber links* or *user links.* These classes of nodes and links are illustrated in Fig. 1.5.

A more detailed modeling of all the communication networks included in this study requires a discussion of the following additional concepts:

1. concepts of network topology and hierarchy dealing with the manner in which the network elements are interconnected
2. concepts of traffic, network identification and numbering plans, traffic flows, routing, and network control
3. concepts dealing with the transmission of information and signaling (control) data
4. concepts of multilevel, iterative modeling, analysis and design of complex, network-based systems
5. concepts of system performance evaluation

The first three concepts, viz., (1) network topology and hierarchy; (2) traffic, network identification, traffic flows, routing, and network control; and (3) transmission define another all-encompassing network attribute known as *network architecture*.

The concepts of multilevel, iterative modeling, analysis, and design are intimately related to the concepts of system performance evaluation.

The chapters that follow within Section I not only discuss the above-mentioned concepts but also describe models of several well-known network systems that use a well-defined structure.

Chapter 2
Concepts of Network Topology, Hierarchy, and Architecture

2.1 INTRODUCTORY REMARKS

Network topology deals with the manner in which the network elements, nodes and links, are interconnected.

Network hierarchy deals with multilevel structures within the network. Such hierarchies are employed for achieving the desired information flows and network controls.

Network architecture deals with the hierarchical structures related to (1) dispersion of physical units within the network, (2) control and flow of information through the network, and (3) representation, interpretation, and transformation of information. Alternatively, a network architecture defines the distribution of communication processing (CP), data processing (DP), and database-management (DBM) functions throughout the network and the hierarchical levels pertaining to such functions and message formats and link protocols.

Network topologies, network hierarchies, and network architectures have always received, and will continue to receive much attention from system scientists who are deeply interested in not only understanding complex systems, but also improving their overall performance and utility. Some network architectures remain on the drawing board until a significant breakthrough occurs in terms of cost versus throughputs of hardware and software modules. To state that one network architecture is the best for all times to come is to ignore the lessons of history. New and unheard of developments in designs of hardware and software modules are destined to help create many novel network architectures, thus providing new and improved services economically.

In the following paragraphs, we try to classify some well-known network topologies and hierarchies. Network architectures are very difficult, if not impossible, to classify. Although each architecture possesses a distinct topology and a hierarchy, the remaining attributes, such as network control, are too complex for classification. All the concepts presented in Chapter 1 to 6 are germane to the study of network architectures. In Chapter 7, we try to describe detailed models of many well-known system architectures. A close study of

Chapter 7 should help the reader grasp the true meaning of network architecture.

2.2 CLASSIFICATION OF NETWORK TOPOLOGIES AND HIERARCHIES

As the number of network elements increases, the number of ways one can interconnect the various elements increases rapidly. Consequently, any attempt to classify all possible topologies for a network is bound to fail. If one has the patience to observe the various networks that are described in the literature, however, one will find only a handful of useful network topologies that are prevalent. Some of the most notable of network topologies follow:

1. fully connected topology
2. generalized tree topology
3. minimal spanning tree (MST) topology
4. bus topology
5. loop, or ring, topology
6. single-center, single-star (SCSS) topology
7. single-center, multidrop (SCMD) topology
8. multicenter, multistar (MCMS) topology
9. multicenter, multidrop (MCMD) topology

A large and complex network may consist of one or more of the above topologies. Special techniques for network design are required for each topology. Networks with mixed topologies require special care during the design cycle. Network design techniques will be surveyed and described in Section III. The above-mentioned network topologies will be discussed in the following paragraphs.

2.2.1 Fully Connected Topology

A fully connected topology provides a direct connection between every pair of nodes in the network. Figure 2.1 illustrates this topology. Such a topology is economically feasible only when there are few nodes in the network. As the number of nodes increases, the number of links required for realizing such a structure increases approximately as the square of n where n is the number of nodes in the network. See Section II for a more detailed analysis. A fully connected network, despite its relatively high costs, provides better response time and throughput than those for other topologies. This topology is especially suitable for a local computer network where the need for responsiveness and throughput is quite acute.

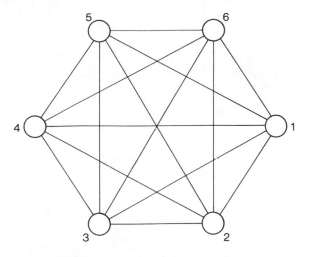

Fig. 2.1. A fully connected network topology.

2.2.2 Generalized Tree Topology

This is a multilevel, hierarchical structure that allows only a single path between any two nodes in the network. Figure 2.2 illustrates a three-level, hierarchical tree topology, which is generally employed to illustrate the logical interrelationships among the elements of a data bank or other abstract networks to show the information, either data or control, flow.

2.2.3 Minimal Spanning Topology

This topology is a subset of the generalized tree topology designed with the constraint to minimize the sum of all links in the network. Figure 2.3 illustrates such a topology, which relates to the physical distribution of the nodes on a

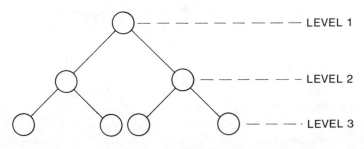

Fig. 2.2. A three-level, hierarchical generalized tree topology.

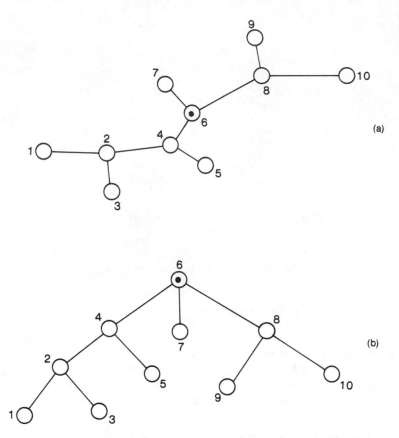

Fig. 2.3. A minimal spanning tree topology (a) and an equivalent four-level hierarchical tree (b).

map. The structure of Fig. 2.3(a) can be translated into a multilevel hierarchy by giving logical importance to the various nodes, as shown in Fig. 2.3(b). According to the existing tariffs, the monthly lease costs of a multipoint (shared) link are generally computed by summing the costs of all individual connections of the MST structure.

2.2.4 Bus Topology

The bus topology employs a shared broadcast transmission facility, called a *bus,* for information exchange between several nodes. Figures 2.4(a) and (b) illustrate distributed and centrally controlled bus topologies. In Fig. 2.4(a), all nodes are identical in nature. In Fig. 2.4(b), a single control node manages the traffic flows between every pair of nodes. Although the structure of Fig. 2.4(a) appears simple, a technique must be developed to eliminate contention for the use of the bus. In Fig. 2.4(b), all nodes communicate with control node C before setting up a call. All the known techniques result in some waste of bus bandwidth, or capacity. The bus topology is usually employed in realizing local computer networks, e.g., multiprocessor systems.

2.2.5 Loop, or Ring, Topology

Two varieties of loop, or ring, topology are illustrated in Figs. 2.5(a) and 2.5(b). In the first structure, each node acts as a message store-and-forward node. In other words, the node does not transmit a new message until it has processed the current message. In the second structure, Fig. 2.5(b), each node receives bits only in assigned time slots. Each node has the capacity of storing a certain number of bits and recognizing some control sequences of bits that enable exchange of information among nodes.

If all nodes of the loop are of the same type, a distributed loop topology results, but if one node is assigned the job of controlling call establishments and traffic flows, a two-level, centrally controlled loop topology results.

The traffic on the loop could, in principle, flow in both directions. In practice, the bidirectional traffic creates many difficulties in term of design and implementation. Consequently, most of the loop designs are based upon a unidirectional information flow.

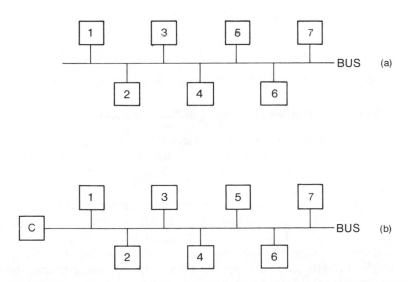

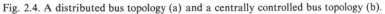

Fig. 2.4. A distributed bus topology (a) and a centrally controlled bus topology (b).

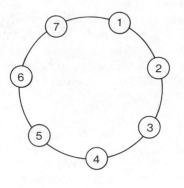

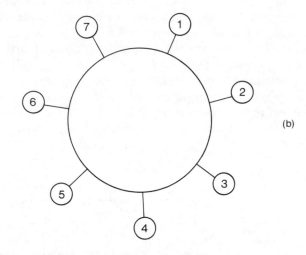

Fig. 2.5. A serial S/F loop topology (a) and a broadcast loop topology (b).

2.2.6 Single-Center, Single-Star (SCSS) Topology

A single-center, single-star (SCSS) topology is a two-level, hierarchical network consisting of a single network node at the higher level and all the subscriber nodes at the lower level, connected to the control node as shown in Fig. 2.6(a) and Fig. 2.6(b).

This topology is commonly employed to connect terminal nodes to either a switching node or to a data processing (DP) node whenever these nodes are situated close together. If this is not the case, the cost of the communication links will tend to be too high and thus economically unjustifiable.

Examples of systems employing the SCSS topology are university-based timesharing systems and telecommunication systems using a single private automatic branch exchange (PABX). Some of the early message switching (MS) systems also employed the SCSS topology even when the terminals were scattered over the entire continent. The justification for such an implementation was based upon the high cost of the switching node.

2.2.7 Single-Center, Multidrop (SCMD) Topology

An SCMD topology is a multi-level, hierarchical network consisting of a single network node at the higher level and several links, each shared by several subscriber nodes. Figure 2.7(a) illustrates a physical structure, and Fig. 2.7(b) illustrates an equivalent multi-level logical structure.

The SCMD topology is usually employed to provide some useful service to a large number of subscriber nodes scattered over a large area. This topology allows a considerable savings by allowing the sharing of transmission facilities among a large number of users. The interconnections of user nodes on a shared link obey the MST topology, as discussed in 2.2.3.

Determining which user node gets connected to what link has always presented great difficulty to system designers. Several algorithms are described in

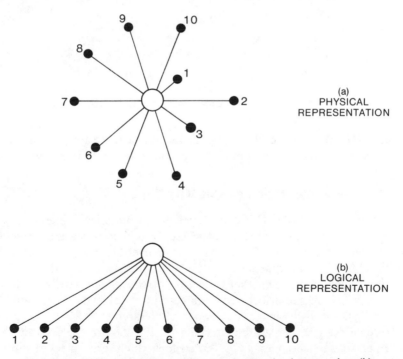

(a)
PHYSICAL
REPRESENTATION

(b)
LOGICAL
REPRESENTATION

Fig. 2.6. An SCSS topology (a) and its equivalent two-level tree topology (b).

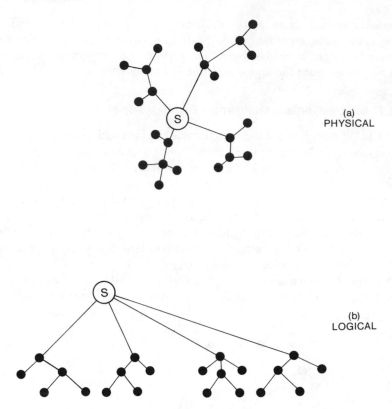

Fig. 2.7. An SCMD topology (a) and its equivalent, multilevel tree topology (b).

Section III. An example of an SCMD topology can be found in a medium-sized message switching system with subscribers scattered over a wide area.

2.2.8 Multicenter, Multistar (MCMS) Topology

A multicenter, multistar (MCMS) topology is a multilevel, hierarchical network consisting of several interconnected switching nodes that collectively serve a large number of subscriber terminals over large distances. According to Fig. 2.8, which illustrates such a topology, four switches, S1, S2, S3, and S4, are connected to one another via network trunks. Additionally, each switch serves a subset of subscriber nodes. In case identical switches are employed, the MCMD topology reduces to a two-level hierarchy.

In some designs, the subscriber nodes of Fig. 2.8 are replaced by the so-called end-of-service nodes (EOSNs), each of which serves a set of subscriber nodes, as shown in Fig. 2.9. Examples of EOSNs are private automatic branch exchanges (PABXs) and public Class 5 central offices (COs).

Figure 2.9 illustrates one way to achieve a three-level, hierarchical network satisfying the MCMS topology. In this illustration, each EOSN is connected to the switch node via access lines (ALs), and each subscriber line is connected to the EOSN via a subscriber line. Examples of MCMS topology are afforded by the private, corporate voice networks. Economical design of such networks also presents many difficulties. Detailed traffic flows among all EOSNs for all hours are essential for a near optimal network. See Section III for a discussion of some useful design techniques.

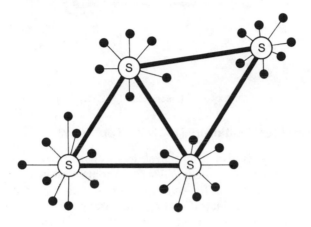

Fig. 2.8. A two-level, hierarchical MCMS topology.

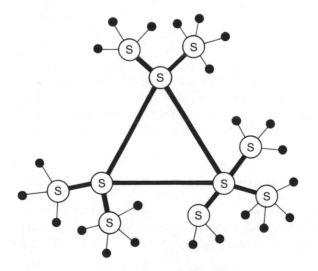

Fig. 2.9. A three-level MCMS topology.

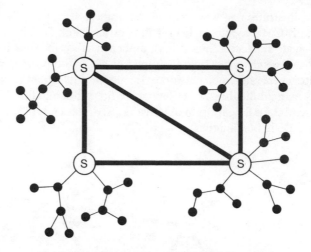

Fig. 2.10. A two-level, hierarchical MCMD topology.

2.2.9 Multicenter, Multidrop (MCMD) Topology

An MCMD topology is also a multilevel, hierarchical network structure that is used to provide service to many subscribers' data terminals scattered over large distances. See Fig. 2.10 for an illustration of such a structure.

According to the multi-level network hierarchy of Fig. 2.10, the four switches are interconnected via network trunks. Furthermore, each switch serves a subset of subscriber nodes connected to some shared links according to SCMD topology. This topology is finding an increasing use in the implementation of private, corporate data networks based upon either the packet switching (PS) or the message switching (MS) techniques.

As the number of switches increases, the cost of shared access links decreases, because the switches are closer to the subscriber nodes. The cost of the backbone trunk network increases with the number of switches, however. Consequently, some form of network optimization is required. These arguments are similar to those required for the design of economical private voice networks, as described in 2.2.8. Section III unifies all the design methodologies for private, corporate networks.

2.3 COMPOSITE NETWORKS

A complex network may be hard to understand if more than a single topology is involved. The concept of superimposition is usually employed for either modeling or designing a large network when it is composed of several component networks.

Most of the multinational networks can be generally modeled as composite networks. To illustrate, an international telephone call is completed over a composite network consisting of two or more component networks, each of which may or may not possess an identical network architecture or topology or hierarchy. Similarly, a multinational, corporate network handling both voice and data is generally composed of two or more component networks, each of which possesses a unique topology.

Two or more component networks can be combined to yield a composite network through the use of gateway switches, as shown in Fig. 2.11. The gateway switches, G_1 and G_2, provide all the required concentration, code translation, physical and logical interfacing, and required switching functions. Of course, no gateway switches are needed if no internetwork communication is provided.

2.4 ON-NET AND OFF-NET NODES

The subscriber nodes of a corporation or a public network may be scattered over the entire globe. For that case, to connect all the user nodes to the shared, backbone network will be too costly. A detailed economic analysis, based upon traffic patterns and intensities and cost of access lines, is generally required to select subscriber nodes that should be connected to the network and subscriber nodes that should be accessed through the other public networks. The sub-

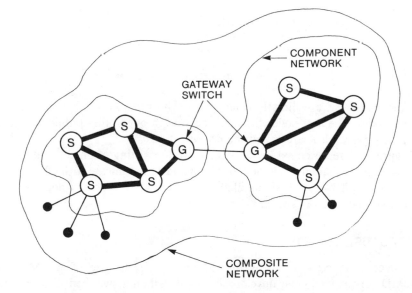

Fig. 2.11. Use of gateway switches to obtain a composite network.

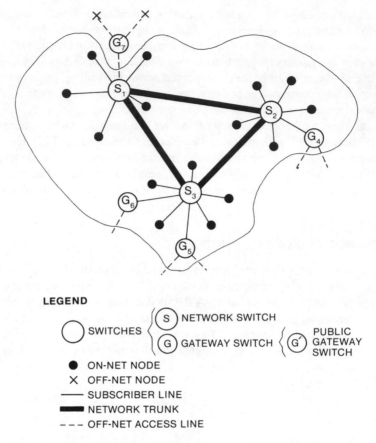

LEGEND

⭘ SWITCHES
{ Ⓢ NETWORK SWITCH
Ⓖ GATEWAY SWITCH
{ Ⓖ′ PUBLIC GATEWAY SWITCH

● ON-NET NODE
× OFF-NET NODE
—— SUBSCRIBER LINE
▬▬ NETWORK TRUNK
– – – OFF-NET ACCESS LINE

Fig. 2.12. A representation of on-net and off-net nodes.

scriber nodes that are directly connected to the given network are called the *on-net nodes*. The user nodes that are accessed through other public networks, via gateway switches, are called the *off-net nodes*.

Figure 2.12 represents a network structure consisting of on-net and off-net nodes. Suppose that on-net node No. 1 wants to communicate with off-net node No. 7: the call will be first handled by the originating switch node S1 and routed via the gateway switch G7 en route to off-net node No. 7.

2.5 FUTURE TRENDS

The decreasing cost of hardware will encourage the use of MCMS and MCMD topologies in the development of distributed switched networks for large corporations. During the early days of computer-controlled, network-based systems, the cost of the MS or the DP node was so high that only the SCMD topology was economically feasible.

The bus topology will continue to be popular for the realization of single processor architectures. The bus structure provides a simple and an economical interconnection between processing elements and memory modules in a multiprocessor architecture. The bus topology is also popular in the design of local computer networks based upon distributed control. Nevertheless, performance degradation due to contention of the bus and propagation delay on the bus must be taken into consideration before endorsing the design.

The loop topology has been used in the design of some well-known multicomputer systems, such as the C-System of Rockwell International and the Distributed System of the University of California at Irvine. Its associated complexity and cost, however, will continue to prevent its widespread use in the realization of local multicomputer networks.

Chapter 3
Concepts of Traffic Flows and Network Control

3.1 INTRODUCTORY REMARKS

The design of an economical network that satisfies the user's needs requires a complete understanding of (1) traffic entities that flow within the network, (2) traffic flow patterns for all pairs of subscriber pairs, and (3) techniques employed for controlling network flows and performance. In case the network spans a large geographic area, distribution of traffic flows for all significant hours also becomes essential.

Although traffic entities and traffic flows are quite important by themselves, smooth operation of the network is impossible without network control. Network control provides the means for not only dynamic traffic routing, to avoid congestion and failed network resources, but also fault monitoring, fault isolation, nodal/network recovery, traffic protection, and reporting of all operational events.

Network control is an important element of a network architecture. A good deal of effort must be expended in the design of network control techniques that may determine the difference between success or failure of a multimillion dollar program.

3.2 CONCEPTS OF TRAFFIC ENTITIES

All communication networks are characterized by flows of discrete traffic units from one node to another via the available links. One can model these traffic entities in the form of traffic units as defined below.

Discrete Traffic Unit. A discrete traffic unit is defined as having the shortest fixed length in a given component network. A typical unit may be a *bit* for a synchronous link or a *byte* for an asynchronous link.

Data Record. A data record is a traffic element consisting of an integral number of discrete traffic units. A traffic record may have different values for different users or for different applications of a given user.

Data Block.   A data block consists of an integral number of data records. A data block may be partially filled with null records in order to fix a block length. In some systems, the length of data blocks may be a variable number.

Data File.   A data file is equivalent to a related set of discrete blocks. The length of a data file is generally variable and is generally defined in terms of data blocks.

Data Bank.   A data bank is generally a network node that provides long-term storage for a large number of data files. Data files are generally stored in the form of directed traffic to and from the data bank. References to the data files in a data bank are in the form of directed messages to that data bank.

Data Message.   Data messages, or simply messages, are user's data that is directed from the originating subscriber node toward the destination node. Network elements, such as network nodes and links, are generally transparent to data messages. A message is generally a single transmission of user data between two nodes, and it could denote a simple one-way message with no requirements for acknowledgment. In some systems, a message could be in the form of an inquiry, which is always followed by a response from the destination node to the node that originated the message. Thus, a message may be classified as an inquiry message or a response message.

Control Message.   The control and supervisory codes, which may or may not be embedded with the data message, also propagate through the network. These control and supervisory messages direct the network nodes to perform the required network control, management, and special communication processing functions.

Transaction.   A transaction generally involves a series of messages in both directions relative to the subscriber and network nodes. A transaction is simply a characteristic of the particular application handled by the network-based system. To illustrate, in the airline reservation application, the transaction consists of (1) an inquiry message originated by the reservation clerk and (2) the response message generated by the network node and transmitted toward the reservation clerk. In the circuit-switched networks, transaction requires that a path be set up, consisting of physical links between the calling subscriber and the called party. In the PS and MS networks, the transaction may require the establishment of only logical paths between the two subscriber nodes.

Call.   A call is an unstructured sequence of intelligence between the calling subscriber and the called subscriber(s) in both directions. In CS networks, a call requires the establishment of a path consisting of physical links. In PS networks, a call generally requires the establishment of a virtual path consisting of logical channels.

Session. A session is a two-way communication process between a terminal and a host or between two hosts in a DP or a DDP network. Either a virtual or a permanent virtual circuit needs to be established through the communication network.

Data Structure. Data structure deals with the hierarchical structures of stored data in nodal storages. It deals with such aspects as the message segment units stored in storage, the type of chaining employed for message segments, the representation of message fields, and the addressing employed.

Bin or Buffer. A bin is a unit of primary storage within a network node. A buffer or a bin provides short-term storage for message segments. The duration of storage is measured between the moments of message segment arrival and its subsequent storage in secondary storage within a MS node or its transmission toward the destination node, as applicable in a PS system. The size of the bin or the buffer is generally fixed and is determined by the average message length and the amount of overhead information required for chaining and other network management functions.

Message Segment. A message segment is a fixed portion of a data message that is stored not only in the primary storage for a short duration, but also in the secondary storage for long-term retention. The size of the message segment should be carefully chosen because it influences the total storage requirements within every node.

Chaining Information. Each buffer and secondary storage cell consists of both user data and chaining information. Chaining information may consist of the following:

1. time of receipt
2. identification of the subscriber or the inlet link
3. address of previous segment of the same message now stored on the secondary storage
4. address of the next segment of the same message, generally preassigned in an MS system
5. information about whether the acknowledgment has been received from the destination node

The chaining information is sometimes completely created by the network node, and sometimes it is provided partially by the received packet or segment. In any case, the amount of information in the chain depends upon the particular application and system design.

Message Fields. A data message, as defined earlier, consists of a user-defined field and one or more control fields that are demarcated and indicated by the use of special codes as shown below:

1. Initial field, which consists of
   a. start of message (SOM) indicator
   b. state of transmitting node (idle/busy/out)
2. Address field: This may include the address of both the sending and destination nodes.
3. Operation field: This denotes the length and meaning of the data field.
4. Data field: This consists of user data that usually requires complete network transparency except perhaps its length.
5. Check field: This may consist of one or more of the following elements: checksum plus message string count and link stream count. The checksum provides error detection for the user data portion. The message string count provides a check for the entire message string, and the link stream count provides a message-by-message correlation for any given link.

The actual implementation of these message fields is achieved differently for different network systems. CS systems differ drastically from PS and MS systems. Even the PS systems vary from one to another in terms of message fields.

3.3 TRAFFIC ATTRIBUTES

The purpose of any network-based system is to provide service to subscribers who input their requests, unique signals, or messages. Thus, a primary concern in the design of a communication system is the specification of the input traffic a network can handle while providing all subscribers a desired grade of service (GOS) and quality of service (QOS). Chapter 6 defines these terms and describes techniques for analyzing GOS and QOS for any system. Input traffic can be characterized by the message/call arrival rates, message lengths or call durations, and traffic intensities.

Message/Call Arrival Rate. Message/call arrival rate is a measure of how often calls/messages are arriving at any network node during a unit of time, usually a second. It is also described as the calling rate in a CS or PS system.

The interarrival time for calls arriving in a system that has a large number of subscribers is generally represented by a negative exponential distribution. In practice, the calling rate varies significantly over different periods of time, such as the hours of the day, days of the month, or months of the year. Furthermore, the calling rate distribution is also influenced by the number of samples or the periods of observation. The calling rate is generally denoted by the symbol λ, and it is generally associated with the average second of a typical peak hour.

Message Length or Call Holding Time.   The length of an entire message string is generally measured in terms of discrete traffic units, and the call duration is measured in terms of occupancy of the associated link. Message lengths or call durations are characterized by probability distributions.

In CS systems, a session may involve several different types of calls. At the start of the session, a subscriber indicates its desire to be served through a very short message. After the system acknowledges the request by a dial tone, the subscriber sends a second message in the form of dial pulses denoting the address of the called party. These special messages and their arrival rates influence the use of special common-control equipment in the switching node. The call arrival rates and their durations determine the sizing of the transmission links. The call duration is generally denoted by *TH*.

Traffic Intensity.   Traffic intensity is a measure of the total traffic being handled at any given time by the entire system or any of its subsystem. Consequently, it is a function of both the calling rate and the call duration. Traffic intensity is generally measured in terms of units named after A. K. Erlang, the famous Danish mathematician. Traffic intensity in erlangs is a product of the call arrival rate, as seen by the subsystem, and the average call holding time. The following expression denotes such a relationship:

$$A = \lambda * TH \text{ erlangs}$$

An alternative representation of traffic intensity, as seen by any subsystem, is in terms of hundred call seconds, or simply CCSs. To illustrate, 100 CCSs can be realized by a system having one call arriving per second, each call lasting for 100 seconds or a system having 100 calls arriving per second, each call lasting for 1 second.

Erlangs are equivalent to the average number of user links that are concurrently busy at any one time. A CCS does not provide such an understanding. One can obtain erlangs from CCSs as follows:

$$\text{erlangs} = \frac{\text{CCSs}}{36}$$

In case a subsystem consists of a single resource, such as a link or CPU or disk file, the traffic load, or intensity, in that resource can not exceed 1 erlang. In practice, most individual resources do not experience traffic loads exceeding 0.7 or 0.8 erlangs. In the literature, the resource load is generally represented by the following expression:

$$\rho = \lambda * TH$$

Section II will expand upon techniques for analyzing the performance of subsystems consisting of one or more servers interconnected to form a unique network. Performance parameters, such as average queue lengths, waiting times, and subsystem utilization, are defined, and techniques for computing these quantities will be developed.

3.4 NETWORK CONNECTION MATRIX

Graph theory provides a rather simple means of visualizing the connectivity of a network. A *zero connectivity* means that all nodes are not connected to any other node within the network. A *full connectivity* implies that each network node is connected to each and every node of the network. By allowing 1 to represent a direct connection and 0 to represent an absence of any connection between the two nodes, one can obtain a connection matrix C_5 for a fully connected network consisting of five nodes, as illustrated in Fig. 3.1.

C_5 suggests that each node is connected to all other nodes via FDX links. In other words, the connection matrix of Fig. 3.1 is a fully connected, directed graph, meaning that traffic flows in both directions among all nodes. Furthermore, C_5 also suggests that each node can also communicate with itself. This notion of branching on to itself (this is also known as *looping around itself*)

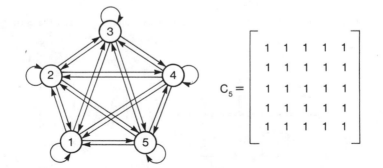

$$C_5 = \begin{bmatrix} 1 & 1 & 1 & 1 & 1 \\ 1 & 1 & 1 & 1 & 1 \\ 1 & 1 & 1 & 1 & 1 \\ 1 & 1 & 1 & 1 & 1 \\ 1 & 1 & 1 & 1 & 1 \end{bmatrix}$$

Fig. 3.1. A fully connected five-node network and the corresponding connection matrix, C_5.

can be used to represent the intranodal traffic among subscribers served by the same network node or it can represent reliability states of a network system. The notion may be unnecessary for the study of those switched communication networks that are concerned only with traffic flows among different nodes. A fully connected, five-node network for this case is illustrated in Fig. 3.2. The connection matrix for a five-node network characterized by only simplex links is illustrated in Fig. 3.3. Figures 3.4(a) through 3.4(f) illustrate the connection matrices for various network topologies discussed in the previous chapter.

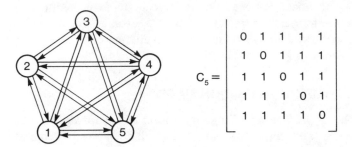

$$C_5 = \begin{bmatrix} 0 & 1 & 1 & 1 & 1 \\ 1 & 0 & 1 & 1 & 1 \\ 1 & 1 & 0 & 1 & 1 \\ 1 & 1 & 1 & 0 & 1 \\ 1 & 1 & 1 & 1 & 0 \end{bmatrix}$$

Fig. 3.2. A useful form of a fully connected network and the corresponding connection matrix, C_5.

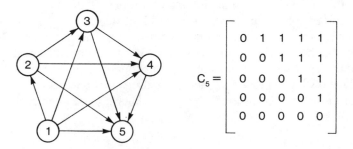

$$C_5 = \begin{bmatrix} 0 & 1 & 1 & 1 & 1 \\ 0 & 0 & 1 & 1 & 1 \\ 0 & 0 & 0 & 1 & 1 \\ 0 & 0 & 0 & 0 & 1 \\ 0 & 0 & 0 & 0 & 0 \end{bmatrix}$$

Fig. 3.3. A fully connected five-node network using only simplex lines and the corresponding connection matrix, C_5.

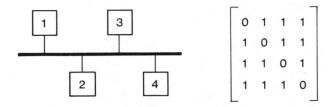

$$\begin{bmatrix} 0 & 1 & 1 & 1 \\ 1 & 0 & 1 & 1 \\ 1 & 1 & 0 & 1 \\ 1 & 1 & 1 & 0 \end{bmatrix}$$

Fig. 3.4(a). Bus topology and the corresponding connection matrix.

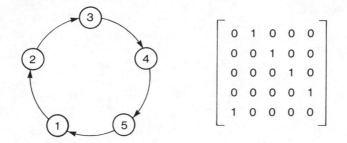

Fig. 3.4(b). Serial loop topology and the corresponding connection matrix.

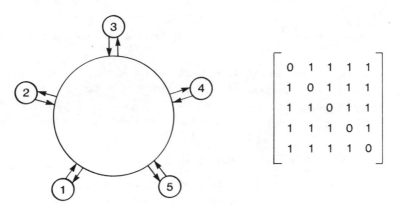

Fig. 3.4(c). Broadcast loop topology and the corresponding connection matrix.

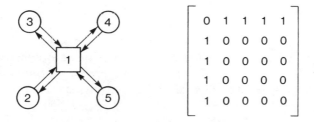

Fig. 3.4(d). An SCSS topology and the corresponding connection matrix.

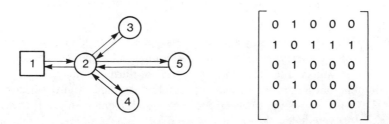

Fig. 3.4(e). An SCMD topology and the corresponding connection matrix.

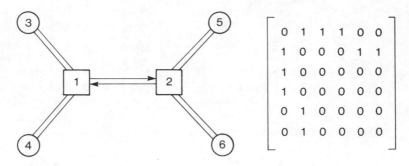

Fig. 3.4(f). A two-center, two-star topology and the corresponding connection matrix.

The above examples should be sufficient to give an insight into the relationship between the connection matrix and the physical network structure, or topology. Once the concept of network topology is understood, the concepts of traffic paths, routes, and traffic flow control become easier to understand.

3.5 TRAFFIC PATHS AND ROUTES

A simple representation of the directed path, or route, a message follows through the network is a directed vector whose elements are the nodes encountered by the message en route. This is illustrated as follows:

$$P_i = (n_1, n_2, n_3, \ldots n_j)$$

where P_i is the ith path, and n_j is the jth node in the path.

Several different types of paths encountered within a switched communication system for an airline, as shown in Fig. 3.5, are unique for message switching, inquiry response, and DP sessions, respectively, as listed below:

$$P_{ms} = (7,4,1,3,8) \qquad \text{MS}$$
$$P_{ir} = (7,4,1,2,1,4,7) \qquad \text{IR}$$
$$P_{dp} = (8,3,,1,,2,,1,3,8,3,,1,2,,1,3,8, \ldots) \qquad \text{DP}$$

The first path involves only a single message. The second path is for a transaction involving two types of messages—inquiry and response. The third type of path is established for the entire DP session, during which many incoming and outgoing messages may travel between the user node and the host processor (HP). It is interesting to observe that though the end nodes in the MS path are two different nodes, the end nodes for the IR type path are the same nodes. The path for the DP session consists of job entry phase (session establishment), first output, subsequent changes in the input data, as dictated by the earlier outputs from the DP node, and subsequent outputs and the exit phase, depending upon the particular protocol. All the inputs and outputs are generally highly structured, and a departure from the norm results in an aborted session.

The method of representing paths as suggested earlier is not very elegant, mathematically speaking. The earlier representation describes only the network nodes and the sequence of functions performed in the path. It does not say anything about the links that are involved in the path. The attributes of the links—name, type, and bandwidth/capacity—tell a great deal about the path traversed by the transaction.

An alternative method of defining network paths is to define a directed vector. Its elements are directed branches, $C(i,j)$ where $C(i,j)$ is the element of a connection matrix, Cn, of an n-node network. Many paths starting from node 2 and ending at node 1 in the three-node network of Fig. 3.6 can be defined as follows:

$$P(2,1) = (C(2,1)) \qquad \text{path of length 1}$$
$$P(2,1) = (C(2,3), C(3,1)) \qquad \text{path of length 2}$$
$$P(2,1) = (C(2,3), C(3,1), C(1,2), C(2,1)) \quad \text{path of length 4}$$

and so on.

In other words, the path length is simply the number of branches, $C(i,j)$, in the path.

Algorithms exist that can enable one to use a high-speed computer to enumerate all the paths that are of length q or less for a given connection matrix. One such algorithm will be discussed in Section II. After these paths are enum-

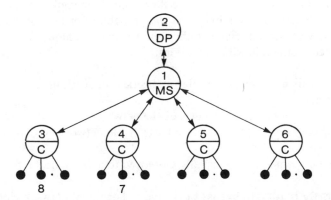

Fig. 3.5. An airline reservation network representation consisting of MS, DP, and concentrator (c) nodes.

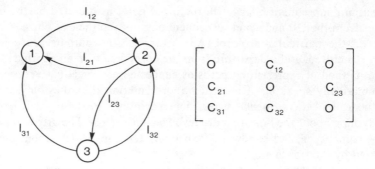

Fig. 3.6. A representation of a directed graph corresponding to a three-node network and its connection matrix.

erated, one can then choose only those paths that will be allowed according to the functions provided by the network nodes.

3.6 TRAFFIC FLOW CONTROL

During periods of heavy traffic, congestion may appear at certain network elements, giving rise to a degradation in network performance (see Chapter 6 for a discussion of network performance concepts). In some cases, either the request for service or the traffic data may get lost due to the unavailability of some critical nodal resources, such as common-control equipment or traffic buffers. Consequently, it is important to employ some traffic flow control techniques in the design of network service nodes, such as the CS, PS, and MS nodes. Only through the use of traffic flow control techniques can one hope to maximize the system throughput and the probability of providing the desired grade of service (GOS). Such traffic flow control techniques must overcome the ill effects of the following conditions:

1. statistical peaking of traffic intensities at certain critical network elements
2. degraded service in some parts of the network
3. complete failure of one or more parts of the network system

Two major techniques are usually employed to achieve traffic flow control:

1. alternate routing to bypass the congested or failed network elements
2. inhibition or delay of input requests for service until the congestion has subsided below a certain threshold

Of the two solutions, alternate routing is preferred, as it is transparent to the subscribers. Inhibition of input requests for network services will tend to irritate the network users. Most large national telephone networks employ a combination of the two techniques, with an emphasis on the alternate routing technique. Some of the new emerging public data networks, e.g., Telenet in the United States and Datapac in Canada, tend to provide dynamic alternate routing generously. Alternate routing is also appealing because it actually helps a better utilization of network resources.

A successful implementation of the two techniques requires the availability of pertinent data at the network control node(s). Feedback of real-time data dealing with performance and traffic intensities at all critical network elements to the control node(s) is required periodically to reduce the additional communication costs. The number of control nodes, the amount of feedback information required, and the extent of control desired are important design considerations, and these are intimately related to one another and to the particular design philosophy employed. Performance evaluation of several techniques will be discussed in Section II. Various network routing techniques and control strategies will be discussed here.

3.6.1 Network Routing and Control Techniques

Three methods of network routing are generally employed in systems with alternate routing capabilities.

1. Deterministic Method: This is the simplest routing control method that involves the use of fixed primary, or high usage, and a certain number of alternate, or final, routes, as determined through several tables stored in the memory of either the originating network node or every network node in the path of the transaction. Whereas the former approach is known as the OSRA (originating station routing approach), the latter approach is generally called the ESRA (en route station routing approach). Of course, each approach implies a fixed routing scheme.
2. Synoptic Method: The Network Management Center (NMC) measures the overall traffic flow patterns using some statistical sampling techniques. Based upon the information collected periodically and the network connectivity, the NMC creates optimum routing tables for the system using either the OSRA or the ESRA approaches. This method, although simple to comprehend, requires an additional overlayed data network for collecting traffic statistics.
3. Adaptive Method: This technique requires that each network node gather traffic statistics from all its neighboring network nodes and then determine the optimum route a transaction must follow toward the destination

node. Utmost care is taken to prevent looping around within a part of the network. In the literature, many different names have been given to this technique, but they all do the same thing.

Generally speaking, the fixed routing schemes are quite simple to implement. They are generally useful in networks characterized by uniform traffic intensities and nonvarying topology achieved through highly reliable components within the network.

The implementation of the synoptic method requires a complex NMC and an additional overlaid data network for collecting traffic statistics from all the network nodes. Such a method is already finding increasing use, due to decreasing hardware costs.

Implementing the adaptive routing method requires each network node to be complex enough to gather traffic statistics, perform traffic analyses, and adaptively compute optimum routes to all other network nodes. The gathering of traffic statistics is generally accomplished through the reading of messages floating around in the network, messages that are stamped with time and path-traces. As the cost of hardware decreases further, this method is bound to replace the synoptic method.

3.7 OTHER NETWORK CONTROL CONCEPTS

Network control requires the use of not only traffic flow control techniques, as described earlier, but also (1) fault detection, fault isolation, and fault reporting and recovery techniques, and (2) traffic protection through network partitioning and traffic buffering and/or feedback control.

Implementation of any useful network-based system requires an implicit or explicit use of error detection and retransmission, fault detection and fault isolation, initialization, and restart of hardware and software functions, and traffic protection throughout the network. A consistent design plan must be adhered to if uniformly good network control and network performance are desired.

3.7.1 Fault Detection, Fault Isolation, and Fault Reporting and Recovery

There are three types of disturbances that could degrade the performance of any network based system:

1. Catastrophic failure that results in a complete loss of system capacity.
2. Minor failure that results in a sudden loss of only a portion of the system capacity.

3. Transient failure in hardware or software that may or may not cause an immediate or measurable loss of system performance. A transient failure or disturbance can cause an error in stored data, e.g., a routing table, that may result in a slow attrition of system performance. Then again, a transient failure in a network element may not cause any perceptible degradation in the system.

When a Type 1 or Type 2 disturbance occurs, it is imperative that the system detect the malfunction quickly to prevent either excessive loss of user requests for service or propagation of erroneous messages throughout the system. Steps that must be taken are (1) isolation of the defective subsystem, (2) removal of the defective subsystem, and (3) initiation of restart and recovery procedures. Traffic protection techniques are essential for preventing loss of traffic caused by Type 1 or Type 2 disturbances in the network.

When a Type 3 disturbance occurs quite frequently, fault detection, fault isolation, malfunctioning subsystem removal, and restart and recovery procedures should be invoked through the use of diagnostics. Nonetheless, there are many variations of Type 3 disturbances, e.g., additive random noise on the transmission links, that do not result in any isolation of hardware or software subsystem malfunctions. For these cases, some error control, e.g., error detection and retransmission or forward error correction, procedures are essential. In several emerging new system architectures, e.g., X.25-based PS systems, an efficient error control procedure involving error detection and retransmission is automatically provided for every transmission link, whether network or subscriber, in the intelligent network. As a consequence, the life of a system designer is now becoming much easier, although the design of complex diagnostics for validating the health of various subsystems still poses many challenges to all system engineers.

Fault detection is generally accomplished through the use of the following techniques:

1. The system realizes that it is unable to communicate with a malfunctioning subsystem.
2. A malfunctioning subsystem realizes that one of its elements has failed, and this results in a message to a control point in the system.
3. The subsystem software or firmware notifies the system of a hardware failure in some unknown element(s).

Once a network fault is detected by the system or NMC, the system has three responsibilities:

1. Isolate the faulty element and remove the failed element from the system.
2. Take steps to restart all the affected jobs and procedures.

3. Report the fault through an alarm report at the NMC, causing an action by the repair and maintenance crew.

Many large, network-based systems suffer from the lack of such reports, a situation that makes it difficult to maintain the system and assess its true performance on a real-time basis.

The responsibility for recovering from the failure rests jointly on the system and the system users. The division of responsibility depends upon the type of traffic handled, the type of failures encountered, and the particular system design philosophy employed. To illustrate, in a public telephone system, the user redials the number after a delay hoping that the malfunctioning exchange may have been repaired.

In the case of a distributed system with alternate routing capability, the system should restructure its routing tables to avoid the failed network element, e.g., a switching node or a trunk bundle. In the case of a user node becoming defective, the user must either use another nearby unit or simply inform the utility company and ask it to repair or replace the defective unit.

If traffic data is actually handled by the network service node, e.g., an MS node, checkpointing data or providing redundant storage techniques can be employed to allow a more extensive recovery by the system when needed. For the case of a public telephone system, its CS node does not actively handle the traffic data—it simply maintains a connection during the duration of the conversation. A sudden breakdown of the established path through the switch module will require the user to enter its call request again. In this example, the system is not directly involved in the recovery procedure except for honoring the user complaints. In case the number of complaints becomes excessive, the system may invoke elaborate diagnostics of the particular CS node for fault location and fault isolation within the node. In some sophisticated systems, validating software is always operating to automatically locate the faulty element within the CS node. The system should be capable of initiating recovery procedures in case the number of Type 3 malfunctions exceeds a certain number within a unit of time or when Type 1 or 2 malfunctions occur.

3.7.2 Traffic Protection

An important function of network control is to provide end-to-end traffic protection. Without such protection, the system will be unable to deliver the traffic data to the destination if traffic is lost due to (1) failure of network elements, (2) system noise, and (3) user errors, etc. The probability of loss of traffic passing through the network-based system is inversly related to the degree of traffic protection designed into the system. Several techniques for analyzing the effectiveness of various traffic protection schemes are discussed in Section II. It is imperative, however, to introduce here some well-known techniques for enhancing traffic protection, which can be understood only in terms of network partitions.

A partition may include the entire network, in which case the traffic protection boundary is external to the network. Also, there may be a bounded partition internal to the system. In case no measures are taken to prevent traffic loss within a given partition, then the responsibility for traffic protection lies within the contiguous partitions. To accomplish this, feedback paths must be provided to either acknowledge completions or receive requests for retransmission of lost or mutilated data. In the extreme case when the system has no protection at all, the users must report to one another receipts or nonreceipts of correct data.

Traffic protection internal to the network requires storing data on redundant storage devices, e.g., disk files), retrieving traffic data from a correctly functioning subsystem when a traffic loss is detected, and reinitiating all recovery procedures.

Selecting protection boundaries for a given system is clearly an economic consideration, and it also depends upon the particular application.

3.8 FUTURE TRENDS

The availability of inexpensive computing and storage elements will encourage the use of adaptive techniques for controlling traffic flows in future systems. This trend is quite consistent with the trend to distribute intelligence throughout the network, wherever it might be most effective.

The availability of inexpensive computing and storage elements will definitely encourage the emergence of intelligent networks that will provide the required amount of not only traffic protection for each of the many applications it handles, but also security or privacy to users of distributed systems. The problems related to security and privacy are, however, quite complex.

Chapter 4
Concepts of Transmission and Signaling

4.1 INTRODUCTORY REMARKS

Although Chapter 1 discussed simple attributes of network nodes and links, to understand the operations of a network system, a deeper understanding of the transmission and signaling techniques employed throughout the system is necessary. It is clear to us that a link is used for transmitting intelligence from one node to another, but there are many additional aspects of transmission that are significant. One can point to the modulation techniques employed for encoding data prior to transmission, multiplexing techniques used for increasing the utilization of the links, transmission of control data at appropriate points within the entire session, and synchronization techniques employed for preserving the bit and message boundaries. These are some of the most important design criteria one must contend with when designing a network system.

Basically, there are two types of intelligence generated by the user node and later handled by one or more of the network nodes in a very structured manner:

1. user information, which may or may not be transparent to the network nodes, that must be transported to another node
2. control information that enables the network node to provide the service requested by the user

Whereas transmission deals with both the user data and control data, signaling deals with only the transmission of control information in the system. Both concepts—transmission and signaling—will now be discussed in as much detail as necessary for understanding the workings of any network-based system.

4.2 CONCEPTS OF TRANSMISSION

An optimum design of a network-based system requires an integrated plan for transmitting both user and control data from one node to another within the network. A knowledge of transmission techniques and characteristics is required. There are several concepts associated with links, both user and network trunks, that must be understood.

4.2.1 Transmission Links

A fundamental concept related to a link is its *capacity,* which is defined as the maximum rate of information transmission achievable on the link for a given network environment. Link capacity is measured as *bits per second* (BPS), and it is generally denoted by R. A related attribute is link bandwidth B, which is related to R as shown below:

$$R = B*\log_2(n)$$

where n is the number of levels associated with the transmitted waveform. Note that n cannot be increased without discrimination because noise has a limiting effect on it. Link capacity is sometimes expressed according to Hartley's criterion as follows:

$$R = \frac{1}{t} \log_2(n)$$

where t is the duration of the modulated and keyed pulse waveform.

Transmission on a link can be characterized by the type of signals transmitted on the link. Basically, there are two types of transmitted signals:

1. analog signals
2. digital signals

An *analog signal* is generally realized by multiplying a modulating function with a high-frequency carrier waveform centered at F_c. Figure 4.1 illustrates several forms of modulated analog signals.

A *digital signal* is simply a digital pulse train whose frequency spectrum is centered at baseband, 0 Hertz (Hz). For this reason, a digital signal is sometimes simply termed a *baseband signal*. It is interesting to note that with the availability of cheap computing elements, there is a great deal of interest in digital signals because they are easier to interface with computers directly and are less prone to distortion and noise than their analog counterparts.

4.2.2 Dependence of Transmission Techniques on Switching Technology

A CS system receives some control signals, e.g., off-hook signal and dial pulses, at the start of the session and determines the type of service required by the user. Later the system provides a permanent path between the originating node and destination node(s) during the entire conversation.

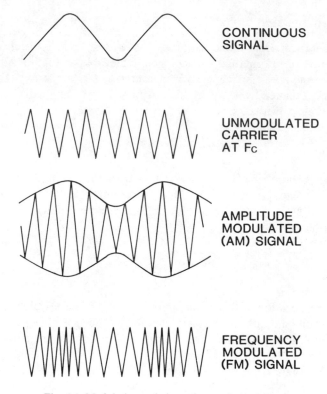

Fig. 4.1. Modulation techniques for continuous signals.

A user link in a CS system is also known as the *local loop*. It is generally a two-wire loop. The use of four-wire local loops would have doubled the need for copper in the public telephone systems. The local loop connects the user node to the network node. The local loops must be cheap and always ready for use. The local loop is capable of handling both voice and data and control signals. The electrical characteristics of the loop must be such as to pass bandwidths associated with voice and dial/ringing pulses. Special design considerations are required for implementing local loops for either the analog or the digital systems. In the analog system, a two-wire loop is sufficient for providing a half duplex (HDX) link between the subscriber node and the network node. This works out fine, as only one person talks at a time. In contrast, the digital system generally employs two two-wire loops, each pair dedicated to a particular direction of transmission. In digital systems, shared synchronization circuitry is also employed at the network node to handle both the incoming and outgoing digital data streams.

The network service nodes in the CS environments also employ multiplexing techniques for increasing the utilization of network trunks. At present, both voice and data streams are handled as the multiplexed sum of individual channels.

PS systems usually provide virtual circuits among the packet mode terminals during a conversation. No permanent, dedicated physical links are allowed throughout the networks. Permanent virtual circuits can be assigned to eliminate the need for frequent call setups and cleardowns. All the physical network links are thus fully shared by all the users of the networks. Another characteristic of the PS network is that each PS node provides a short-term storage, just a few milliseconds long, to each received packet of a call before sending it toward the destination node. For this reason, only the primary storage is generally employed by the PS node.

The nonpacket mode terminal, e.g., asynchronous, low-speed type, are generally connected to a network node, e.g., a PS node or a concentrator, via a two-wire loop, as in a CS system. A host processor is generally a packet mode terminal. Therefore, it is always connected to the PS node directly via a four-wire loop to achieve a full-duplex (FDX) communication. Because most PS systems of today are used for data communication only, care must be taken in choosing the user link bandwidths, as these effectively determine the system response times.

PS systems employ a very simple and yet a powerful technique for increasing the utilization of network trunks whose bandwidths are much higher than that for the user links or trunks connecting the concentrators to the PS nodes. In most existing PS systems, 56,000-BPS trunks are usually employed. With the availability of leased digital channels, higher bandwidths are in store. The network nodes transmit packets at the highest transmission rates allowable on the network trunks, using the first-in-first-out (FIFO) scheme. This transmission scheme is also known as the *asynchronous time division multiplexing* (ATDM) *technique,* in which the smallest unit of transmission is a packet, instead of the message, as is the case for MS systems. The preceding schemes will be referred to hereafter as PATDM and MATDM, respectively. As ATDM and statistical concentration are synonymous, ATDM can be shown to be more efficient than any other conventional multiplexing techniques, such as frequency division multiplexing (FDM) and time division multiplexing (TDM). Section II will present a detailed performance evaluation of the various multiplexing techniques.

Another advantage of PS systems is that error control is a part of system architecture. This applies especially to PS systems that are based on the recently adopted CCITT X.25 standard. In contrast, the users of the CS systems for data transmission are responsible for developing special solutions for achieving a desired error rate.

Most MS systems differ from the CS and PS systems in three respects:

1. There are no permanent or temporary virtual connections between two subscribers assigned during the communication session. Only the network node talks either to the originating node or to the destination node(s). Only in those cases where a concentrator is employed, can PS techniques be employed on the trunk connecting a concentrator to the MS node.
2. User nodes are generally connected to a network service node, concentrator or MS node, according to either the SCSS or the SCMD topologies.
3. High utilization of the user links is achieved through the use of MATDM and long-term message queuing provided at the MS node.

The last point is particularly significant in that the CS and PS systems do not allow such a capability. In those systems, only the high utilization of network trunks is achievable. Such high utilization of network trunks is also realized in MS systems consisting of many MS and concentrator nodes, through the use of ATDM or PS techniques discussed earlier.

DP and DBM systems do not generally employ switching techniques and, as a result, present fewer challenges to the designer of transmission equipment. To illustrate, a timesharing (TS) system situated on the campus of a university will usually employ an SCSS topology for interconnections. The user links generally employ digital transmission at baseband. One can extend the distances of all links through the use of either analog modems or digital repeaters. In case some form of switching is employed on the DP and DBM systems, and an NMC is employed for an elaborate control of the network, design considerations valid for CS and PS will then apply.

The previous paragraphs illustrate how transmission techniques are influenced by the type of switching employed in the network. Nevertheless, several aspects of transmission, such as modulation, multiplexing, and synchronization, need to be explored even further to gain a better understanding of the transmission techniques.

4.2.3 Various Aspects of Transmission

The underlying purpose of this section is to equip the reader with all the major transmission-related concepts, definitions, and critical variables required for detailed modeling of a network-based system and for evaluating the performance of the system.

4.2.3.1 Modulation

During the last 50 years, several modulation techniques have been developed for transmitting information over individual physical links and network trunks, each consisting of many logical channels, e.g., multiplexed trunks of a telephone system. Some of these modulation techniques are good for only continuous signals, e.g., voice over dedicated circuits, but most of the modulation techniques are useful for the transmission of discrete units of information. Of course, some modulation techniques are good for both continuous and discrete signals. Some of the most common modulation techniques are enumerated as follows:

1. amplitude modulation (AM)
2. frequency modulation (FM)
3. phase modulation (PM)
4. pulse amplitude modulation (PAM)
5. pulse width or duration modulation (PWM or PDM)
6. pulse position modulation (PPM)
7. pulse code modulation (PCM)
8. delta modulation (DM)

The first three modulation techniques involve a multiplication between a modulation function representing intelligence and a sinusoidal carrier wave centered at F_c. The AM technique is generally used by broadcasting stations to transmit analog or continuous voice or music signals over large distances. This involves direct modulation of the voice or music signal and a high frequency carrier.

AM, FM, and PM are also employed for transmitting data, intelligence in discrete form, through the use of pulse keying of a carrier wave.

Figure 4.1 illustrates the manner in which continuous signals are modulated, and Fig. 4.2 illustrates the manner in which discrete signals are modulated, using the above-mentioned modulation schemes. It should be observed that AM, FM, and PM have been renamed *amplitude shift keying* (ASK), *frequency shift keying* (FSK), and *phase shift keying* (PSK), respectively, for digital transmission.

Because our interest lies primarily in SPC network systems, our emphasis in the book will remain on digital data modulation techniques only.

Several variations of the above-mentioned modulated signals are employed to achieve economy of transmitted bandwidth, simplicity in demodulator design, and better signal-to-noise performance. For example, *coherent FSK*, which requires two synchronized carriers at both the transmitter and the receiver, is employed to achieve lower error rate. Another variation of FSK is *minimum shift keying* (MSK), which requires: (1) no phase transitions at pulse boundaries and (2) coherent detection, resulting in a lower transmitted bandwidth.

A variation of the PSK, known as *differentially coherent phase shift keying* (DCPSK), is also commonly employed to transmit digital signals over large

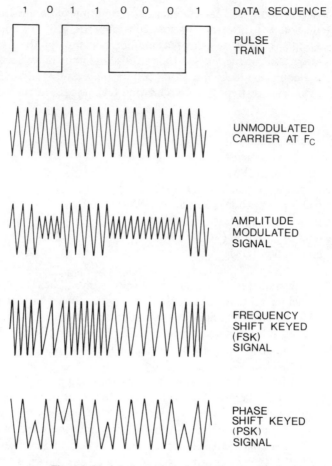

Fig. 4.2. Modulation techniques for discrete signals.

distances and simplify detection. The transmitted phase shift is relative to the previous pulse and not to the absolute carrier at the transmitter.

All transmitted signals using a carrier frequency and some form of keying belong to a family of analog signals, despite the fact that they carry digital information. Only baseband digital waveforms can be classified as digital signals. A link carrying analog modulated signals or just continuous waveforms is called an *analog link*. A link carrying baseband digital signals is called a *digital link*. A link could be both an analog and a digital link at different times. For example, a local loop, when carrying signaling data in the form of baseband digital waveform, acts as a digital link and, when carrying the analog voice waveform, acts as an analog channel.

The sampled data technique is another modulation scheme to convert a continuous signal into a sequence of digital pulses. See Fig. 4.3 for an illustration of this technique. A sampling rate of twice the bandwidth of the incoming signal is required to preserve the information contents and to re-create the original waveform at the receiver with minimum distortion. This technique allows one to derive the benefits of digital transmission even when user terminals output a continuous waveform, e.g., voice.

Some common forms of pulse modulation systems are known as *pulse amplitude modulation* (PAM), *pulse width/duration modulation* (PWM or PDM), and *pulse position modulation* (PPM). These modulation systems lend themselves very well to multiplexing of many continuous signals by simply increasing the sampling rate that is determined by the total bandwidth of all incoming signals. This process is illustrated in Fig. 4.4.

In practice, a transmission system may utilize both pulse modulation and carrier wave modulation prior to high-frequency (HF) radio transmission to achieve long-haul capabilities.

An extremely popular form of pulse modulation is known as *pulse code mod-*

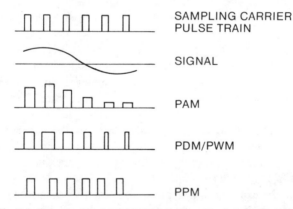

Fig. 4.3. Pulse modulation systems based on sampled data principles.

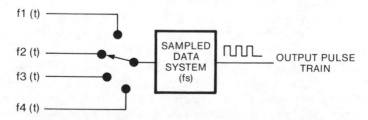

Fig. 4.4. Use of pulse modulation for multiplexing where $Fs \geq 2\ (B_1 + B_2 + B_3 + B_4)$.

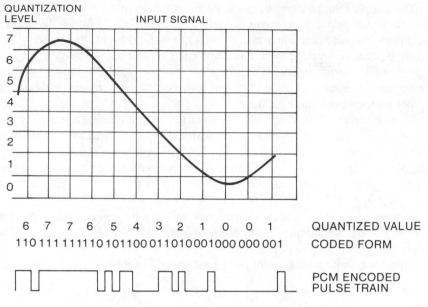

Fig.4.5. Steps in making a PCM encoded pulse train.

ulation (PCM). In this form of pulse modulation, sampled values of the input signals are first quantized into discrete amplitude levels, and then a fixed number of binary pulses, consisting of 0s and 1s, are generated for each sampled value. The number of pulses generated for each sampled value is related to the maximum number of quantization levels. The larger the number of quantization levels, the higher is the resulting fidelity or the lower is the quantization noise. See Fig. 4.5 for an illustration of the various steps that take place before the creation of a PCM pulse train.

According to the example shown in Fig. 4.5, the PCM bit rate is six (a factor of 2 implies a sampling rate of twice the bandwidth, and a factor of 3 implies the number of bits per sample) times the bandwidth of the input signal. The telephone industry has set a higher standard than that shown in Fig. 4.5. For a 4000-Hz voice signal, a 64,000-BPS PCM bit stream is realized, which implies 256 quantization levels. Therefore, for the industry standard, the PCM bit rate is sixteen (= 2∗8) times the bandwidth of the input signal.

A PCM encoded signal has a higher immunity to noise and nonlinear distortions that plague other modulated signals, such as FM, PPM, and other uncoded wideband systems. Furthermore, a PCM encoded signal can be completely regenerated at each repeated node, which results in simpler design for repeater stations than required for analog carrier-based systems. This also prevents accumulation of signal degradation through nonlinear distortion. Because the PCM technique allows an efficient multiplexing of several PCM bit streams, higher utilization of short-haul terrestrial and long-haul satellite links can be achieved.

The *delta modulation* (DM) scheme also employs PCM-like encoding. It is characterized by a single binary digit representing the difference between the present and the previously sampled values. Thus, the output bit stream simply conveys the polarity of the difference signal at each sample point.

See Fig. 4.6 for an illustration of a DM encoding process. A close examination of the figure shows that the output bit stream simply represents a derivative of the input signal at each sample point. A 1 represents an increment change above the previous sample, a 0 represents an decrement below the previous sample, and an alternating 0 and 1 represents no change in the signal value.

Because each sample in DM results in only one bit, the sampling rate equals the output bit rate. Therefore, the sampling rate must be selected according to the maximum slope and the dynamic range of the incoming waveform, instead of merely the waveform's bandwidth. Due to this reasoning, DM generally uses much less bandwidth than PCM for the same efficiency. Furthermore, its simplicity and ease of implementation make DM an excellent candidate for replacing PCM in the long run, despite the large existing PCM base all over the world.

No discussion of modulation techniques should be complete without describing the *bipolar* signals (see Fig. 4.7 for an illustration) that are replacing the rectangular pulse trains at baseband. A bipolar signal tends to concentrate the transmitted power below the signaling frequency in comparison with a rectangular pulse train.

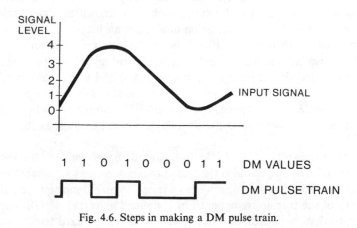

Fig. 4.6. Steps in making a DM pulse train.

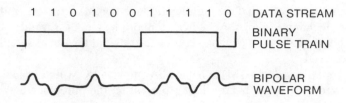

Fig. 4.7. A representation of a bipolar waveform corresponding to a digital data stream.

4.2.3.2 Multiplexing Techniques

Basically, there are three ways to multiplex several independent data streams:

1. space division multiplexing (SDM)
2. frequency division multiplexing (FDM)
3. time division multiplexing (TDM)

Space division multiplexing (SDM) is accomplished by simply bundling the individual physical links together to form a single, larger, physical cable. SDM is feasible only for a system consisting of a few short-haul links. Nevertheless, SDM is rather a simple technique requiring no processing of signals. The only precaution to be taken in SDM system design is regarding distortion resulting from crosstalk caused by wires packed close together. For such reasons, SDM techniques are widely employed in the design of local loop plants.

Frequency division multiplexing (FDM) combines several frequency spectrums used as sublinks to form a larger spectrum for subsequent transmission as a whole. At the receiver, the sublink separation is accomplished through filtering. Different modulations may be used in different parts of the total spectrum. To illustrate, AT&T's Dataphone digital system (DDS) derives the network trunks through an FDM-related technique known as *data under voice* (DUV). See Fig. 4.8 for an illustration of a scheme whereby a baseband digital waveform and modulated voice channels are multiplexed together.

FDM imposes a great many constraints on the design of the component modulated signals and the entire system. Because AM and FM involve double side bands, *Single Side Band* (SSB) techniques are used to eliminate one of the two side bands inside the component spectrums. Assignment of FDM channels must also be done according to the CCITT recommendations, as shown in Fig. 4.9.

The total bandwidth of the FDM link is made up of not only the individual bandwidths of sublinks, but also the guard bands necessary to prevent crosstalk among adjacent sublinks. Assuming N channels to be FD multiplexed, the total bandwidth of the transmitted spectrum is defined as $N*(B + G)$, where B is the bandwidth of each individual sublink, and G is the guard band required to separate the sublinks from one another.

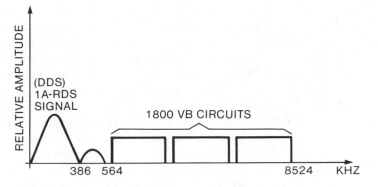

Fig. 4.8. DUV spectrum allocation in TD/TH microwave radio links for combining DDS and multiplexed VB circuits. Copyright (1977) Bell Telephone Laboratories. Reprinted by permission.

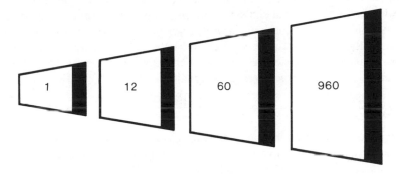

Fig. 4.9. Allocation of FDM channels according to CCITT recommendations.

FDM is quite suitable for multiplexing up to 960 voice channels that need to be transmitted over long distances or for long-haul applications. For this reason, FDM finds its greatest use in satellite communication. Nevertheless, FDM is generally more expensive than other multiplexing schemes used for long-haul applications.

Time division multiplexing (TDM) is achieved through combining several channels of binary information, resulting in a higher-rate channel of binary information. Consequently, pulse modulation (PM) and pulse code modulation (PCM) schemes are ideally suited for TDM. In practice, TDM is employed for short-haul applications. As mentioned earlier, a combination of PM or PCM, TDM, and a form of carrier modulation is generally employed for long-haul applications. The new fiber optics technology may make long-haul TDM economical within the next decade. Because TDM employs a fixed number of time slots, or channels, in each frame of time, some redundant bits must be added to the transmitted bit stream to achieve the various levels of synchronization required for demultiplexing at the receiver. Only through synchronization can one hope to derive the individual bit streams unequivocally.

TDM links are generally organized in a hierarchical fashion. One such hierarchy is illustrated in Fig. 4.10 for PCM-TDM.

The first PCM-TDM hierarchy is widely used in the United States. According to this scheme, 24 voice-grade channels are first pulse code modulated and then multiplexed together to form a T1 carrier at 1.544 MBPS, and then four such T1 carriers are TD multiplexed to form a T2 carrier, and so on. AT&T alone has a good deal of investment tied up in this type of PCM-TDM trunk.

The second hierarchy, which also obeys the CCITT recommendations, is widely used in Europe and Japan. This hierarchy involves 32 voice-grade channels at the lowest level of multiplexing to form a T1 carrier at 2.048 MBPS. It also employs an entirely different synchronization scheme from that used in North America. Consequently, it is not an easy matter to mix these two multiplexing techniques within the same system. Therefore, one can predict that these two schemes will continue to prosper in their birthplaces for some time to come, although the pressures of cheaper hardware, combined with the evolving bandwidth compression techniques, will make delta modulation (DM), TDM, and packetized voice prevail eventually.

4.2.3.3 Synchronization Techniques

Transmission of digital information through a network of digital switches requires special attention in the matters of timing and synchronization. They

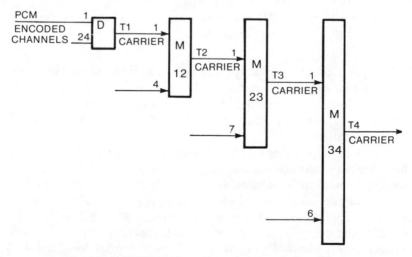

Fig. 4.10. PCM-TDM hierarchy employed in North America.

influence the choice of modulation and switching techniques employed in the network systems. Handling and transmission of analog signals, such as voice in CS systems, does not require any special considerations for timing and synchronization except for those cases that use satellite channels. CS systems designed for digital transmission require by far the most complex network-wide synchronization techniques. Clocks at each switch node must be synchronized at all times to avoid either a bit loss or a bit gain. Special control bits must be derived from the transmitted bit stream to achieve bit and frame synchronization.

To illustrate the PCM-TDM case, 1 bit from the 8-bit code is reserved to denote whether the particular link is on-hook or off-hook. After each sequence of 24 8-bit words, i.e., 192 bits, an additional bit, called the *framing bit*, is added to achieve frame synchronization at the receiver. Thus, each transmitted frame is a 193-bit-long frame, thereby resulting in an effective 193*8000 = 1.544-MBPS T1 carrier.

Several levels of synchronization are generally required in a CS network. These are as follows:

1. bit level synchronization
2. character level synchronization
3. word level synchronization
4. frame level synchronization
5. network level synchronization

Bit level synchronization is achieved through either highly accurate clocks or fully synchronized clocks at network nodes. Other forms of higher level synchronization are achieved through the addition of special bits, e.g., the longer bit in the teletypewriter-based system, or unique bit patterns within the transmitted bit stream.

Packet switching (PS) and message switching (MS) systems designed for digital data transmission are much simpler because they require only node-to-node synchronization. No network level synchronization is required. Use of store-and-forward and error control techniques at each network node simplifies other forms of synchronization significantly.

4.3 CONCEPTS OF SIGNALING

Signaling is a process of transferring information over a distance to control the setup of calls or sessions, to maintain the connection, to gather the billing or cost allocation data, and to terminate the calls or sessions. Basically there are two realms for signaling:

1. user/subscriber links, e.g., local loops in a public telephone network
2. network links or trunks

Signaling over user links implies an interaction between the subscriber node and the network node. Signaling over the network links implies interactions among network service nodes. Each type of network system may use special nomenclature to discuss these two types of signaling. For example, in public telephone systems, signaling over user links is generally called *local loop signaling,* and signaling over trunks may be called common channel interoffice signaling (CCIS).

The primary functions of user-link signaling are as follows:

1. initiate a request for a call
2. demarcate the start of control information
3. transmit the identity of the called node and in some cases the identity of the calling node when the link is shared
4. alert the called node
5. indicate the acceptance of the call or session
6. cease alerting the called, or in some cases the calling, node(s)
7. begin charging for the call
8. indicate the moment when the call is terminated by either the calling or the called subscriber
9. provide feedback to the originating node for one or more of the following items of information:
    a. call cannot be completed
    b. called node is being alerted
    c. called node is busy
    d. request for call is accepted
10. notify the requesting node, if it is a part of the service, the amount of bill

These functions are generally achieved in the public telephone system through DC signaling that is free of any high frequency carrier modulation— just making and breaking of an electrial connection using a DC battery and a switch.

The objective of a good network system design is to make the operation of the user node as simple and as universal as practical while achieving the above design goals. Signaling on the user link often results in appropriate signaling on network trunks. To understand this intimate relationship, one must first get a deeper insight into the various classes of control information, listed below:

1. Supervisory signals: These are used to initiate requests for service, to initiate and hold or release an established call, to request assistance from a network operator, to initiate or terminate billing, and to alert the user nodes.

2. Address signals: These convey information regarding the called and the calling nodes and all other network elements involved during the connection within the network.
3. Information signals: These fixed messages are used to (a) alert the users regarding the call progress, (b) inform the user about any difficulties being experienced by the system in completing the call, or (c) provide any advice made to the users for making another request for service using another approach.
4. Network management signals: These are used to control and manage the network by means of traffic routing, fault isolation, fault reporting and nodal recovery, and traffic protection.

Signaling on the network trunks is required if the called node is served by a separate terminating network node, different from the originating network node, or if network management signals are required. In some small systems, signaling is generally accomplished on the same network trunks that support the transmission of user intelligence. This form of signaling is often called the *in-band* signaling.

If separate links are employed for the transmission of control signals and user intelligence, the two types of links are sometimes called (1) *order wires, or control links,* and (2) *data links,* respectively.

Although a user control link is generally not shared by more than one user, a network of control trunks is shared by all the network users. Particular signaling schemes employed in a network system will, of course, depend upon the switching technology.

4.3.1 Signaling in CS Systems

Basically, there are two major applications for CS, namely voice and synchronous data switching. In both applications, the user goes off-hook, or lifts the receiver, receives a dial tone from the network service node, dials the called party's number, hears the ringing pulses provided by the serving network node, and finally begins conversing with the dialed terminal. Between those two moments, the common control equipment of the originating network node is busy recognizing the off-hook signal, sending the dial pulses to the calling node, receiving and analyzing the dial pulses, alerting the destination node in case it is free, making the connection, and connecting the ringing pulse generator to the calling node until the two terminals begin conversing with one another. The network node also begins the billing process at that time. After the call is finished, the connection is terminated, the call is logged on a permanent storage medium, and the billing process is finalized. In case two or more network nodes are involved in call setup, some form of signaling needs to be accomplished on network trunks.

Most of the older telephone systems employ two-state DC signaling on both user links and interoffice trunks. Rotary telephones generate off-hook and on-hook signals and send address signals in the form of dial pulsing. Each dialed digit results in an equal number of pulses generated at the rate of about 10 pulses per second. Each dialed digit is separated by a relatively long off-hook interval, the length of which depends on how fast the user can rewind and release the dial.

Some modern telephones have a dual-tone multifrequency (DTMF) signaling capability. DTMF uses a two-group code in which each signal is represented by selecting one frequency from each of the two mutually exclusive groups of four. DTMF is still accomplished over two-wire loops, however.

For interoffice signaling over four-wire trunks, a variation of DTMF called *multifrequency* (MF) is generally employed. Decimal digits and five auxiliary signals are each represented by selecting two frequencies out of a group of six frequencies. Maximum transmission rates are about 10 digits per second for either DTMF and MF and about 1 digit per second for dial pulsing. In some private networks, DTMF is also employed for interoffice signaling. The above forms of signaling occur on a *per-channel basis,* whereby signaling takes place first on the end-to-end connection before the called party answers.

A new form of interoffice signaling, called *common channel interoffice signaling,* (CCIS) has been developed by AT&T for use in its public telephone system. The principle of CCIS is to transmit all the signaling information pertaining to a group of voice trunks over a separate, dedicated network consisting of data links connecting switching nodes and special service nodes called *signal transfer points* (STPs). CCIS is particularly attractive for use among an extremely large number of SPC exchanges. CCIS permits a great deal of reduction in call setup times, not only by its inherent speed, but also by signaling the next office in the path before the node has finished switching. CCIS also provides much flexibility and economy for a large public network characterized by a good deal of signaling volume. CCIS has also allowed the introduction of new control signals. CCIS is generally not required for small private networks with three or four nodes. The paths are quite short and do not require any large investment in an overlayed CCIS network.

4.3.2 Signaling in MS Systems

In MS systems, the control information is transmitted as an envelope around each message. The beginning portion of the envelope is called the *header,* and the trailing part of the message is called the *ender.* See Chapter 3 for a description of the components of a message header and ender.

4.3.3 Signaling in a PS System

In packet-switched systems, the control signals are transmitted along with each packet. See the Appendix for a description of the various fields of different types of packets.

4.3.4 Challenges Facing Signaling

Several challenges face the system scientists and designers of PS systems.

Intersystem Compatibility: With the advent of digital and SPC switches, intersystem compatibility poses a major challenge to designers of network systems. Public telephone networks of many countries have overcome this challenge through the help of international standards. Compatibility among several public data networks is a problem at present. Several international standards organizations are helping develop new standard protocols in that area. The situation in the fields of DDP and DDBM is not good because each vendor is inventing a unique panacea for the already confused user community.

Increased Speed of Signaling: The trend toward shorter and shorter call setup times will continue. DTMF, MF, and CCIS for the CS telephone systems are good examples. Fast CS techniques for data communication are in the offing.

Post Dialing Delay Minimization: This is an important parameter for designing a system with minimum time delay between the last digit dialed and the connection made.

Fully Shared Signaling Networks: Greater diversity of control signals will continue to share a common control network. As the number of services provided to the users are bound to increase, a need to develop a network shared by a variety of data and control signals is certain to arise. Consequently, this trend will favor PS and MS technologies.

4.4 FUTURE TRENDS

Trends to transmit information at a faster rate and lower cost per bit will continue. Most transmissions will continue to use the existing terrestrial links in their paths, and benefits of new transmission media, such as optical fibers and satellites, will surface during the next five years.

Although satellites offer distance-independent tariffs, the disadvantages of large two-way transmission delays and the possibilities of international sabotage, via eavesdropping, jamming, or destruction, should pose serious considerations for designers of private networks for large corporations.

Optical fibers could in the near future provide cheap, reliable, and secure transmission facilities for most large private networks.

Several new public offerings, such as private line DDS, switched DDS, ACS, Telenet, Tymnet, and SBS, are bound to provide low-cost and fast-connect services to an increasing number of users.

Chapter 5
Concepts of Multilevel, Iterative Modeling, Analysis, and Design

5.1 INTRODUCTORY REMARKS

The availability of cheap computing elements and the need for faster interchange of messages among locations of a large airline resulted in the development of the first commercially available SPC message switch in 1962. Before that epoch, the computer had mainly served as a stand-alone DP node. The first MSS provided an economical interchange of messages among several hundred teletypewriter terminals. Such a system enabled the airlines to provide excellent service to airline passengers and also to acquire a position of leadership in the area of rapid communication—a position it has not yet relinquished.

The single MS node of early network systems formed a significant component of the entire system cost, which also consisted of the costs of communication facilities and data terminals. The price of the MS node was high because of the high costs of the large core storage required for transient message buffers and the large, redundant secondary storage required for long-term message retention for later retrievals. Costs of the MS nodes were high because of the heavy manpower required to develop the many hardware and software modules necessary to satisfy the special user requirements, such as handling of unique message formats and headers, unique code translations, stringent traffic protection, and elaborate recovery procedures. These were difficult problems.

Much has happened since 1962, however. The dramatic reduction in hardware costs, the availability of high-level languages for software development and management, and a good deal of progress in standards are enabling an accelerating development of distributed systems consisting of many network service nodes interconnected. Some of the network nodes boast of novel computer architectures with such features as shared memories, multiprocessor architectures, and multilayered/structured software. These advances in the design of SPC network nodes have penetrated the fields of not only the traditional CS systems, but also many exotic PS, DDP, and DDBM systems.

The task of developing efficient and meaningful models for detailed system analysis and design has again become challenging and exciting. The next paragraphs present concepts of multilevel, iterative modeling, system analysis, and design.

5.2 CONCEPTS OF MULTILEVEL, ITERATIVE MODELING

Chapter 1 introduced some basic nodal and network concepts. Using such concepts, one can realize some simple network systems. Using the principle of superimposition, one can also realize some very complex network systems that offer myriads of services, such as voice switching, DP, MS, and DBM.

Analysis and design of all network systems require detailed modeling of user requirements and several candidate solutions. The relationship between modeling and system analysis and design is illustrated in Fig. 5.1.

There are basically two approaches in modeling. These are (1) to start with a microscopic model and iteratively simplify it until the required level of modeling is achieved and (2) to start with a highly simplistic macrolevel model and then continue adding complexity until the desired level of modeling is obtained. The former approach is known as the *bottom-up* approach, and the second approach is known as the *top-down* approach.

A microscopic model of even a single node consisting of a computer is almost impossible to construct. The difficulties exist because the number of logical states resulting from all the combinations of inputs and outputs, some of which act as inputs at later times, may exceed all the protons in the entire universe. Consequently, we suggest avoiding the bottom-up approach. Unfortunately, the bottom-up approach is still widely employed, the only difference being that the model begins with logic elements, such as gates and interconnect wires, etc. In many cases, important facts dealing with the various services provided, paths followed by the various transactions, performance attributes, etc. are completely ignored. Instead, hundreds of pages devoted to trivia are not uncommon.

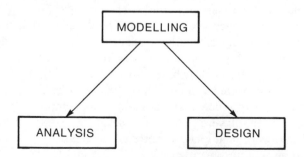

Fig. 5.1. Relationship among modeling, analysis, and design of network systems.

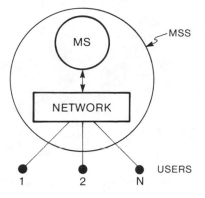

Fig. 5.2. A high-level model of an MSS.

Instead, the top-down modeling approach apppears as the most practical and logical. Experience shows that this approach requires the fewest iterations to achieve the desired level of modeling needed for a meaningful system analysis and design. Such an approach is the quickest way to uncover the critical system resources that limit system performance. The concept of multilevel, iterative modeling naturally fits most systems that also exhibit multilevel and hierarchical organizations. A concept as complicated-looking as multilevel, iterative modeling can be understood only in terms of some useful examples.

Consider, for example, a network system consisting of a single MS node and many user terminals connected to the MS node according to the SCMD topology. A simplistic, top-level model is shown in Fig. 5.2. A description of such a system can run like this: a message is received from the ith user; it is stored on a reliable, redundant storage; when the user link associated with the jth destination node is free, the message is sent; the message is retained for some time for later retrieval if required; the system is capable of handling a specified throughput during a peak period, with each message encountering a maximum delay through the MS node; the costs of MS node, transmission facilities, and terminals are specified.

In case the network cost is much higher than the costs for other subsystems, one may wish to expand on the next-level model of the network. The result may appear as shown in Fig. 5.3, which shows that the network consists of four communication links to which 22 user nodes are connected according to the SCMD topology (see Chapter 2 for details). The process of assigning the various user nodes to particular links is an integral part of the design process that will be discussed in Section III.

Analysis of the model defined in Fig. 5.3 may result in the need to apply the

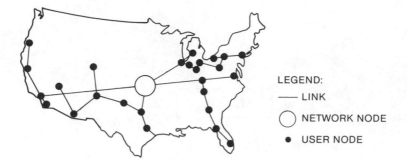

Fig. 5.3. A second-level, iterative model of the network.

multilevel, iterative modeling approach. In the case where analysis indicates that the network resources are lightly loaded and it is the MS node that is the critical element, then the next level would be of the MS node, as shown in Fig. 5.4. The model implies a local network of nodal resources, such as CPU, core memory, disk files (DFs), and magnetic tapes (MTs). Using the system analysis techniques, one can analyze the utilization of every resource shown in Fig. 5.4. Let us assume that the disk files provide only 2 peak hours of traffic retention. This may be a violation of the statement-of-work (SOW), which required 24 peak hours of traffic retention. This problem is easy to fix, however. One can simply add additional spindles of disks to the existing DF controllers.

In case an excessive demand for either traffic buffers or CPU time is suspected, the job of obtaining next level of models becomes more difficult. Both the operating systems and the application software modules need to be studied and effective models built. A close analysis of these models may pinpoint the problem. In case more traffic buffers are needed, one could attach additional core storage if permitted. In the case where the CPU is excessively loaded, it is difficult to replace the slower computer with a faster one. The new computer may use another language, which will require reprogramming of all the software—an extremely expensive proposition. One could refine some of the software modules that were inefficiently coded, but this method is generally incapable of providing sufficient improvement for the effort involved.

Another solution to the above problem may lie in off-loading some of the CPU tasks to minicomputer-controlled communication control units (CCUs) as shown in Fig. 5.5. A CCU performs many of the functions originally executed by the main CPU. A CCU sends polls and calls to user nodes at the command from the main CPU. A CCU also receives contiguous messages, divides these into segments, and forwards them to the main CPU. A reverse process takes place during message transmissions. This technique, which

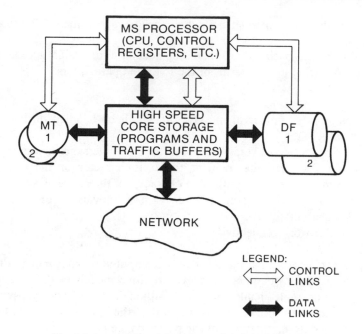

Fig. 5.4. A second-level, iterative model of the MS node.

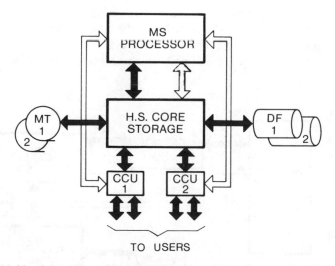

Fig. 5.5. A third-level, iterative model of the MS node consisting of communication control units (CCUs).

implies distributed processing, can reduce the load on the main CPU to a practical level.

The above-mentioned models should be adequate for evaluating the performance of an MS system in terms of the following parameters:

1. cost
2. throughput—number of messages that can be handled during a peak period
3. grade of service—average response time per message measured as the duration between the moment the last character of the message is received and the moment the first character of the message is transmitted
4. quality of service—average recovery times from various forms of failures and probability of data loss
5. overall network connectivity

If these performance parameters can be computed without much difficulty, there is no need for obtaining next-level iterative models of the MS system. The previous example should show that, although the network subsystem of the MS system may cost more than the rest of the system, it is the MS node that generally determines many of the performance parameters.

Another example dealing with a modern CS node should be useful to the reader. A second-level iterative model of an SPC-CS node is illustrated in Fig. 5.6, which shows a local network of a call processor, core memory, common control equipment, magnetic tape, and a switch module.

The common control subsystem consists of the control and supervisory hardware units and storage buffers for holding the dial pulses. The above common control subsystem enables the call processor to recognize the off-hook condi-

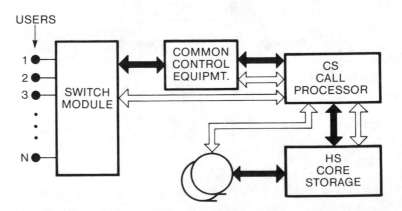

Fig. 5.6. A second-level, iterative model of a CS node.

tion, send the invitation-to-dial tone, make the connection between the originating and destination nodes through the switch module, etc. Because the time spent in the signaling state is quite small compared with the call duration, it is a general practice to share this common control subsystem among all the subscribers that are terminated directly to the switch module.

Analysis of the CS node presents some unique aspects when analyzing the performance of the common control and the switch subsystems; these will be discussed in Section II. A system consisting of many CS nodes also presents some unique problems for analysis and design; These will also be discussed in the next two sections.

Multilevel models of a PS node are almost identical to the MS node, except that large disk files are missing from them. Distributed PS systems also employ similar network topologies as in distributed MS systems. Similarly, multilevel, iterative models of the DDP and DDBM systems can be constructed for system analysis and design. The methodology is the same, only the details differ. Any effort spent on obtaining such models pays for itself—even in the form of providing utmost clarity of the network.

The above methodology will be used later in Chapter 7 to develop meaningful models of some well-known network systems.

5.3 CONCEPTS OF SYSTEM ANALYSIS AND DESIGN

Planning a cost-effective network system requires the execution of several well-defined tasks, as illustrated in Fig. 5.7.

To some readers, many of the milestones listed in Fig. 5.7 may appear either obvious or wishful. Nonetheless, experience shows that a lack of a clear methodology, such as shown in Fig. 5.7, generally results in a system that fails to meet either the user's specifications or the growing needs of the customer within a few years. A failure to implement such a methodology has resulted in many heartaches, user dissatisfactions, and even multimillion dollar lawsuits.

Modeling the existing environments is generally ignored in favor of expediency. If one doesn't understand the existing environments, it is impossible to justify the new system in the first place and then to make a smooth migration to the new system. Too often, it is the current environments that provide pertinent traffic data which must be analyzed to assess the user's true requirements.

Once the models of existing environments are complete, it implies that one is in possession of (1) all pertinent data bases concerning customer vehicles (CVs) and communication facilities, (2) raw traffic data, and (3) user specifications for performance. Based on this data, one can formally specify the user's requirements in terms of (1) communities of interest, (2) distribution of peak periods at various locations, (3) peak period traffic intensities at each CV,

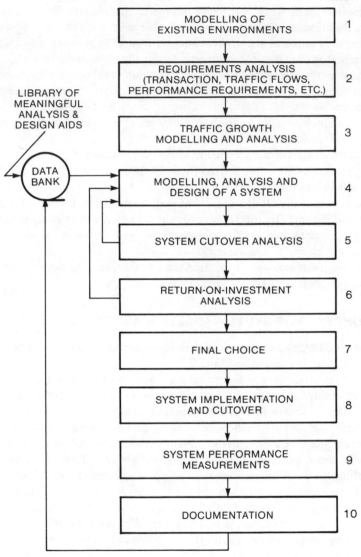

Fig. 5.7. Major tasks executed during the life cycle of a network system.

and (4) existing costs for each completed transaction. If these analyses are not executed, one will always be in the dark about the justifications for the new network. In case the customer has no existing network from which one can derive all the raw data for requirement analysis, a greater effort is required. In any case, one must spend this front-end money, probably less than $50 thousand, to derive all the benefits of the new network, possibly saving millions of dollars over the life of the new network system.

The user's cooperation is also required in making valid models for traffic growth for the period equaling the estimated life of the network system. Without the direct involvement of the customer's top management, this effort is generally meaningless. This effort is essential if one doesn't want the network system to become obsolete within two or three years.

The task of modeling, analysis, and design of all candidate solutions for finding the best solution that meets the user's needs at the lowest cost may be the most time-consuming if done manually. The availability of time-tested and meaningful computer design aids can make this task easy, although experience has shown that most of these design aids are employed in an iterative manner, with the human mind always in control of what is happening, what is expected, and how valid are the final results. Figure 5.7 illustrates many such iterations.

All the steps required to phase out the old system and cut over the new network system must be carefully planned. The original CV data base should come in handy. The challenge lies in avoiding any surprises.

A return-on-investment (ROI) analysis can now be performed. The results will prove the justification of the new network system. Without such an analysis, the job of selling the new system to the top management will remain difficult, if not impossible.

Based upon all the results obtained thus far and all the feedback received from the customer, the time is now ripe to make a final decision about the solution that is "acceptable" to all the parties concerned.

The next task deals with system implementation and cutover, and it is executed by the program manager and his team. They apply a methodology identical to the one described above, except that their design aids consist of scheduling controls and other management tools.

A very important task that is frequently bypassed deals with the measurement of the system's performance. Without this task, one will never know how close the designed system is to meeting the user's requirements. The results can also show the vendor how to fix any possible problems found during measurements, before they are later discovered by the user. The results should also be properly documented. Without a proper documentation of the test results, the entire task of system planning remains unfinished.

The highlight of the methodology being discussed deals with the process by which all the available analytical and design aids are constantly improved through feedback. Of all the tasks listed in Fig. 5.7, the task of system performance measurement stands out as the most critical one.

The tasks of system modeling, analysis, and design require the most expertise of system scientists. They generally follow the methodology shown in Fig. 5.8.

The main idea behind the methodology of Fig. 5.8 is to enumerate the critical resources in a network system, decide upon the related design parameters for such resources, analyze the utilization of such resources, and, based upon these analyses performed recursively, select the optimum system design. Such an approach can be applied to the entire system or any subsystem. A technique used for displaying the utilization of various critical resources is illustrated in Fig. 5.9. All those resources that show high utilization factors should be con-

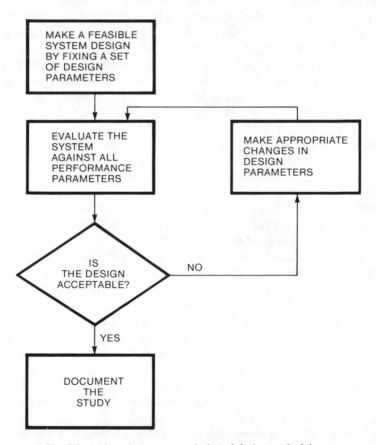

Fig. 5.8. An iterative system analysis and design methodology.

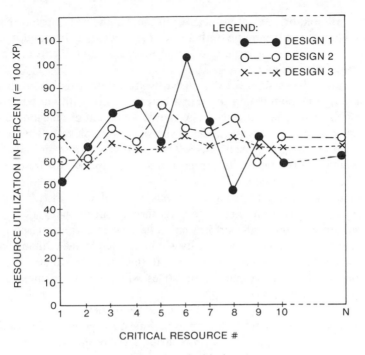

Fig. 5.9. Utilization of critical resources.

sidered critical to performance and subjected to further analysis. There are applications, however, where a resource may be 90 percent utilized, but does not cause any violation of the user's specifications. In general, all design parameters affecting every critical performance requirements should be considered critical.

In case the high utilization of a resource does result in an unacceptable level of system performance, either the resource-related design parameters may be altered until the desired performance is achieved or the entire resource may be replaced with a more efficient one.

5.4 FUTURE TRENDS

System analysis and design methodologies as discussed in the previous paragraphs may appear rather obvious to many readers. We believe, however, that it is the lack of "an approach" that kills the system and not the lack of "one given approach." Minor differences among the several proven methodologies are insignificant for a successful system design. It is the adherence to a proven, structured methodology that counts. Furthermore, the design of large network systems will require an intensive use of the "high-level" structured design methodology at the beginning. Otherwise, a good deal of time and money will be spent in correcting a large number of unexpected problems using the so-called *tweeking* method.

A continual decrease in the cost of hardware elements is bound to simplify system design by eliminating to a great extent the criticality of hardware elements. This trend will also encourage the development of distributed systems with many identical network nodes dispersed geographically wherever most effective in reducing the system costs. This trend should also simplify the software, which had become quite complex in an attempt to squeeze more out of critical hardware subsystems.

Availability of inexpensive logic elements will enable the distribution of special purpose hardware and firmware units throughout the network.

Each hardware unit will perform only one task at a time. Based upon the results of processing, the output results will be queued to one of many hardware units in the system for later execution. If this trend continues, the task of designing an optimum system or its nodes will probably reduce to that of designing an optimum network.

Use of automated analysis and design aids will continue to accelerate with time. Interactive techniques will tend to become quite popular. The availability of cheap personal computers and timesharing services through tariffed PS networks will help the widespread use of sophisticated analysis and design tools in our daily lives.

The availability of cheap microprocessor-controlled and easy to use performance measurement equipment should also encourage the widespread use of performance validation techniques. An indirect benefit of these new performance measurement tools will be the development of efficient and meaningful analytical and design aids.

Chapter 6
Concepts of System Performance

6.1 INTRODUCTORY REMARKS

The subject of system performance is still new, and consequently there is still no general agreement on how to describe the performance of a network system. Although there are some accepted notions of performance for some traditional network systems, such as public telephone systems, international organizations are still engaged in developing valid performance parameters and standards for the emerging public network systems.

Fortunately, enough experience with network systems now exists to help a serious system analyst develop useful concepts required for describing system performance. Basically, there are two types of systems with special performance requirements:

1. public network systems, such as the public telephone networks
2. private network systems developed to satisfy only the unique needs of the particular user. Corporate voice or data networks fall into this category

In general, the public networks have more stringent performance requirements than their private counterparts. Standards set by FCC and CCITT have a great deal to do with the difference. Private network systems are not required to obey such standards.

Performance of a network-based system can be characterized in terms of the following criteria:

1. system cost and its distribution among critical subsystems
2. system throughput measured in terms of messages, calls, transactions, sessions, and some mixes of these handled per unit of time
3. quality of service (QOS) criteria
4. grade of service (GOS) criteria
5. network connectivity

The cost criterion is self-evident. The QOS criteria deal with several subjective aspects of performance, such as speech intelligibility, raw bit error rates (BERs), system reliability or availability, man-machine interfaces, etc. The

GOS criteria deal with system degradation resulting from insufficiently provided network resources, as opposed to failed resources, during peak periods of traffic. Network connectivity specifies the number of user nodes that can be served by the network system. The following paragraphs will attempt to define the above mentioned performance criteria in some detail.

6.2 COST CRITERION

The cost criterion remains one of the most critical performance parameters despite a widespread neglect of it. Only when a system becomes affordable to users, does it become commonplace. The public telephone system is an excellent example of this. Nevertheless, when the telephone company tried to sell the idea of a telephone with pictures in the late sixties, the public rejected it on the basis of cost. DDP systems are here to stay, as they allow the distribution of cheap computing power where it does the most good. Geographically distributed networks with many network nodes are becoming commonplace because they bring service nodes closer to the various communities of users, and, in doing so, the cost of transmission facilities, a major portion of all network systems, is reduced significantly. The cost criterion has two aspects:

1. costs as seen by the users
2. costs as seen by the utility company

To illustrate, a telephone system can be characterized by (1) the telephone bill resulting from the local and long-distance use of the telephone and (2) huge investments in the entire system owned by the utility company. This consists of start-up costs, constant additions and improvements, and round-the-clock maintenance of the entire system. Using some sophisticated accounting procedures, one can derive an equivalent monthly bill for the entire system.

Although the costs incurred by the subscribers are clear-cut, there is a great deal of political maneuvering among the public utility commissions and the utility companies before the final rates are fixed.

For similar reasons, the costs of a private network are hard to determine. Most communication and DP managers still dream of the day when they can find ways to allocate the true costs to each and every user of the network and, in the process, discover the day-to-day, bottom-line costs of the network. At present, everyone is banking on the SPC network systems to perform the miracle soon. What is needed, however, is a clear-cut methodology.

Using the multilevel, iterative modeling approach, one should first break the system down into large but distinct components. To illustrate, a large network system can be partitioned into the communication network and the nodal hardware. Because the cost of the communication network is generally determined by the monthly lease cost of all the facilities, and because it forms about 70 to 80 percent of the total system costs, one gets a good start at finding the system costs.

The costs of the nodal hardware should be combined with the costs of sites, maintenance, and support. By projecting such costs over the life of the system, and considering the depreciation allowances and investment tax credits, it is possible to obtain an equivalent monthly charge for all the nodal hardware. On the other hand, if the switching or DP services are also leased from the specialized or common carrier, the task of computing the monthly costs of nodal hardware is greatly simplified.

System costs can be further divided among smaller components or subsystems by the use of next-level iterative models of the network service nodes. One may be forced to use such facts as year of CPU introduction, cost-per-bit data for the various types of memories or storages, etc.

If the system costs are displayed in a manner similar to the one discussed above, network planning and vendor selection become extremely straightforward. Of course, the additional performance criteria, as discussed in the following paragraphs, cannot be ignored.

6.3 SYSTEM THROUGHPUT CRITERIA

System throughput is also an important measure for system performance, and it directly influences the cost per transaction. This criterion varies slightly from the one discussed earlier, depending upon the type of switching technology or the particular application of the network system.

6.3.1 Throughput of a CS System

The following parameters define the system throughputs:

1. maximum number of arriving calls that can be handled during an average second of a busy hour
2. maximum number of calls that are concurrently being handled within the system during a busy hour

6.3.2 Throughputs of PS, MS, DDP, and DDBM Systems

The following parameters define the system throughput:

1. maximum number of input packets or messages that can be handled during an average second of a peak hour. It is assumed that all the resulting input and output processes are combined for each incoming packet or message

2. maximum number of transactions that can be handled by all the DP/ DBM nodes in the network during an average second of a peak hour. Again, each input transaction may result in secondary input and output messages that must also be handled
3. maximum number of sessions that can be handled by the system during a peak hour

6.4 QUALITY OF SERVICE (QOS) CRITERIA

Nonlinear signal distortion, transmission loss, random noise, and random component—hardware or software—failures affect the quality of transmission and service in ways different from those caused by contention of operational system resources.

6.4.1 Effects of Distortion

QOS, in terms of protection against crosstalk in analog systems, is specified as percentage of transmitted power lost. To illustrate, in public telephone systems it is defined by the percentage of power lost due to crosstalk on the various types of network trunks.

QOS, in terms of distortion caused by frequency shift resulting from differences in the carrier generators, is specified by the tolerated differences in Hertz (e.g., + 2Hz).

QOS, in terms of protection against echo distortion and loss, whether planned or not, is specified in terms of (1) transmission loss and via net loss (VNL) plans adopted for each type of network link and path and (2) availability of echo suppressors and their dynamic ranges.

The effects of distortion, attenuation or loss, and impulsive noise can also be represented by curves obtained through a series of subjective tests. These curves relate acoustic-to-acoustic loudness loss, in decibels (DB), to noise level, as measured at the end terminal and as defined as decibels relative to reference noise (typically at 10^{-12} watts).

The above measures apply to CS systems using analog transmission techniques for voice applications. Distortion will affect the bit error rate (BER) of a CS system used for data transmission achieved through the use of analog modulation techniques.

6.4.2 Effects of Noise

BER will also be affected by the additive random noise and impulsive random noise present everywhere in the network employed for data transmission. Specification of BER and mean-time-between-error bursts (MTBEB) should be sufficient for the specification of system's protection against noise for most applications.

Effects of distortion in a network system employing digital transmission techniques are minimum due to the nature of transmission. The effects of additive random and impulsive noises will remain significant.

6.4.3 Effects of Random Component Failures

A loss of degradation of service caused by random component failures can be specified as follows:

1. MTB major failures (MTBMF) of the entire network caused by one or more malfunctions in the system
2. MTB nodal failures (MTBNF) of any one network node caused by one or more hardware or software malfunctions within the node
3. MTB nodal subsystem failures (MTBSF) of any one nodal subsystem causing a loss of service to a specified number of subscribers. The specified number is generally related to modularity employed in the nodal hardware or software design

Not only must the above-mentioned MTBFs be specified to assess the QOS of the network system, but also the average duration of each failure.

6.5 GRADE OF SERVICE (GOS) CRITERIA

The GOS criteria deal with the degradation in service caused by contention for critical resources, assuming that all the resources are functioning properly. GOS criteria differ for CS, MS, PS, DDP, and DDBM systems.

6.5.1 GOS for Circuit-Switched Systems

GOS for a CS system can be specified in terms of the following design parameters:

1. Statistical distribution of system response time measured as the duration between the moment the user goes off-hook and the moment the user hears the dial tone that invites the user to dial the address digits. System response time is characterized by a probability distribution caused by the contention for common control equipment among the requests for service

arriving randomly. Because a detailed specification of the distribution is difficult to state, only the first two moments are generally specified, as follows: (a) mean response time and (b) 90 percentile value of response time, defined as the value of response time that is not exceeded 90 percent of the time. Similar considerations apply to the system response times during the disconnect phase. Some private CS systems specify 99 percentile values for such response times.

2. Statistical distribution of the connection time between the moment the last digit is dialed and the moment the hard connection between the originating and destination nodes is made through the switch module. Again, a practical way to specify this parameter is to define the mean and 90 percentile values for connection times.

3. Statistical distribution of the call setup time, defined as the sum of the above two items and the average times to dial the digits and execute signaling wherever necessary. Again, the mean and 90 percentile values of connection time are specified.

4. Probability of a call loss is caused by the unavailability of the common control equipment at the originating switching node. It is denoted by B.XX or P.XX, representing XX percent of first-call attempts being blocked, computed according to the Erlang-B or Poisson formula, respectively.

6.5.2 GOS of Packet-Switched Systems

Although there are yet no accepted standards for specifying the GOS of PS systems, the following suggestions should be useful for planning PS network systems:

1. Distribution of switching time spent per packet inside each type of PS node. Packet switching time is measured as the elapsed time between the moment the last bit, or character in some systems, of the packet is received and the moment the first bit of the same packet is transmitted toward the destination node on a network trunk. The mean and the 90 percentile values should be sufficient to specify the distribution.

2. Distribution of the call, or session, setup time, measured as the elapsed time from the moment the last character of the call setup packet is transmitted by the packet mode terminal and the moment the first character of the acknowledgment packet is received by the originating packet mode terminal (PMT). The mean and the 90 percentile values of call setup times should be specified.

3. Distribution of the call disconnect time is specified in a manner similar to that for call setup time.

6.5.3 GOS of Message-Switched Systems

As MS systems are primarily used by private corporations, no acceptable standards for GOS are yet available. The following criteria are suggested for planning a MS system:

1. Mean and 90 percentile values of the message switch time, measured as the moment the last character of a message is received in the MS node and the moment the first character of the same message is transmitted on the output link toward the destination user terminal. This time is the sum of input processing of incoming segments, editing of the message, resulting in a separation of header and data portions, routing analysis for finding the destination, queuing of the message for a particular output link, storing of the message on a secondary storage device—segment by segment, retrieval of the message, and outputting of the first segment. In general, the queuing time spent on waiting for the output link to become free is not included because this time is only a function of the network subsystem.
2. Average value of the message retention time provided by the MS node. Its value is determined by the average message length, traffic load distribution throughout the day, data structure employed for storage, and the secondary storage available for traffic retention.

6.5.4 GOS of DDP and DDBM Systems

The GOS of DDP and DDBM systems can be defined by the mean and the 90 percentile values of the system response time, measured as the elapsed time between the moment the last character of the input request is transmitted and the moment the first character of the output is received by the user. The concept dealing with the GOS of DDP and DDBM systems is relatively new to the industry. The number of parameters required to specify the GOS of such systems may grow in the future, but this suggested parameter should suffice for the present.

6.6 NETWORK CONNECTIVITY CRITERION

Most network systems are also judged by the number of subscribers that can be directly serviced as on-net subscribers.

In CS systems, the number of user links and the number of subscribers served are usually identical. The total system connectivity will be determined by the type of switch module used in network nodes and the number of network nodes employed in the system.

Connectivity of PS and MS systems is a function of the number of subscriber links and the number of user nodes serviced by each subscriber link. The reader should recall that PS and MS systems generally employ the MCMD network topology.

For some network systems, e.g., the PABX-based system, network connectivity can become an overriding performance criterion. Other criteria, such as cost, QOS, and GOS, become of secondary importance.

6.7 FUTURE TRENDS

We hope that, during the next few years, several organizations, such as the International Standards Organization (ISO) and the Consultative Committee for International Telephone and Telecommunication (CCITT), will succeed in developing recommendations for public data networks.

The advent of SPC nodes and digital transmission switching or transmission techniques in the design of CS systems will require some revisions in the existing international standards of performance. We also expect that many international organizations concerned with DDP and DDBM systems will begin considering recommendations for system performance. There is bound to be a great deal of resistance to standards in areas that have been historically influenced by a few large vendors.

Interconnection, or interfacing, of diverse public networks will continue receiving the attention of such organizations as ISO and CCITT as long as component networks are architecturally different.

Specifications and recommendations for performance of network systems are meaningless unless and until capabilities for measuring the performance parameters are available. Performance measurements for a network system are far more difficult than for a system with only one node. Very little experience exists in the field of designing hypotheses and testing them in the network environments.

Chapter 7
Models of Some Well-known Network Systems

7.1 INTRODUCTORY REMARKS

The objectives of the previous chapters were to introduce to the reader all the basic concepts required to model and understand the behavior of any network system. The beginning chapters presented concepts dealing with network elements and architectural considerations. The later chapters showed the concepts of multilevel iterative modeling to be prerequisites for analyzing and designing a network system. We believe the concepts of multilevel, iterative modeling are essential for the total network planning task.

Before tackling the difficult subjects of system analysis and design, it should be highly instructive to apply the concepts of the previous chapters and obtain clear and concise models of some well-known network systems. CS, PS, and MS technologies provide a good source of operating systems. DDP and DDBM technologies are still in the early stages of development. Nonetheless, there are several computer network architectures and data base systems that employ some form of physical dispersion of computers and data elements.

These exercises will not only prove the usefulness of the methodology presented in this book, but will also produce a wealth of network-system-related data in a form ideal for constant future reference by the reader engaged in this fast-growing field.

An attempt will be made to discuss the following items of each system:

1. an application summary
2. basic network topology
3. identification scheme employed
4. user's interfaces
5. traffic statistics
6. traffic flows and routing schemes employed
7. transmission and signaling techniques
8. a useful model of a network node
9. performance parameters
10. concluding remarks

7.2 CIRCUIT-SWITCHED (CS) SYSTEMS

Some well-known examples of CS systems are as follows:

1. Bell's public telephone system (PTS)
2. ITT's public switched voice network
3. Royal Netherlands Air Force's private network
4. an airline's private network
5. Bell's DDS and DSDS

7.2.1 Bell's PTS

AT&T's direct distance dialing (DDD) network is probably the most complex and the costliest network system in the world. The network has been evolving since 1878 when the first manual switchboard was installed in New Haven, Connecticut. The first automatic, step-by-step Strowger switch was installed in 1892 in La Porte, Indiana. The electromechanical crossbar type switch came later, and these are still being installed along with digital switches. As a result, PTS has some unique attributes that have helped it to provide an excellent service for a long time.

7.2.1.1 An Application Summary

The Bell System provides public telephone service, also known as *message tele-communications service* (MTS), among subscribers located at private residences, business premises, and coin-operated public telephone booths scattered throughout the continental United States. The service makes use of the individual subscriber lines and includes both local and long distance dialing services.

7.2.1.2 Network Topology

The Bell System consists of subscriber loops, network trunks, and many varieties of CS nodes that provide a hierarchical switching function, as described below and as shown in Fig. 7.1:

1. Class 5 central office (CO) switch node acts as an end office (EO) for subscriber line terminations. Such COs usually employ the electromechanical crossbar switches.
2. Class 4 switch node acts as a toll center (TC) and provides a tandem service for making any long distance connections and taking care of toll charges and billing.

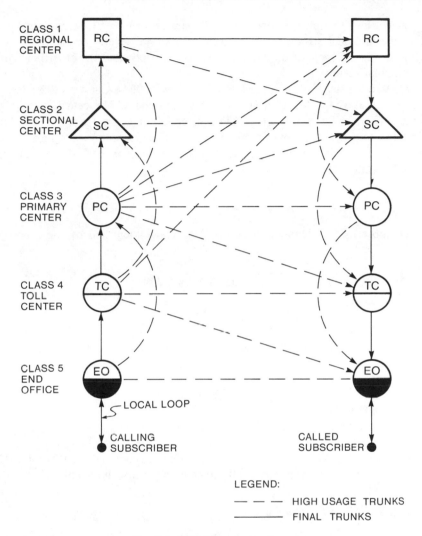

Fig. 7.1. PTS network topology.

3. Class 3 switch node acts as a primary center (PC) and provides tandem routing capabilities.
4. Class 2 switch node acts as a sectional center (SC) and provides high-level, tandem routing functions.
5. Class 1 switch node acts as a regional center (RC) and provides the highest level, tandem routing functions.

Thus, the PTS network topology, as illustrated in Fig. 7.1, represents a five-level hierarchical structure. The figure also shows several levels of network trunks, some of them of the high-usage (HU) variety, and the other belonging to the final variety.

A 1976 census (Ref. 2) shows that there were 9944 Class 5, 802 Class 4, 233 Class 3, 67 Class 2, and 10 Class 1 switch nodes. The census also shows that only 822 of Class 5, 21 of Class 4, and 2 of Class 3 are of SPC type switches that may employ digital switching. The remaining nodes are of the hardwired variety that employ either the old Strowger or the EM crossbar type switching modules.

7.2.1.3 Identification Scheme

Each subscriber's telephone in North America is identified by the following code:

$$(NPX)(NNX)(XXXX)$$

or

(Area code)(end office No.)(subscriber link No.)

where

$N =$ any of the 8 decimal values 2 through 9
$P =$ either 0 or 1
$X =$ any of the 10 decimal values 0 through 9

Consequently, the above numbering plan can accommodate at most 1.024 billion subscribers, if and only if all the codes are fully and evenly filled.

7.2.1.4 User's Interfaces

When the user is ready to make a call to another subscriber possessing a telephone leased from any telephone company (TELCO), he or she goes through the following dialogue with the system:

1. User picks up the receiver and goes off-hook.
2. PTS send a dial tone that invites the user to dial the digits corresponding to the ID code of the called party.
3. User dials the called party's code according to the following rules:
    a. $(NNX)(XXXX)$ if the called party is a toll-free, local number

b. 1(*NNX*)(*XXXX*) if the called party's number is a toll number within the same area code

c. 1(*NPX*)(*NNX*)(*XXXX*) if the called party's number is a toll number and in another area code

d. 011(*W*) (international telephone number) if the called party is in another country with an assigned code *W* as specified by CCITT. Of course, international DDD demands an end office properly enhanced for this service

4. User may hear all kinds of signaling sounds until the PTS sends to the calling party either a ringing tone or a busy tone, depending upon whether the called party is free or busy.

5. As soon as the called party picks up the receiver, the conversation can start.

6. After the conversation is complete, either of the parties can go on-hook. This causes a disconnected path.

7. User is billed for all the calls made during a billing period as specified by the TELCO.

8. If the user fails to get service as described above, a complaint is lodged with the operator or the business office. If the user's telephone instrument is malfunctioning, the user has to use another available telephone to lodge the complaint.

9. TELCO corrects the situation by sending a serviceman to the location.

7.2.1.5 Traffic Flows and Routing Schemes

Using the data of Fig. 7.1, one can express the path of a local call within the same NPA as follows:

(Local loop—Class 5 EO—local loop) or (LL-C5EO-LL)

A long distance call will have the following shortest path:

(LL-C5EO-toll connecting trunk-C4TC-HU ICT-C5EO-LL)

This path has only two trunks in the path. A closer study of Fig. 7.1 shows that the longest path of a long distance call could have nine trunks in the paths.

The PTS employs the principle of traffic concentration on the high usage (HU) trunks and traffic overflows on the intermediate HU or the final trunks as a basis for alternate routing. This approach yields an economy-of-scale and cost savings for the PTS network system, which provide an end-to-end blocking probability of 1% for the first call attempt, denoted by *P*.01.

7.2.1.6 Traffic Statistics

The following parameters characterize some of the salient features of the traffic statistics within the Bell System:

1. The average duration of a completed call is about 300 seconds.
2. The total number of busy hour erlangs handled by Class 1, 2, 3, and 4 switch nodes is approximately 720,000.
3. The average carried load by each local loop is about 0.1 erlangs.
4. The total number of call attempts during an average second of a busy hour is about 13,000.
5. The total number of completed calls handled during an average second of a busy period is about 10,000.

7.2.1.7 Transmission, Multiplexing, and Signaling Techniques

7.2.1.7.1 Transmission and Multiplexing Techniques. Baseband signaling is employed on all local loops with DC loop resistance less than 1300 ohms and loop lengths less than 75,000 feet. For longer, noisy loops, loop carrier systems involving both analog and digital transmission techniques are employed. Fortunately, only 3 percent of PTS local loops require special carrier-based transmission techniques.

Several types of transmission and multiplexing techniques are employed to achieve higher trunk efficiencies and to cope with different trunk lengths, e.g., short-haul and long-haul trunks). See Table 7.1 for a tabulation of such techniques.

7.2.1.7.2 Signaling Techniques. The following data attempts to define the various signaling techniques employed in the PTS:

1. On-hook, off-hook conditions on the local loops are achieved through two states of DC current.
2. Dialing on the local loops is achieved through one of the following two methods:
   a. Each dial digit of the rotary telephone is converted into DC pulses in the form of on-hook intervals transmitted at the approximate rate of 10 pulses per second. Dialed digits are separated by relatively long off-hook intervals. See Fig. 7.2 for an illustration.
   b. In the dual-tone multifrequency (DTMF) approach, the dial digit is converted into a sum of two frequency tones, each a member of two distinct groups—one high group and one lower group, as shown

Table 7.1. Transmission Techniques

MODULATION METHOD	APPLICATION	CARRIER/ MULTIPLEX SYSTEM	XMSSN. MEDIA
DSBAM	A/voice	N1,N2	P.Cable
SSBAM	A/voice	N3,	P.Cable
		L1,L3,	C.Cable
		L4,L5	
SSBAM-FM	A/voice	TD2/3,	4-, 6-, 11-
FM		TH1/3	gHz
		TN1,TL2,	Radio
		TM1	
PCM	A/voice	T1,T2,	P.Cable
		T4M	C.Cable
PCM-PSK	A/voice	WT4	Waveguide
DM	A/voice	SLM,	P.Cable
		SLC-40	
PSK	D/data	43A,43B	4 kHz-VG
DPSK	D/data	DS-201	4 kHz-VG
QAM	D/data	DS-209	4 kHz-VG
VSBAM	D/data	DS-203	4 kHz-VG
		LMDT	2.5 MHZ
			C.Cable
			M.GP.CH
FM-DPSK	D/data	1A-RDT	DUV ON
			TD or TH
			Radios
FM-DPSK	D/data	2A-RDT	20 mHz TD

NOTES: A = analog; AM = amplitude modulation; D = digital; DUV = data under voice; P = paired; C = coaxial; VG = voice-grade channel; QAM = quadrature AM; SSB = single side band; VSB = vestigial side band; DSB = double sideband; RDT = radio digital terminal; LMDT = L mastergroup digital terminal; DPSK = differential coherent PSK.

SOURCE: *Engineering and Operations in the Bell Systems.* Copyright 1977 by Bell Telephone Laboratories; reprinted by permission.

in Fig. 7.3. Because the high group consists of three frequencies and the lower group consists of four frequencies, up to 12 digits can now be dialed in the newer telephones. As shown in Fig. 7.3, the minimum duration of the digit code is 50 milliseconds, and the interdigit time is approximately 45 milliseconds. This results in a signaling speed about 10 times faster than that of rotary telephones.

3. Signaling over the network trunks is achieved through one of the four following methods:

   a. through DC signaling over simple, older trunks
   b. through DC to AC converted signal frequency (SF) signals trans-

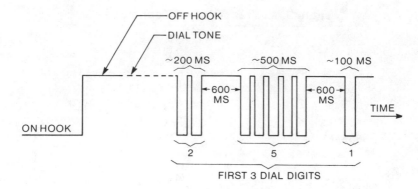

Fig. 7.2. A representation of DC signaling on a subscriber link.

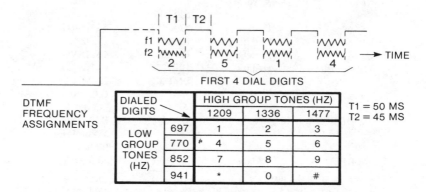

Fig. 7.3. DTMF signaling on a subscriber loop and DTMF frequency assignments for dialed digits.

mitted over the carrier-derived trunks. This scheme is also called the *in-band signal frequency,* or AC signaling

c. through out-of-band signaling over PCM encoded digital transmission facilities, e.g., T carrier, where supervisory and control bits required for signaling are multiplexed with the PCM encoded voice bit streams before transmission

d. through common channel interoffice signaling (CCIS) whereby the signaling data is transmitted between PTS switch nodes over a shared but separate network of CCIS trunks. It is particularly efficient when a good deal of signaling is required over a path that may consist of up to nine trunks. It is also attractive for ESS type Class 5 CO switches offering many new user options

7.2.1.8 Multilevel, Iterative Modeling of PTS Switch Nodes

A lower level, iterative model of the network shown in Fig. 7.1 will not yield additional data on the various network links, but a lower level, iterative model of PTS switch nodes should enhance our understanding of the system.

The high-level switch node model of Fig. 5.6 is general enough to apply to any PTS switch node. It shows that N links (local loops or trunks) terminate on a switch module, each of which has a certain capacity. A next-level, iterative model of the switch module is in order.

PTS consists of several types of switch modules. We still lack closed-form solutions for designing an optimum switch module with (1) a given termination capacity, (2) a given switching speed or delay, and (3) a given blocking probability. Approximate solutions are generally adequate, however.

The rectangular N-by-K switching network within a module and its sym-representation are illustrated in Figs. 7.4(a) and (b), respectively. Such a switch module enables any inlet to any outlet connection through a crosspoint switch element $\times$. Thus, an N-by-K coordinate switch requires N-by-K switch elements. Because a 10,000-line end office will require 100 million switch elements, such a design is an impractical one. We need a few modifications to the above figure. A diagonal element is meaningless because it serves to connect a port to itself. Furthermore, as most local loops are of the two-wire variety, allowing only one direction of signal flow at a time, half the crosspoint matrix is not applicable. Therefore, a single-stage, N-by-K coordinate switch requires approximately $(N*K)/2$ crosspoints. An EO with a one-stage coordinate

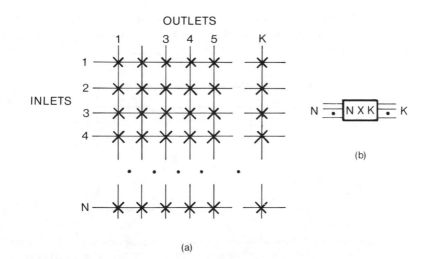

(a)

Fig. 7.4. An NXK coordinate switch.

switch including 50 million crosspoints still remains impractical. It is interesting to reflect on the first switch module installed at New Haven in 1878. It had 24 crosspoints for a 1-stage, 8-by-8 coordinate switch.

The Clos three-stage, nonblocking, space division switching network, as shown in Fig. 7.5, represents a good deal of improvement over the 1-stage, coordinate switching network. It can be shown that only $2\,NK + k(N/n)^2$ crosspoints are required for the case $k \ll N$. See Ref. 15 for a mathematical treatment of such a design.

Large, nonblocking, space division, multistage switching networks are seldom built, for the number of crosspoints is still too high. The number of crosspoints can be decreased significantly if one allows a low probability of blocking in the design of such networks. Jacobeous (Ref. 17) and Lee (Ref. 18) have developed algorithms for computing the blocking probability for given values of N, n, k (see Fig. 7.5), and u, which represent an average utilization of terminating user links.

An SPC switching node, also called an ESS in the Bell System, of today generally employs economical, multistage, time-space, digital switching modules. An example of a three-stage time-space-time switching network is shown in Fig. 7.6. Stages 1 and 3 provide time storage for the incoming and outgoing bits, respectively, from a given PCM-TDM frame, and Stage 2 provides a time-division-based switching mechanism for interchanging bits between inlet and outlet ports of the switch module.

7.2.1.9 Performance Parameters

7.2.1.9.1 Cost Parameters. FCC Tariff 263 prescribes the cost of the interstate LD message telecommunications service (MTS) provided by PTS. The charges for a call depend upon the call duration, airline distance between the

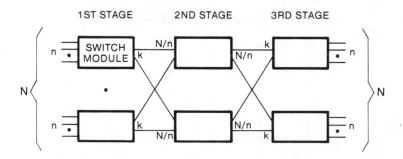

Fig. 7.5. A three-stage, space division switching network, or module, where n = array size of first stage, (N/n) = number of arrays in Stages 1 and 3, and k = number of arrays in second stage.

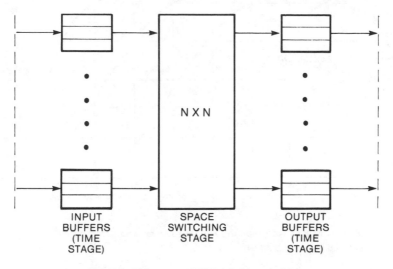

Fig. 7.6. A three-stage TST switching module.

two EOs, and the time of the call. The charges for an intrastate call are generally determined by the public utility commission (PUC) of each state. Examples representing both types of calls and their charges are generally published in the ubiquitous telephone directories. An overall average of $2 for a 5-minute business day call is generally used by most consultants.

In terms of the costs incurred by AT&T for the PTS, a 1974 survey states that 91% of AT&T's total revenues, approximately $28 billion, was derived from MTS. The survey also stated that AT&T's total investment in PTS amounts to about $78 billion, broken down as follows: 45 percent for transmission facilities, 23 percent for switching facilities, 20 percent for station equipment, and 12 percent for land, buildings, and general equipment.

7.2.1.9.2 System Throughput.   The PTS is capable of handling about 55 million call attempts and about 40 million completed calls during a busy hour. The above numbers are quite sensitive to the type of calls (distance and duration) handled by PTS.

7.2.1.9.3 Quality of Service (QOS) Parameters.   During the early seventies, two surveys (see Refs. 19 and 20) were made to measure the various QOS parameters. The first discusses the effects of nonlinear distortion, transmission loss and delay, and random noise on speech quality. Reference 20 analyzes the effect of random noise on the quality of data transmission in PTS. It is quite difficult to summarize the results of these excellent studies in a short space. Figures 7.7 and 7.8 attempt to illustrate the effects of echo distortion and noise

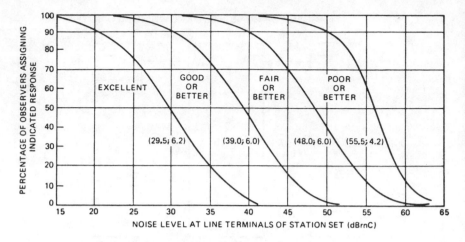

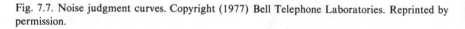

NOTES:
1. VALUES IN PARENTHESES INDICATE AVERAGE AND STANDARD DEVIATION.
2. RECEIVED VOLUME CONSTANT, – 28 VU.

Fig. 7.7. Noise judgment curves. Copyright (1977) Bell Telephone Laboratories. Reprinted by permission.

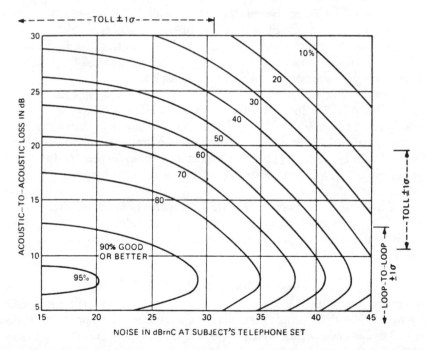

Fig. 7.8. Summary of subjective listener evaluation of effects of noise and loss. The values shown are percentages rating circuit "Good or Better." Copyright (1977) Bell Telephone Laboratories. Reprinted by permission.

on speech quality. The planned transmission losses on PTS trunks used for combating the effects of echo distortion, in PTS are illustrated in Fig. 7.9. As shown, the two-wire terminations on Class 5 EO cause the greatest loss. The use of four-wire trunks in the path of a call is the most desirable.

The effects of crosstalk are minimized by maintaining a crosstalk level of 1 percent or less for trunks connecting Class 1, 2, and 3 offices and 0.5 percent or less for Class 4 and 5 offices.

The impairment caused by frequency shift is minimized by allowing the shift not to exceed 2 Hertz on the longest connection.

The error rate performance on data transmission depends on whether analog or digital transmission facilities are used. The number of connections in the path and the time of transmission also affect BER, which varies anywhere between 10^{-3} and 10^{-6}.

The degradation of system performance caused by component failures within PTS has not been much written about. It is known, however, that modern ESSs were designed to offer a mean time between catastrophic failures (MTBCF) of about 40 years. It is difficult to assess how close the ESS designs have come to the goals. Furthermore, due to the size and complexity of PTS, it is difficult to design an experiment to measure the actual degradation of MTS service resulting from one or more component failures.

7.2.1.9.4 Grade of Service (GOS) Parameters. Due to constant upgrading of the Bell System and the continual but nonuniform growth of traffic within the PTS components, a simple characterization of GOS parameters is quite difficult if not impossible. Nevertheless, several reliable sources (see Ref. 21) constantly review GOS in PTS. A summary of some of the GOS parameters follows:

1. Ninety percent of all off-hooks are responded to by a dial tone within 3 seconds.
2. Ninety percent of all connections within a CO are made within 200 milliseconds.
3. Call set-up time distribution, including the 100 milliseconds for the automatic answering equipment to apply the ringing tone to the user link, can be specified as shown in Table 7.2
4. PTS is designed to block only 1 percent of all the call attempts, represented as *P*.01. Furthermore, only 10 percent of all the subscribers can be simultaneously accommodated in the PTS.

7.2.1.10 Concluding Remarks

The PTS network is the largest of its kind in the world, and it is constantly growing. As shown in 7.2.1.3, up to 1024 million subscribers can be serviced

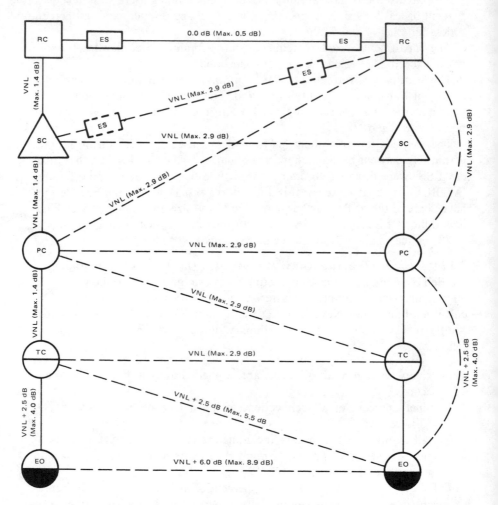

Fig. 7.9. Transmission loss plan for the PTS links. Copyright (1977) Bell Telephone Laboratories. Reprinted by permission.

Table 7.2. Call Setup
Distribution

CONNECTION LENGTH, MILES	MEAN TIME, SECONDS	STANDARD DEVIATION
All	11.7 ± 1.8	4.3
0–180	10.8 ± 1.5	3.7
180–725	14.7 ± 3.2	5.0
725–2900	13.8 ± 2.6	4.5

SOURCE: *1969-1970 Switched Telecommunication Network Connection Survey.* Copyright 1971 by American Telephone and Telegraph.; reprinted by permission.

if all the NPAs are fully and equally occupied by user numbers. In reality, only 120 million or so subscribers are now being served by PTS. It may appear that a fantastic growth capability exists, but unfortunately, that is not true. Difficulties are caused by a nonuniform growth in the 160 NPAs. When an NPA grows beyond 6.4 million subscribers, a further subdivision of the NPA must occur. But this is a difficult and a traumatic transition for both the TELCO and the subscribers. This was clearly shown in 1973, when a split of the existing "703" NPA occurred followed by the entry of a new, unused "804" NPA.

Another difficulty is now surfacing: this has to do with the limitation of only 640 COs (or NNXs) per NPA. Many NPAs are starting to be of concern to TELCOs.

Despite the above difficulties, we expect that the 10-digit numbering plan will probably last until the year 2000. It is interesting to note that in 1962, when the 10-digit plan was incorporated, many experts thought that all the 160 available NPAs would be exhausted by 1975. The population did not explode, however, and the numbering plan was saved. What surprises us is that, if these facts were known in 1962, why a better numbering plan was not developed earlier. Perhaps, the planners did not want us to dial more than 10 digits for a couple of decades. Or perhaps, they were thinking of an entirely new plant that was to replace the existing one. Collins and Pederson, in an excellent treatise (Ref. 15), describe an all-digital plan that can reduce costs, provide more user options, enhance performance, and reduce the space and maintenance requirements.

A bigger challenge to PTS may come from another offshoot of telecommunications—data communications. Because the basis for most existing voice communication is a desire to exchange information, not just to hear someone's voice, new and existing public data networks are bound to take some of the traffic loads away from PTS. This could extend the life of PTS even longer than imaginable today.

7.2.2 Royal Netherlands Air Force's ASCON

7.2.2.1 An Application Summary

The Automatic Switched Communication Network (ASCON) of the Royal Netherlands Air Force is a totally integrated, switched PCM-digital voice network, and it was the first of its kind in the world. With the recent addition of the Royal Netherlands Army as a user, the system is now a 10-node private network that serves about 10,000 voice and about 170 data/facsimile subscribers.

7.2.2.2 Network Topology

The original network consisted of 8 CS nodes, and the new network will consist of 10 CS nodes interconnected according to the overconnected topology of Fig. 7.10.

As illustrated in Fig. 7.10, several customer vehicles (CVs) are connected to two CS nodes, and each CS node is connected to at least two other CS nodes.

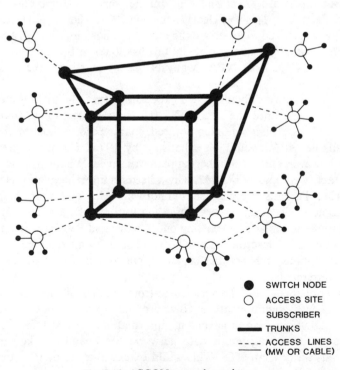

● SWITCH NODE
○ ACCESS SITE
• SUBSCRIBER
▬ TRUNKS
---- ACCESS LINES
── (MW OR CABLE)

Fig. 7.10. ASCON network topology.

In some cases, a CV, although connected to a single CS node, is provided a permanent path through its switch module to an adjacent CS node. These features provide a rich variety of alternate routing, not only between CS nodes, but also between CV nodes during CS-nodal failures. Thus, ASCON possesses unique survivability. At any given time, ASCON obeys the MCMS topology (see Chapter 2) because alternate paths are invoked only when network nodes fail. All CS nodes are hierarchically the same. The network also consists of 1700 VG trunks, access lines, and about 10,000 local loops.

7.2.2.3 Identification Scheme

A uniform seven-digit numbering plan is employed to represent each subscriber and all network elements. This scheme is illustrated as follows:

$$(NNX)(XXXX)$$

where

N = a decimal value between 2 through 9
X = a decimal value between 0 through 9

Each CV is represented by the (NNX) code, which allows 640 combinations. Thus, the network can ideally serve 6.4 million subscribers. The user loops, network access lines, and trunks can be identified accordingly.

7.2.2.4 User Interfaces

To use ASCON, a subscriber lifts the receiver and dials 8 to access the network. The appropriate CS node provides the dial tone. The subscriber then dials the seven-digit code to reach any other subscriber within the allowable closed user group(s). The system also provides several levels of priority and service restrictions. Some subscribers are provided *hot line* capability, which allows an automatic connection to a single subscriber immediately after going off-hook. The remaining user-system interfaces are identical to those in the Bell System described earlier in 7.2.1.

7.2.2.5 Traffic Flows and Routing Control

Each CS node collects pertinent traffic congestion data from all other CS nodes and develops optimum routes dynamically.

Consequently, a fully adaptive routing technique is employed, in contrast to the hierarchical "HU and final" synoptic routing plan used in public telephone systems. In some rare cases, four or five network nodes may be involved in the path of a call connection. The average path length, however, is only 1.5 trunks.

7.2.2.6 Traffic Statistics

From the first day after cutover in 1977, the traffic loads have been increasing. ASCON has provided a great stimulation to the subscribers for two reasons: lower blocking and better intelligibility. Its operational success has attracted the Royal Netherlands Army to have its subscribers served by the network. It will take some time for traffic to settle down. A traffic intensity of eight calls per second and about 1200 erlangs are anticipated during busy hours.

7.2.2.7 Transmission and Signaling Techniques

The transmission interfaces to a CS node are illustrated in Fig. 7.11. These are summarized as follows:

1. Transmission on a direct subscriber loop is via direct voice band transmission.

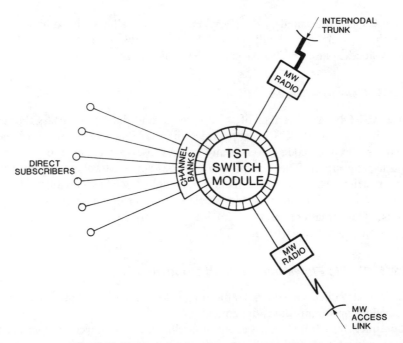

Fig. 7.11. Transmission interfaces to ASCON CS node.

2. Transmission on interswitch trunks is via the MW MULDEM-radio technique that employs four PCM encoded/multiplexed T1 carriers.
3. Subscriber loops employ DC signaling. Most of the telephones in the network employ rotary dialing.
4. Common channel signaling is employed over a separate outshared network consisting of derived 2400-BPS channels.
5. Networkwide synchronization is achieved. Each CS node derives its clock from the several T1 streams being received from adjacent nodes and implements a scheme known as *elastic bit synchronization*.

7.2.2.8 Iterative Modeling of a CS Node

The network employs two network control nodes, each with dual processors, two nodes with dual processors, and six nodes with a single processor. Each node employs a TST switch module originally developed by Rockwell's Collins Division. The TST digital switch is similar to that described in 7.2.1.8. Each of the redundant nodes consists of two minicomputers—one acting as a call processor (CP) in conjunction with common control equipment, and the other acting as a reports processor. In case the call processor fails, the report processor immediately becomes a call processor while the failed processor is either replaced by a spare one or repaired. In case the CP fails, the connected calls are not affected. When a dual control node fails, the second control node assumes network management.

7.2.2.9 Performance Parameters

Some salient performance parameters are as follows:

1. No estimate of cost per completed call is available for this highly survivable DOD type network. The need, rather than cost considerations, created this highly sophisticated network.
2. Each CS node is capable of handling about four call arrivals per second.
3. The average value of BER is .0001.
4. Average speech intelligibility of 95% is achieved.
5. Mean time between catastrophic failures is one failure during 10 years, with average failure duration of 1/2 hour.
6. The network provides a blocking factor of $B.001$ (as compared with $B.01$ for PTS).
7. The network is capable of providing 14,350 terminations (trunks, access lines, direct subscribers). The numbering plan allows a connectivity of 6.4 million subscribers.

7.2.2.10 Concluding Remarks

The ASCON network system is an excellent example of a well-planned system that employs state-of-the-art digital switching and transmission techniques. It employs a fully distributed system architecture characterized by common channel signaling and fully adaptive routing. Such an architecture allows an orderly growth. This aspect of the network architecture was tested recently when two redundant CS nodes were added to the existing eight-node network characterized by a cubic shape. Consequently, ASCON is bound to enjoy a long life while providing excellent service.

7.2.3 ITT's Public Switched Voice Network

7.2.3.1 An Application Summary

This is an interesting example of a network system that provides three types of services: (1) City Call Service (CCS) for the small user of DDD, (2) Switched Private Network Service (SPNS) for low to medium volume interstate business communication, and (3) Corporate Communication Switching Equipment (CCSE) for the high-volume business telephone users, such as large corporations. The three services provide the subscribers the advantages of shared stored program controlled (SPC) digital switches, four-wire private networking with uniform dialing, and significant economies-of-scale.

7.2.3.2 Network Topology

The existing network consists of 11 CS nodes located in 7 distinct sites: New York, Los Angeles, Chicago, Dallas, Cleveland, Memphis, and Atlanta. A network management center (NMC) is colocated with other CS nodes at New York. The topology of the original network was of the fully connected variety. This topology has, however, been going through constant changes, as dictated by the demands for various services since the original cutover in 1976.

7.2.3.3 Identification Scheme

A uniform seven-digit numbering plan is employed, as in most of the modern private networks, e.g., see 7.2.2.3.

Although the seven-digit numbering plan is valid for any private network, the existing PTS 10-digit numbering plan remains valid for the users of the *City Call* service.

7.2.3.4 User Interfaces

A subscriber of the City Call service will make an access through dialing 9 and, upon hearing the dial tone, dials 23 digits, the called 10-digit number, a 6-digit authorization number, and his own 7-digit number.

A subscriber of the SPNS and CCSE services makes an access by dialing 8 and, upon hearing a dial tone, dials seven digits for the on-net called party. Both SPNS and CCSE offer conference calls, abbreviated dialing, hot lines, alternate routing, privacy, usage statistics, and detailed per-call accounting.

CCSE allows dedicated access lines and trunks for each customer, SPNS allows only dedicated access lines for each customer, and both allow shared switching facilities. For these reasons, only CCSE allows on-net to off-net calling. SPNS allows only on-net to on-net calling. Future tariff regulations may make CCSE and SPNS identical.

7.2.3.5 Traffic Flows and Routing

The network employs *synoptic routing,* and the NMC alters the originally defined alternate routing tables whenever required.

7.2.3.6 Traffic Statistics

The mix of so many customers and services makes it difficult to summarize detailed traffic statistics.

7.2.3.7 Transmission and Signaling Techniques

Because most of the CVs and access lines are leased from the common or specialized carriers, the transmission and signaling techniques on local loops and access lines are similar to those in the PTS.

At present, the network trunks are also of the analog variety. When digital transmission facilities, e.g., T1 carrier, are available, however, these will be used. Their use will eliminate the use of A/D converters required to terminate analog facilities on the digital switch employed in all the CS nodes. The use of four-wire digital facilities will also reduce the end-to-end losses and thus enhance the quality of voice everywhere in the network.

At present, the MF type signaling scheme is employed on the trunks.

7.2.3.8 Iterative Modeling of Network Nodes

Each of the CS nodes is identical to that employed in the ASCON network described in 7.2.2. Therefore, all the remarks made in 7.2.2 apply.

7.2.3.9 Performance Parameters

The City Call service costs a minimum monthly charge of $50 and a usage rate of $0.30 per minute, with billing starting at 1.5 minutes followed by 6-second increments.

The net cost per call for SPNS and CCSE services will depend upon the exact network configuration and GOS as specified by the customer. Nonetheless, the FCC-approved tariffs do determine the switch termination costs for SPNS and CCSE as described below:

SPNS: $30 per switch port and $0.153 per minute of network trunk usage. A minimum of $150 on port charges also applies.

CCSE: $60 per switch port and nothing for network usage, because all access lines and trunks belong to the customer. A minimum of $600 on port charges also applies.

System throughput can be computed by knowing the duration of each call, the average path length, and that each CS node can handle four completed calls per second.

QOS and GOS for each of the component networks will depend upon the configuration of each subnetwork of a customer.

Overall network connectivity is approximately 11 times 1400 = 15,400 trunks, access lines, and direct subscriber lines, if applicable.

7.2.3.10 Concluding Remarks

The system architecture is based upon a fully distributed concept in which all the CS nodes are at the same level. Consequently, this network is adaptable to changes and additions. Its history clearly shows its strength. It should be mentioned that at cutover in 1976, the networks provided only two services, i.e., SPNS and CCSE. After MCI's EXECUNET service was approved by the FCC in 1978, however, ITT applied for City Call and won approval. Such a service required quite a reconfiguration of the original network.

7.2.4 A Typical Airline Network

7.2.4.1 An Application Summary

Due to the pioneering efforts made by the major U.S. airlines during the last decade, some unique voice switched networks have been developed to meet their exacting needs. The example chosen here typifies many existing networks, each of which evolved from a set of separate networks to an integrated one.

Each component network was initially designed to provide a capability for automatic distribution of incoming telephone calls to a group of airline agents hired to provide instant reservations or flight-related information to prospective customers. Each component network obeys the SCSS topology centered around an automatic call distribution (ACD) node based upon the CS principles. Many such CS nodes were employed to serve the various geographical areas while minimizing the transmission costs and hence the cost per call.

As the need for efficient corporate communication also grew, it became obvious to the airline management that the two services, i.e., ACD and corporate communication, must be integrated to achieve economies-of-scale. A multinode corporate network obeying the MCMS topology resulted.

Such a network allows the airline personnel to make both on-net and off-net calls and also serve the public. In the process, both high quality of voice and complete call accountability and resource management were achieved.

7.2.4.2 Network Topology

Each of the component ACD network is based upon the single-center, single-star (SCSS) topology, as shown in Fig. 7.12. Accordingly, the ACD node serves many intercity trunks, or FX type access lines, and several four-wire type agent trunks.

The corporate network is based upon the multicenter, multistar (MCMS) topology as illustrated in Fig. 7.13. This figure shows the two-level structure of the network that interconnects the airline's vehicles (e.g., PABXs), Class 5 central offices (COs) and the CS nodes.

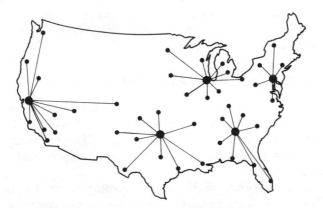

Fig. 7.12. SCSS topologies of individual ACD networks of a typical airline.

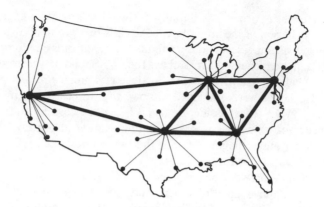

Fig. 7.13. The MCMS topology of a typical airline corporate network consisting of several ACD networks.

7.2.4.3 Identification Scheme

All prospective customers maintain the 10-digit PTS numbering plan. The local 7-digit airline numbers are listed in directories of the cities it serves. All the airline's on-net telephones are identified by the 7-digit code ($NXX\text{-}XXXX$). All the airline's off-net telephones are identified by the 10-digit PTS code.

7.2.4.4 User Interfaces

The prospective customers' interfaces to the network are identical to those for the PTS network, except for the announcement that is played asking the subscriber to wait for a FIFO-based service. In some cases, music is played after the announcement. When all trunks from a city are busy, a busy signal is heard. The user interfaces for the airline employees are identical to those described in 7.2.2.4.

7.2.4.5 Traffic Flows and Routing Control

When all trunks to a city or a CO are busy, a prospective customer's call will be blocked, and the customer will be notified by a busy tone. No alternate routing is provided to ACD customers. When an ACD node is congested, however, some airlines provide a capability for overflowing the calls to another ACD node for service.

The corporate network traffic is routed according to the synoptic approach in case an NMC node is employed. Otherwise, the routing control is distributed to all the nodes, each of which is provided with fixed primary and alternate routing tables.

7.2.4.6 Traffic Statistics

Although a network can be configured to handle any traffic intensity, most airline networks handle traffic intensities in the range of one to five calls per second of a peak hour. The average duration of a call is between 100 and 300 seconds.

7.2.4.7 Transmission and Signaling Techniques

Because all the users' two-wire loops, two-wire intercity links, and the four-wire internodal trunks are leased from the common and specialized carriers, the transmission techniques described for the PTS apply. When four-wire digital T1 trunks become available, their use should simplify the nodal hardware through the elimination of A/D converters from the all-digital CS nodes. Digital trunks should also enhance the network QOS.

As the agents' headsets are connected to the digital switch via four-wire loop, a two- to four-wire hybrid is eliminated from the path of each ACD call. This fact, coupled with a no-noise digital switch, results in an unusually high-quality voice. It was not surprising to see the productivity of each ACD agent increase abruptly after the ACD network cutover.

Signaling on the two-wire subscriber loops and the two-wire intercity trunks are through DC current closures and openings. Signaling over the internodal trunks is via DTMF (see 7.2.1.7).

7.2.4.8 Multilevel, Iterative Modeling of CS Nodes

Each CS node is equipped with an integrated software package that provides both ACD and digital tandem switching (DTS) functions. The hardware structure is identical to that discussed in 7.2.2.8. Each CS node provides detailed reports for ACD resources management. Half-hourly reports that describe call statistics in detail and "Average agents positions required" also help the communication manager to plan his resources dynamically. Real-time link and trunk monitoring reports also enable airlines to save a significant amount of money by eliminating defective trunks.

7.2.4.9 Performance Parameters

As each network system is a private network, it is hard to summarize the actual costs per call incurred on all networks.

Intelligibility on ACD networks is far superior to that for the PTS. Unfortunately, no measured results have been published thus far. Nevertheless, a consensus appears to exist in the minds of the communication managers we interviewed.

Most of the intercity trunk-bundles for the ACD are designed using the blocking criterion of *B*.05.

The ACD agent positions are computed for each half-hour period using the criterion that 85 percent of the incoming calls will not be delayed more than 20 seconds.

Private networks are generally sized using the end-to-end blocking probability of 10 percent for the first attempt.

The reliability of each CS node is better than 0.995. Through the use of internodal call overflows, almost 100 percent service availability can be achieved.

7.2.4.10 Concluding Remarks

One can continue to look toward the U.S. airlines for challenges in the area of cost-effective, integrated network systems that handle not only voice, data, and DDP but also DDBM. Several airlines are already looking into the feasibility of corporate data processing networks for sharing of DP resources, MS, DDBM, and, of course, handling their office-of-tomorrow requirements, including voice communication.

7.2.5 AT&T's Digital Data Service (DDS) and Dataphone Switched DDS

7.2.5.1 An Application Summary

This is a major, new, all-digital CS network designed to provide high-quality, leased, synchronous digital circuits operating at the speeds of 2400, 4800, 9600, 56,000, and 1.544 million bits per second. DDS, when started in December 1974, covered only five metropolitan areas. When fully operational in 1980, it should span approximately a hundred metropolitan areas. DDS provides not only point-to-point, but also multipoint, private leased lines accommodating HDX and FDX data terminal equipment (DTE). DSDDS provides switched DDS at 56,000 BPS to begin with.

7.2.5.2 Network Topology

DDS employs a four-level network hierarchy as illustrated in Fig. 7.14. The entire country is divided into digital service areas (DSAs), each equipped with a number of digital CS nodes called *hubs*. See Refs. 62 and 63 for details.

Each CS hub serves a number of local service offices (LSOs). Each user's DTE is provided with a data service unit (DSU) or channel service unit (CSU)

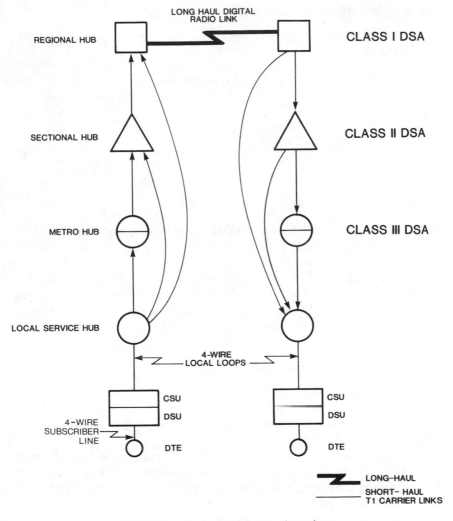

Fig. 7.14. The four-level DDS network topology.

for providing the necessary interfaces between the DDS network and industry-standard DTEs.

Each LSO is primarily a multiplexing and demultiplexing node. Interconnections among the LSOs and the various-level CS hubs is via T1 encoded trunks. HU and final trunks are employed for alternate routing and better utilization of trunk groups.

7.2.5.3 Identification Scheme

The DDS/DSDDS numbering plan is similar to the one employed in the PTS. It is defined as follows:

$$(DSA)(NNX)(XXXX)$$

where
  (DSA)   is a three-digit DSA code
  (NNX)   is a three-digit hub code
  (XXXX) is a four-digit station code

7.2.5.4 User Interface

DTEs are interfaced with the DDS/DSDDS network through the use of DSUs or CSUs placed at the user's premises. These units are connected to the DDS network via four-wire user loops.

The call setups and disconnects are identical to those employed in the PTS. Automatic calling units and multiline hunting group arrangements can be provided to achieve fast call setups. Many other options, such as conferencing and hot lines, are also available. See Ref. 63 for details.

7.2.5.5 Traffic Flows and Routing Control

Proximity to the hub determines the level of the CS hub or DSA that directly serves a particular DTE. Several T1 trunks may be involved in the path of a call. The actual number depends upon the actual locations of the communicating DTEs and the amount of traffic generated.

The routing control is of a fixed, hierarchical type, employing HU trunks and overflow to final trunks. The network management center has the capability of changing the routes, if required, thus providing a synoptic technique.

7.2.5.6 Traffic Statistics

Because the network is still being expanded, no data regarding the traffic statistics is available.

7.2.5.7 Transmission and Signaling Techniques

User DTE to local service office (LSO) transmission is via four-wire baseband, bipolar digital signals. Inband signaling employed on the user loop is similar to

CCITT's X.21 recommendation. Transmission between LSOs and metro hubs, between metro hubs and sectional hubs, and between sectional hubs and regional hubs is via T1 bipolar signals. Network utilization is enhanced through the use of T-carrier multiplexing/demultiplexing techniques, as described in Chapter 4.

Transmission between the regional hubs is accomplished through the use of a data under voice (DUV) technique, as described in Chapter 4.

Network synchronization is achieved through the use of a technique called the *tree subnetwork approach*. According to this technique, all the network links that carry user data are used to distribute the synchronization signals throughout the network in a treelike manner, all the way down to the individual DSUs at the user's premises. A new Bell System reference frequency standard is located near St. Louis, Missouri, and it sets the synchronization frequency for all Bell networks, including DDS.

7.2.5.8 Iterative Modeling of Network Nodes

The local service office (LSO) contains office channel units (OCUs) that regenerate the loop signal and prepare it for transmission through the multiplexing hierarchy. The OCU also contains a loopback switch that can be actuated remotely for facilitating fault location.

Each LSO and all the hub offices contain a family of new TDM units for DDS and DSDDS. One TDM unit is designed to handle the lower three customer speeds, either 20 customer signals at 2400 BPS or 10 customer signals at 4800 BPS or 5 customer signals at 9600 BPS, into a single bit stream of 64,000 BPS. The output of this first-stage multiplexer is fed into a second-stage TDM unit that combines 23 of these 64-KBPS channels into a single T1 stream of 1.544 MBPS. Another second-stage data multiplexer, called a *data/voice multiplexer,* is employed to operate with a D-channel bank or in a stand-alone mode. When operating with the D-channel bank, the data/voice multiplexer allows 64-KBPS data channels and digitized voice circuits to share T1 lines.

A hub office node consists of not only hierarchies of multiplexers, but also TST type digital switch modules, CPUs, primary, secondary, and tertiary storage units, and precision timing devices required for network synchronization. All hub offices also consist of multipoint junction units (MJUs), which enable several DTEs to share a single digital circuit.

The regional hub office (RHO) consists of not only the above-mentioned equipment, but also the long-haul transmission facilities required to communicate with other RHOs.

Extensive use of test equipment is made in every hub office for handling customers' complaints.

7.2.5.9 Performance Parameters

Only the costs for DDS service are known at present. The charges are for mileage, service terminals, and network interface equipment. These are summarized in Table 7.3.

Throughput figures for DDS and DSDDS are not yet known.

7.2.5.9.1 QOS Parameters

1. DDS provides high-quality data communication with objectives of 99.5 percent error-free seconds.
2. DDS provides high service availability by automatic switchover to standby T1 facilities. The design objective is 99.96 percent availability during every day of the year.

7.2.5.9.2 GOS Parameters

1. DSDDS provides an average call connect time of 1 second or less.
2. For multipoint circuits, the polling delays vary from 5 to 60 milliseconds for 56-KBPS lines and from 30 to 75 milliseconds, depending upon the distance between the control and remote stations. See Refs. 62 and 63 for details.

Table 7.3. Monthly Lease Costs for DDS

| | PER MILE | PER MONTH | |
MILEAGE RANGE	2.4–9.6 KBPS	56 KBPS	T_1
Basic	$49.20	$246.00	NA
2–15	$1.80	$9.00	$64.00
16–25	$1.50	$7.50	$64.00
26–100	$1.12	$5.60	$64.00
101–200	$0.66	$3.30	$64.00
201–500	$0.66	$3.30	$50.00
501–1000	$0.66	$3.30	$40.00
over 1000	$0.40	$2.00	$40.00
CTU	$25–$32.33	$125.00	$100.
DSU	$15.45	$20.60	$200
off. NA	$150–$300	$450	–

NOTES: CTU = Chan. Term. Unit; DSU = data svc. unit; DAL = data access line. (1979 Tariffs)

7.2.5.10 Future Plans

DDS and DSDDS represent definite improvements in the state of art for digital transmission and communication. In this respect, these are major AT&T undertakings. Vast outlays of capital will be needed before all the phases of DDS and DSDDS are completed.

7.2.6 Summary Models of Other CS Systems

In the preceding pages, we tried to present detailed models of some well-known CS systems. Lack of intimate familiarity with every CS system and available space limited the number of CS systems modeled. Summary models of other well-known CS systems will be described in the following paragraphs.

MCI's EXECUNET network system made history through a prolonged battle with AT&T and FCC regarding MCI's right to share off-net facilities (e.g., FX and LONAL) among a large number of EXECUNET subscribers. MCI finally won the battle. Its victory influenced other specialized common carriers to offer similar services. In the beginning, EXECUNET consisted of unconnected single-center, single-star (SCSS) type networks. The purpose of EXECUNET was to reduce the cost of long distance calls to certain metropolitan areas served by MCI. The subscriber dials the 10-digit number and his authorization code. The MCI switch then connects the calling party to the called party using one of the off-net access lines that connect the switch to the particular metropolitan CO. Several bundles of such off-net access lines emanate from each switch, thus giving rise to the SCSS topology. As the business grew, MCI soon discovered the inefficiency of unconnected SCSS subnetworks. All the switch nodes are now being interconnected via intermachine trunks, and the entire network is being redesigned to yield an MCMS topology similar to the ones discussed in 7.2.2, 7.2.3, and 7.2.4.

MCI's EXECUNET service is similar to the City Call service of ITT discussed in 7.2.2. MCI also provides other network system services, such as QUICKLINE, CCSA, and SPLS. QUICKLINE provides a metered private line, whereby the subscriber gets a monthly bill based upon usage. In some cases, a user can achieve significant savings with respect to AT&T's multipoint private line (MPL) leased offering. CCSA is a leased switching arrangement permitting the interconnection of subscriber's dedicated circuits terminated on the SCC's common control switching machines. CCSA is similar to AT&T's CCSA and ITT's CCSE (see 7.2.2) offerings. SPLS (shared private line service) allows the sharing of switches and IMTs as provided by MCI. Thus, SPLS is identical to ITT's SPNS (see 7.2.2) offering.

Another major, specialized common carrier (SCC), Southern Pacific Communication, also offers a network system service called SPRINT, which is identical to EXECUNET and City Call.

Another CS system, known as the *Telex* system, has been a household word since the 1950s. Most of the Telex systems allow interchange of digital data at 50 bauds between asynchronous terminals. Most of the countries of the world boast an MCMS type telex network. Dialing is similar to that for the PTS, and conversation is achieved through a keyboard and a printer. Most of the private networks are interconnected, allowing a worldwide interchange of information.

There are faster types of Telex networks that allow interchange of digital data at speeds up to 200 bauds. The DATEX 200 network of West Germany and a proposed DATEX network for Italy are some examples.

Several CS networks have recently sprung up in France, West Germany, and the nordic countries, Denmark, Norway, Sweden, and Finland, for the interchange of synchronous digital data. These networks are thus similar to AT&T's DDS/DSDDS network. The Conducee network of France handles speeds of 2400, 4800, and 9600 BPS. Another Conducee network within the Paris area can handle speeds of 48 k, 64 k, and 72 KBPS. The EDS network of West Germany can handle speeds of 2400, 4800, and 9600 BPS. The nordic network can handle only 2400 and 4800 BPS. Analog subscriber links and trunks are used only in the nationwide Conducee networks. Digital access links and trunks are employed in all other networks. Digital switching techniques are employed in all the synchronous networks discussed above. All the synchronous digital networks, except the nordic network, employ a single node. The nordic network employs four switching nodes, one in each country involved.

An interesting aspect of the public telephone and Telex and data networks is that they are all separate networks. There is no economy-of-scale available, and the latest multifunction subscriber terminals cannot be used. The PS technology is thus superior in these regards. PS systems form the basis for the next subsection.

7.3 PACKET-SWITCHED (PS) SYSTEMS

Whereas CS systems were developed sometime during the late 19th century, PS systems are of recent origin. Paul Baran (see Ref. 22) was the first to describe what we now call a PS system. Because the 11-volume work was done at the Rand Corporation for the U.S. Air Force, survivability was the prime design consideration. But no developmental work was done.

Licklider of the Advanced Research Projects Agency (ARPA) promoted the PS concepts by applying PS to the design of highly responsive timesharing (TS) systems. Although no concrete PS systems resulted, his ideas were picked up by Davies of Great Britain's National Physical Laboratories (NPL) and Roberts of ARPA.

Davies conceptualized a store-and-forward PS system (see Ref. 23) and coined the term *packet* to describe the 128-byte blocks to be used for information interchange throughout the network. But his ideas also fell on deaf ears in the U.K. administration, although he was ultimately able to implement a one-node private PS network for NPL by 1973.

It was Roberts who eventually succeeded in implementing a multinode Arpanet PSS for true resource sharing (see Ref. 24). Since then, many other PS systems have sprung up throughout the world.

At present, much progress is being made in developing international standards for PS. Ultimately, such standards will mean cost savings to all users through terminal interchangeability and hence independence from vendors.

Only a few PS networks will be modeled in detail. Architectural uniqueness will be the basis of network selection. The following well-known networks are selected for a detailed description:

1. Arpanet
2. Telenet
3. Tymnet
4. Pacuit

7.3.1 Arpanet

ARPA published the Arpanet plan in 1967. The design consisted of a PS network that employs minicomputers at each computer site for both packet switching and computer interfacing. The network nodes were to be interconnected via 50-KBPS trunks. A request for proposal (RFP) was issued in 1968 for developing the system. Bolt, Beranek and Newman (BBN) won the contract in January 1969. A four-node network was operational in December 1969. The network was expanded rapidly thereafter to support 23 host computers by April 1971, 62 hosts by June 1974, and 111 hosts by March 1977. In 1975, responsibility for the network was transferred from ARPA to the Defence Communication Agency (DCA). Arpanet is, therefore, no longer an experimental network.

7.3.1.1 An Application Summary

The initial application of Arpanet dealt with research and experimention in packet switching technology. The ultimate application, however, deals with the distribution and sharing of data bases and computing resources among the thousands of users situated at many university communities in the United States.

7.3.1.2 Network Topology

As the existing Arpanet has too many nodes, and each node employs a different number of minicomputers for packet switching and HP interfacing, no attempt will be made to illustrate the exact topology. Instead, only a basic topology will be illustrated, as shown in Fig. 7.15.

The example network consists of three network nodes interconnected by 50-KBPS trunks. Each node consists of a minicomputer-based interface message processor (IMP) and several terminal interface processors (TIPs). The IMP is a PS subnode that provides interface to one or more packet-mode host processors (HPs). The TIP provides an interface between asynchronous terminals and the IMP. The TIP assembles characters from the user terminals and creates packets for transmission. The TIP also performs the reverse of the above function. The network node may or may not consist of a TIP. The IMP receives and transmits only packets. Each network node has at least one HP.

All network nodes are at the same level hierarchically. This results in a single-level backbone, network hierarchy.

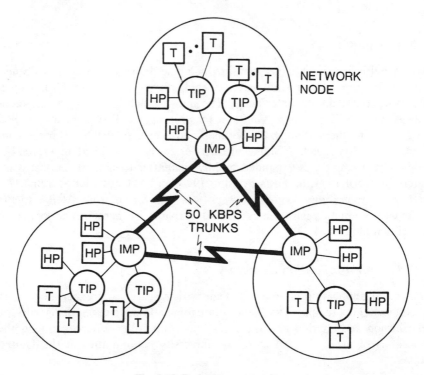

Fig. 7.15. Basic Arpanet topology.

7.3.1.3 Identification Scheme

Each HP and TIP has a four-character identification on the network level. The TIP maintains a lower-level terminal address for local network management only. The IDs are limited to suggestive combinations, such as UCBA (the Ath HP at the University of California, Berkeley node).

7.3.1.4 User's Interface

At first, each user logs in. The user then specifies the destination ID and the structured command(s) required for resource sharing. Each packet flows through the Arpanet according to the so-called *Datagram protocol*, whereby each packet carries the calling and called IDs. The user then waits for the reply from the called host. In this manner the session continues until the user logs out.

7.3.1.5 Traffic Flows and Routing

Arpanet employs the so-called *distributed adaptive scheme*, whereby each node in the path of a packet determines the next trunk on which the packet must travel toward the destination. As the network is not fully connected, a packet may travel over several trunks. Each IMP node sends to each of its immediate neighbors a routing table every 640 milliseconds. The routing table lists the number of trunks in the path and the approximate delay for reaching every other IMP in the network. The receiving IMPs use these tables to update their own tables that they employ for routing. Many experts have questioned the complex routing scheme employed in Arpanet. Although it imposes an overhead of about 4 percent on network capacity, the proponents claim high dividends during periods of congestion.

The Datagram protocol employed in the Arpanet allows an independent routing of each packet through the network. Consequently, the receiving IMP may have to reorder the packets before they reach the user.

7.3.1.6 Traffic Statistics

Arpanet is handling about 10 million packets a day, which are generated by about 100 hosts and 1000 terminals. Although the majority of the messages are one packet long, quite a few messages are two, four, and eight packets long. Most of the very long messages, e.g., files, are sent at night or on Sundays.

Each packet in Arpanet can contain up to 1008 bits of user information plus 96 bits of overhead. Actual observations show, however, that the average packet length is only 27 characters, including overhead.

About 60 percent of the Arpanet messages are sent by users to a favorite destination, which signifies predictable communities-of-interest. Furthermore, 22 percent of Arpanet traffic is local, which implies that it is switched within the same network node or it is between hosts within the same node.

7.3.1.7 Transmission and Signaling

The capacity of each internodal trunk is 50 KBPS. An analog transmission technique is employed on leased lines from common carriers.

An in-band signaling scheme, whereby the control information is contained in each packet, is employed.

All user lines that connect asynchronous terminals to a TIP employ start-stop baseband transmission techniques and a well-defined signaling protocol for accessing any network HP.

7.3.1.8 Iterative Modeling of Network Node

The first 15 nodes employed IMPs based on the Honeywell H516R minicomputer. It was then decided to change to the newer and cheaper Honeywell H316 minicomputer, and all later IMPs except one were based upon this. The TIP developed in 1971 also employs a H316 with up to 32 k words of primary storage.

In late 1974, BBN started the development of a new multiprocessor IMP called *Pluribus,* with higher throughputs and reliability as goals. BBN chose the Lockheed SUE as the basic CPU module, and the Pluribus was a working entity by 1975. Four Pluribuses have now been installed in Arpanet as an IMP, communication and control processor (CCP), TIP and/or Pluribus private line (PPL) interface for secure front ending. A fifth Pluribus application, Pluribus satellite IMP (PSI), is scheduled to be employed in Arpanet soon.

There are five levels to the network control protocol as developed by BBN. The levels are as follows: Level 1 as physical/electrical interface equivalent to the EIA RS 232-C or CCITT V.24 standards; Level 2 for link control; Level 3 for packet control; Level 4 for call control; and Level 5 for process-to-process control, e.g., open, close file. Interfaces among the various levels had to be precisely defined.

The initial capacity of the H516R was such that only one HP could be colocated with each IMP. A TIP now allows many hosts to be connected to an IMP. To accomplish this, a new host-to-host protocol had to be developed.

7.3.1.9 Performance Parameters

It is difficult to compute the total costs that have been incurred on Arpanet due to its complexity and originality as a research tool. Furthermore, because

Arpanet is a private network, no cost accounting is available. Nevertheless, we will make an attempt to assess some of the costs for its components.

Each of the original IMPs costs $100,000. The cost of a later IMP is somewhat lower.

The throughput of each original IMP is about 750 kbps. This figure has not changed much, although the capabilities of each IMP or TIP have increased significantly.

The average shortest path had grown to be 6.5 hops and the longest, 15. Some recent increases in network connectivity have reduced these numbers to 5.4 and 11, respectively. Using the above data, and assuming 58 nodes and a bell-shaped curve for traffic intensity during a 24-hour period, one should arrive at the peak hour loading of 30 percent. At this loading, an average response time is observed to be about 300 milliseconds.

The overall trunk availability has been observed to be 99.7 percent. The average availability of a network node is 99.6 percent. When only hardware and software failures were considered, the nodes had an average availability of 99.96 percent, with a mean time between failures of 840 hours and a mean time to repair of under 1 hour.

7.3.1.10 Concluding Remarks

Arpanet has been a great stimulus for PS technology. It has made believers of most critics of PS. Arpanet has been an effective test bed for many of the concepts now being employed in public PS systems.

Arpanet architecture has allowed a rather orderly growth ever since 1972. Without the distributed adaptive routing philosophy, it would have been very difficult to achieve manifold growth.

Although the predominant use of Arpanet is for access to remote interactive computer resources, an interesting application dealing with "network mail" has sprung up. Each user has an "electronic mail box" in a suitable HP. Anyone desiring to communicate with another user simply provides addresses of HPs and mail boxes and types in the message. It is surprising that other public PS networks do not provide this useful service.

The addition of Pluribus hardware is constantly providing additional capabilities, such as satellite channel interfaces and secure front ending, e.g., for HPs whose messages must be encrypted before transmission over the insecure Arpanet, for DOD users.

There have been several updates in Arpanet software. The most significant was related to IMP-to-IMP and IMP-to-host formats to allow more than 63 nodes and more than 4 HPs per IMP. This also involved changes in the packet format. Similar improvements in the TIP design are being implemented. Interfaces with other public PS networks are also planned.

7.3.2 Telenet

Telenet Communication Corp. was the first value-added common carrier to offer a public PS service in the United States. It began operation in August 1975. That event culminated three years of development that began in 1972 when BBN formed Telenet. Telenet president, Dr. Roberts, whose expertise strongly influenced the development of Arpanet, was again instrumental in making a success of Telenet. Telenet was acquired by GTE in 1979 and was made a part of the newly formed Communication Network Systems (CNS) group.

Unlike the public PS networks promoted by the PTTs in other countries, in the United States, Telenet must compete with other vendors of similar services.

7.3.2.1 An Application Summary

Basically, Telenet offers timesharing capability to widely scattered user terminals. The first two customers were timesharing services. Because Telenet

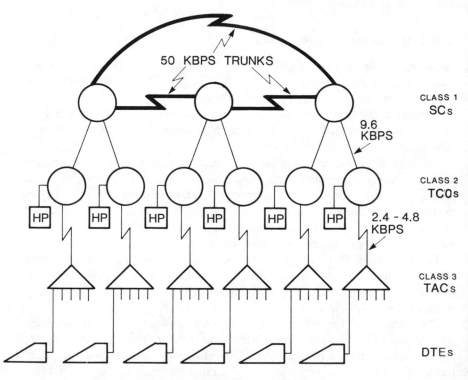

Fig. 7.16. Basic Telenet topology.

maintains many gateway switches, hosts and user terminals may now be distributed over many countries and interconnected, separate networks.

7.3.2.2 Network Topology

Telenet consists of nine major switching nodes called *Class 1 COs,* over 90 network access centers called *Class 2 Telenet central offices* (TCOs), transmission facilities leased from common carriers, a network control center (NCC), and network access equipment located on customer premises. Due to the network complexity, only the basic network topology is illustrated in Fig. 7.16.

The nine major COs are interconnected by 50-KBPS trunks. Class 2 COs serve as concentrators to provide economical network access nodes at some cities that do not justify the costs of establishing a major CO. The Class 2 CO (also TCO) is connected to the nearest Class 1 CO via one or more medium-speed access lines (2400 to 9600 BPS). A Class 3 node is a Telenet terminal access controller (TAC) generally situated at the customer's premises, and it provides concentration for local low-speed terminals. A Class 3 TAC is connected to the nearest Class 2 CO via one or more medium-speed lines. A TAC also provides the Packet Assembly/Disassembly (PAD) functions for asynchronous, low-speed terminals when required.

7.3.2.3 Identification Scheme

Telenet has a plan to implement the CCITT recommendation X.121 for a numbering plan for public data networks. It is as follows:

$$(P + \text{DNIC} + \text{national DTE No.})$$

where P = international prefix, DNIC = data network identification code $zxxx$—z = a digit between 2 and 7, x = a digit from 0 to 9—and national DTE No. is the actual code assigned to each DTE within the national public data network (PDN).

7.3.2.4 User Interfaces

Telenet offers several different types of access ports, as follows:

1. Public dial ports: asynchronous terminals that use the network occasionally to gain access by dialing a public telephone number. The operator selects the number according to the terminal speed.
2. Private dial ports: these may be either the dial-in type or capable of

dialing out to customer terminals or hosts. The ports could also be of either the local or foreign exchange (FX) type with speeds of 110 to 300 BPS for asynchronous communication and 2400 to 4800 BPS for synchronous application.

3. Dedicated access ports: hosts and heavily used terminals normally access Telenet through dedicated ports for 50 to 1800 BPS asynchronous and 2400 to 56,000 BPS synchronous applications. Telenet assumes end-to-end performance for this service.

4. Private packet exchange (PPX) access: for customers with 400 or more hours of terminal usage, it may be economical to lease a PPX consisting of multiplexer/concentrator and a PS node. PPX accesses Telenet via a public dial-in or dedicated port.

A host can be interfaced to Telenet in a variety of ways. There are over 200 (80 IBM, 60 CDC) hosts in Telenet. A host can act as a terminal by connecting it to a TCO via one or more asynchronous lines. A host can also be interfaced via a Telenet processor (TP) or a TAC, requiring no change in host software. The most powerful interface occurs when a special software package (THI or X.25) converts the host into a packet-mode terminal.

Telenet provides a comprehensive set of interfaces for almost all types of terminals, and it supports more than 10,000 terminals, most of them asynchronous.

A user's terminal can be interfaced via a TAC or TP. The latter interface allows a simple call setup procedure, as the TP provides all the necessary parameters. Otherwise, when the terminal makes a connection through a public dial port, an initial session is necessary before the TP becomes transparent during the session between the terminal and host. Several types of prompts and commands are available, making interactive session setup easy.

7.3.2.5 Traffic Flows and Routing

Because the key developers of Telenet are the same people who developed Arpanet, some similarities are bound to persist. One of them deals with the *distributed adaptive* routing within the backbone network consisting of Class 1 nodes. Telenet, however, has adopted the *virtual-circuit* concept, as required by the X.25 protocol, for network accessing. It provides facilities, such as message ordering, end-to-end error control, hot line (permanent virtual circuit), and private network (closed user group). These facilities would tend to create traffic flows closely related to the user communities in an Arpanet-like system, but the existence of a backbone network in Telenet allows a good deal of trunk sharing. For this reason, Telenet is more cost-effective than Arpanet.

7.3.2.6 Traffic Statistics

Unavailable.

7.3.2.7 Transmission and Signaling Techniques

All the remarks made for Arpanet also apply to Telenet. Both Arpanet and Telenet have the capability to employ the digital transmission facilities as they become available.

7.3.2.8 Iterative Modeling of Network Nodes

Earlier TIPs using Prime 200 minicomputers employed communication handling cards and up to 128 kbytes of storage. Several types of communication controllers, such as AMLC (asynchronous multiline controller), SMLC (synchronous multiline controller), and N-SMLC (network SMLC) for high-speed trunks, were developed.

Telenet Access Controller (TAC) was also developed for asynchronous access, using the principles of character-interleaved, time division multiplexing. The character stream from the TACs was demultiplexed in TIPs.

It was soon discovered that a minicomputer is not suitable for packet switching. The third generation nodes now employ the multimicroprocessor systems known as the Telenet Processor (TP) series.

A generalized model of a third generation PS node can be shown as in Fig. 7.17. A CO differs from another CO in terms of the number of TIPs employed in the node. The TP family was originally manufactured by Digital Communication Corp. It can realize nodal processing rates in the range of 0.6 to 35 MIPS (million instructions per second). Both private and shared memories can be configured to total 2 million bytes.

Telenet plans to gradually replace all Prime minicomputers in COs and TACs with TP hardware.

Three TP series are available. TP1000 has the capability of supporting 3, 7, or 14 asynchronous host or terminal ports at 75-300 BPS. TP1000s are replacing the old TACs as Class 3 COs to interface a small number of users to Telenet. TP2200 provides a network interface to host asynchronous ports at 75 to 9600 BPS. The majority of the hosts will be connected this way. Therefore, TP2200 will not be a part of a TCO. TP4000 is a multifunction node acting as a switch and TIP (host/terminal concentrator). It can handle both asynchronous and synchronous ports operating at 75 to 9600 BPS and 2400 to 56,000 BPS, respectively. TP1000 can now be easily upgraded to a TP4000 when growth demands it.

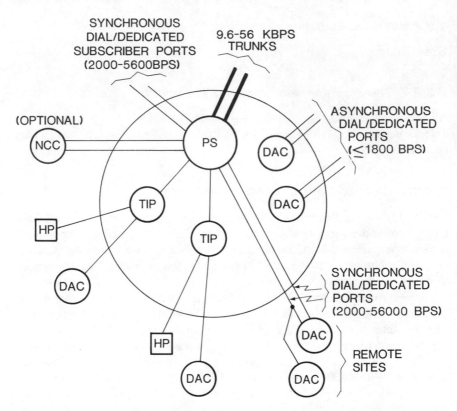

Fig. 7.17. A generalized model of a third generation Telenet central office.

Telenet NCC consists of two Prime 350s with 516 kbytes of core and more than 25 million bytes of disk storage.

Telenet employs X.25 protocol as an access method for packet-mode terminals and their TP-based nodes. The interchange between asynchronous terminals and TP nodes does not follow CCITT's X.28. Telenet has, however, implemented X.3 and X.29. The interchange between Class 1 switches is similar to that used in Arpanet. Telenet intends to employ X.75 protocol for interchange between its gateway switches and the gateway switches of other public data networks.

7.3.2.9 Performance Parameters

Telenet offers a tariffed service to users. According to the July 1, 1978 tariffs, monthly costs for a dedicated access port range from $300 for 50 to 300 BPS to $1100 for 9600 BPS. The charge includes a port at the TCO, access line, and the necessary modems. A dial-in terminal user pays a flat rate of $3.25 per hour in all cities directly served by Telenet. Private dial-in service costs $160 per month for 110 to 300 BPS and $450 per month for 4800 BPS. Traffic-dependent charges are $0.50 for 1000 packets, each containing up to 1024 bits of user data. Fixed charges of $100 per account and $10 per ID/Password Account are also levied. See Ref. 25 for further details on this tariff and a tariff related to private packet service (PPS).

No figures for throughput are available. According to Ref. 27, the trunks are 70 percent loaded during peak hours, which is higher than the 30 percent load estimated for Arpanet.

The high connectivity for the backbone network results in fewer hops and shorter response times when compared with Arpanet. The average path length is 1.4 hops within the backbone network and 0.7 hops for each end of the lower level subnetworks, resulting in a total average length of 2.8 hops.

The average time spent by the packet within the network is about 200 milliseconds. A change from 35 to 70 percent loading causes only a 5 percent increase in the network transit time—an unperceptible change.

Reliability of Telenet meets all the specified goals of the French public PS system, called TRANSPAC. The major switches have been observed to yield 99.99 percent availability. A single host connected to a TP has a reduced availability of about 99.9 percent due to local loop problems.

7.3.2.10 Concluding Remarks

Telenet is now a common name, and its service has met an extremely wide acceptance in the United States. Traffic and revenues have been continuously growing at the rate of at least 15 percent per month. The recent merger of Telenet with GTE is destined to provide the additional capital that will be required to increase the Telenet plant to meet the growing demand. The number of TCOs were recently increased to approximately 250, and the local service is now available in about 400 U.S. cities by 1980. The availability of TP1000 hardware will definitely accelerate the growth of Telenet without sacrificing availability and performance.

An increased availability of packet-mode, synchronous hosts and terminals from several vendors will boost Telenet business even further.

Because other countries are also developing public data networks (PDNs), interworking between their networks and Telenet will also grow. Telenet is already connected to six European countries, Canada, and Mexico.

7.3.3 Tymnet

Tymnet is a public data network that has been in service since 1971. It employs a unique variety of packet switching.

The network was originally used exclusively by the subscribers of Tymshare Inc., but in 1972, others were allowed to make use of its excess capacity. To do this, Tymshare offered service under an existing AT&T joint-use tariff according to which AT&T billed the users for their share of the line cost and Tymshare billed its users only for usage. In 1976, Tymnet Inc. was created as an independent subsidiary of Tymshare Inc., and it filed an application with the FCC to become a value-added network (VAN).

7.3.3.1 An Application Summary

About 40 percent of the Tymnet traffic deals with Tymshare services performed on their 55 host computers attached to Tymnet. The remaining traffic deals with many other service bureaus that also attach their hosts and data bases to Tymnet. About 179 data bases are available at present on such diverse topics as patents, mortality data, Japanese economy, and thoroughbred horses. Other users of Tymnet access their own private data bases or perform data processing services (e.g., payroll, inventory control, and MIS). Tymnet also offers a message switching service provided through its own hosts. Some users of this service send sales orders from all branches to a single headquarters.

7.3.3.2 Network Topology

Tymnet consists of four types of nodes: (1) Tymsat, (2) Tymcom, (3) supervisor node, and (4) composite node that performs all the functions previously mentioned. Tymsat interfaces 8 to 128 dial-up terminals to the network, and it is generally situated at Tymnet sites. An asynchronous Tymcom interfaces hosts to the network, and it is usually located at the user site. The synchronous Tymcom interfaces user host(s) to the network via 1 to 256 virtual ports, and it may be located at either Tymnet or user site. Tymnet consists of four supervisor nodes, only one being in control of the network at any one time. The network consists of about 335 intelligent nodes (communication processors), each of which is capable of switching data to any of the nodes to which it is connected. The network is not fully connected, but its connectivity is such that each node can be reached via at least two ways.

The network nodes are linked together via two or more 4800 BPS (mostly) and 9600-BPS trunks. A few connections are of higher capacity. Tymnet's policy is to add another 4800-BPS trunk whenever a trunk bundle is getting congested, instead of upgrading the capacity of the individual trunks.

Due to the complexity of the network, it is difficult to show the entire network topology. Figure 7.18 attempts to illustrate the basic network topology having only a two-level hierarchy.

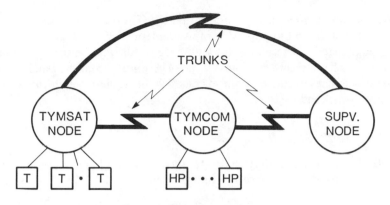

Fig. 7.18. Basic Tymnet topology.

7.3.3.3 Identification Scheme

Unavailable. In any case, it is a unique one applicable only to Tymnet.

7.3.3.4 User Interfaces

The internal protocols used in Tymnet are unique. Once the call is established through the help of a supervisory node, the user is unaware of such protocols, and the network appears transparent. The user-host interaction is solely determined by the particular host.

Tymnet provides the software in each of its nodes that interfaces the user terminal or host, with little or no change in the workings of user equipment. Part of the Tymnet protocol deals with the log-in procedure. This is straightforward and can be learned in a short time.

7.3.3.5 Traffic Flows and Routing

Only the supervisory node has the capability of establishing the virtual path, or route, between the user and the host during the entire call duration. The en route Tymnet nodes are responsible only for switching data. Each node can select any one of the individual trunks out of a given bundle connecting it to the next node in the path.

Tymnet has chosen a unique method of traffic flow. The basic unit of data is a byte consisting of 8 bits. The next higher-level traffic unit is a packet, which is packed with data from several users active at that time. Each physical packet has 2 bytes of overhead, up to 60 bytes of user data, and 4 bytes of checksum.

Each subpacket contains 2 bytes of header, which specifies the logical channel number and the number of information bytes in the subpacket. This technique allows statistical multiplexing of a number of independent data streams into a single packet. Therefore, this technique results in a better utilization of trunks and a shorter network transit time. The routing control, which is not a dynamic one, does enable a homogeneous flow of traffic through the network on a call-by-call basis.

7.3.3.6 Traffic Statistics

The 200 hosts on the network generate about 400,000 hours of connect time per month. This activity also results in processing of about 12 billion I/O characters each month.

7.3.3.7 Transmission and Signaling Techniques

Only analog transmission techniques are employed for the transmission of digital data on all long access lines and trunks. In-band signaling is employed on trunks. Signaling on user loops connecting terminals to a colocated Tymsat is via baseband signals.

7.3.3.8 Iterative Modeling of Network Nodes

The original Tymsats and Tymcoms employed Varian 620 minicomputers with 16 kbytes of storage each. A new minicomputer called "Tymnet Engine," designed and constructed by Tymshare, is providing more capabilities for a given cost.

The new minicomputer is a 32-bit machine that can support 1 million bytes of primary storage, 300 million bytes of secondary storage, 32 high-speed, synchronous I/O channels, and 256 medium-speed asynchronous I/O channels. The CPU operates on a 750-nanosecond cycle time.

The original supervisory node employed the SDS 940 computer. The new one employs the Interdata 7/32 minicomputer, which is more powerful and less expensive. The supervisor node has responsibility for keeping track of Tymnet topology, failures, and resource utilization levels, establishing optimal routes, gathering accounting and diagnostic data, and checking user-access profiles. Consequently, the supervisor node accounts for all the log-ins. It provides more detailed monthly bills to users than most other public data networks.

Tymnet offers many facilities to users, notably, restricted host usage and host level loading, which allows the movement of user identities from one host to another. Tymnet does not offer closed user groups.

A new node called the "ISIS" has been delivered to Manila, Singapore, Tokyo, and the international record carriers (IRCs). ISIS performs the functions of a Tymsat, Tymcom, Supervisor, X.25, and X.75 interfaces. An ISIS can thus manage a separate network.

Several Tymnet nodes employ hosts to provide message switching (MS) service (see the subsection 7.4 for models of MS nodes).

7.3.3.9 Performance Data

Tymnet is a tariffed service. The charges are made up of (1) usage charges based upon the bytes transmitted without consideration of distance, (2) either connect charge for dial-up access or a monthly rental for terminal access ports, and (3) a monthly bill for host connection via a Tymcom. A fixed bill for installation and change orders is also levied. Terminal access charges depend upon the speed and location of the terminal. Tymnet has about 145 local access cities—28 high-density, 54 low-density, and 37 FX locations. For example, a high-density, 1200-BPS host access port for teletypewriters will cost $100 a month. Forty hours of connect time will cost $40 per month ($1/hour). Five hundred kilobytes sent at 300 BPS and 5000 kilobytes received at 1200 BPS will cost another $50 and $150 per month, respectively. This totals $340 per month. For any computation, the latest FCC tariffs must be studied in detail.

Tymnet throughput capacity should be in the range of 15 to 18 billion characters per month, although Tymnet can easily upgrade its network to match any demand.

The unique packet transmission and switching technique costs a network-wide overhead of about 16 percent.

Despite the attempt to reduce the delay through the network by using the unique packet transmission technique, an average response time of 750 milliseconds is observed for an interactive user.

Tymnet doesn't guarantee any error rate or availability. Tymnet nodes fail on an average once every two years. Considering the large number of nodes in Tymnet, a nodal failure occurs once every two to three days. Because each node is at least doubly connected, the network availability is not much affected. When a supervisor node fails, it takes 2.5 minutes for another supervisor to assume control. This failure has no effect on the calls in progress. Only the calls being set up have to be routed again. The control on the four supervisory nodes is rotated once every week without any regard to failures.

The weakest point in Tymnet (as in any public network) is the single access line or a Tymsat node without backup.

Transmission error rate on Tymnet is about 1 in 4 billion bits.

7.3.3.10 Concluding Remarks

Tymnet has grown 10-fold since 1972. It is more or less a matured offering. Competition from Telenet, AT&T's ACS, and ITT's COM-PAK is bound to slow its growth rate. To maintain its dominant position, Tymnet is introducing new services, such as (1) ACT (advanced communication technology) for supporting both synchronous (e.g., IBM 3270s and X.25 packet-mode terminals) and asynchronous terminals/hosts, and (2) ON-TYME II electronic mail.

7.3.4 Pacuit Network Architecture

Packet switching was developed to reduce the delays involved with message switching. The other benefits, such as trunk concentration through ATDM, node-to-node error control, concurrently active virtual ports for timesharing or inquiry/response applications, and compatibility with diverse DTEs obtained via pads, etc., were really by-products. Pacuit switching is a hybrid packet and circuit switching technique developed by Tran Telecommunication Corp. It attempts to carry the above trend a little further, by using a technique that combines the concepts of TDM circuit switching and *composite packets*. As the reader will recall, Tymnet also uses the concept of composite packets to reduce node-to-node delays within the network. See Refs. 28 and 29 for more details.

7.3.4.1 An Application Summary

Although no existing public data network employs Pacuit switching at this time, one can still project several applications. A private or a public data network based on Pacuit switching can be synthesized to provide such applications as resource sharing, timesharing, inquiry/response, message switching, DBM service(s), host-to-host bulk data transfers, remote-job-entry (RJE) batch transfers and digitized voice. Pacuit is especially useful in a large, distributed network where delays could get too high for an inquiry/response or transaction processing environ.

7.3.4.3 Network Topology

A three-level hierarchical network topology can be synthesized using three types of nodes: (1) major nodes for a backbone subnetwork, (2) minor nodes for user entry and exit, and (3) remote terminal interface unit (RTIU) nodes. See Fig. 7.19 for an illustration of a generalized network topology. Major nodes are interconnected via 64 KBPS trunks. The minor nodes can be interconnected to each other or to major nodes via 1.2- to 64-KBPS trunks. Synchronous terminals with speeds ranging from 1.2 to 19.2 KBPS and asynchronous terminals with speeds ranging from 50 to 1200 BPS can be accommodated.

7.3.4.4 User Interfaces

Asynchronous terminal operation: the terminal operator "rings" the network using standard protocol; the operator enters the autobaud character; the net-

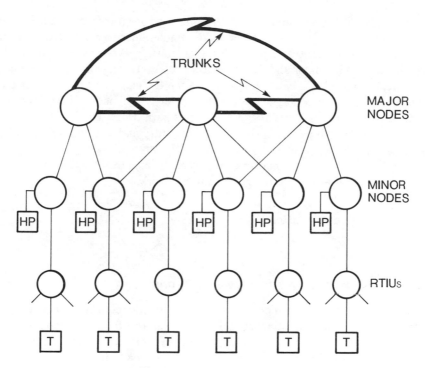

Fig. 7.19. Basic Pacuit topology.

work sets up for speed and code of terminal; the operator enters a password; the network prompts "res"; the operator enters the address of a specific terminal/host; the network sends a "/" if a connection is made; if the destination is busy, the network sends "RESOURCE BUSY"; from this point on, the network is transparent to data transfer operations.

Synchronous terminal operation via an RTIU (the RTIU provides status display and 12-key touch pad for operator addressing): the operator presses "*" to ring network; the network sends "CONTINUE" to the display; the operator enters the address of a resource; the network sends "CONNECTED" to the display; transmission now takes place, with network as a transparent medium.

7.3.4.5 Traffic Flows and Routing

A fixed route is assigned by the master node at the time of call establishment. For each call, there is an entry minor node and an exit minor node. The source and destination terminals are connected to these nodes, respectively. Composite packets are constructed at small, regular intervals at the entry minor node and disassembled at the exit minor node. All intermediate minor and major nodes operate in the TDM-circuit switched mode. Each minor or major node has the capability of flow control through instantaneous, per call basis, bandwidth management. The minor and major nodes have also the capability of assigning transmission method or bandwidth, based upon the class mark of the user terminals. To illustrate, a host-to-host bulk transfer is assigned a TDM-CS path, and a timesharing session is assigned a Pacuit path if desired.

Error control on a packet basis between the entry and exit nodes is provided for Pacuit mode of transmission, using an SDLC-like protocol.

A higher-level backbone network can be constructed to achieve greater sharing of trunk facilities in a large public data network.

7.3.4.6 Traffic Statistics

Not available.

7.3.4.7 Transmission and Signaling Techniques

The Pacuit network is a synchronous digital network requiring a master network clock. Consequently, the network is quite suitable for synchronous digital applications, unlike the Tymnet network. Tran's principle and technique of master clocking have been operationally proven in many installations, including the trans-Canada telephone system, DATAROUTE, the world's first public digital network.

Signaling over trunk facilities is accomplished via a separate subnetwork assigned to common channel, internode signaling. Baseband signaling is employed over four-wire user links, which are also shared by user data.

7.3.4.8 Iterative Modeling of Network Nodes

Each minor and major node employs a Tran M3200 computer that is based on a modular, multibus architecture (see Ref. 29 for details). It employs a 16-bit word structure and can support 512 kbytes of core storage.

Through the use of utility function modules and switch modules dedicated to specific tasks, incompatible terminals or computer ports may communicate through the network in a transparent mode. Two or more of these specialized modules may be appended to the network to provide conversion services to otherwise incompatible protocols, codes, and data rates. Similar techniques may be employed to establish connections with other public or private data networks.

The network also provides centralized network management and partitioning for control and cost accounting.

7.3.4.9 Performance Parameters

A basic Pacuit node has a base price of about $50,000. A satellite Pacuit node starts at $12,500. Multinode network hardware can cost approximately $300,000 or more.

Maximum throughput of an M3200-based node is estimated at 400,000 BPS. The node can support up to 2048 low-speed channels and up to 64 high-speed trunks.

The network boasts (see Ref. 29) a lower network delay for messages with lengths of 1500 bits or less, when comparing Pacuit and conventional packet switching technologies (e.g., X.25).

No data on availability for existing systems could be obtained at the time of writing.

7.3.4.10 Concluding Remarks

The developers of Pacuit are hopeful that their technology will ultimately replace packet switching (e.g., X.25) just as packet switching replaced message switching for interactive/transaction processing applications. They also believe their technology to be optimum for handling a mix of digitized voice, bulk data transfer, and bursty interactive traffic. The issues are very complex, however. Multiple virtual circuits, conferencing, multiple deliveries, and dynamic packet-by-packet routing through the network are still major advantages of PS. Transmission of digitized voice through the network is still an open issue. No existing hardware can handle the packet switching loads associated with a PCM-encoded large voice switch.

7.3.5 Summary Models of Other PS Systems

In the previous pages, we tried to model some basic PS network architectures. Their features form the basis of many other PS systems to be described here briefly. We will start with the North American PS systems and conclude with the remaining PS systems.

7.3.5.1 AT&T's Advanced Communication Service (ACS)

According to current plans, ACS will probably be offered in 1983. It is a PS data communication service based on digital facilities already in place for Dataphone digital service (DDS) and Dataphone switched digital service (DSDS); see subsection 7.3.2. The current timetable calls for 3 major message processing nodes—in Chicago, Los Angeles, and New York—and 100 minor service nodes scattered throughout the nation. ACS is an ambitious service, for it offers utmost compatibility, flexibility, network partitioning, network transparency, and low start-up costs.

7.3.5.2 ITT's COM-PAK Network

COM-PAK is a nationwide network that will support CCITT's X.25, X.3, X.28, and X.29 recommendations. In the beginning, ITT plans to offer FAX-PAK service for the transmission of facsimile data. Incompatible facsimile machines will be accommodated. Later, a general data service is scheduled to be offered for both synchronous and asynchronous terminals based on X.25 and IBM standards. Two sizes of packets, up to 8192 or 2048 bits, will be employed to achieve better utilizations of facilities or lower response times.

7.3.5.3 Trans-Canada Telephone System's (TCTS) Datapac

Datapac is a PS network with eight high-level switching nodes, each of which is connected to at least two other nodes. TCTS's Dataroute network's digital facilities are used in the backbone network. The minor nodes are called *network interface machines* (NIMs). Whereas the BNR's SL-10 computers are employed in each major node, either an SL-10 multiprocessor or an NCR 721 minicomputer is used in NIMs. Originally, TCTS had developed a standard network access protocol (SNAP), which was based on the Datagram philosophy, as used in Arpanet, but later SNAP was modified to conform to the X.25's virtual circuit concept.

Datapac offers many services: (1) 3000 service is for synchronous terminals that support SNAP protocol, which is similar to X.25, but allows BSC framing. TCTS supplies X.25/SNAP software package for IBM 3704/5 front ends; (2) 3101 service is for start/stop, asynchronous terminals connected to an NIM. Access to the NIM can also be made through dial-up ports; (3) 3301 service is for point-of-sale (POS) terminals connected to an NCR721-based NIM; (4) 3203 service is for large organizations in need of an extensive inquiry/response application available to its many customers.

Interworking to other PS networks is offered, although the priority mode, which has the smaller packet size of 128 bytes instead of the normal 256 bytes, may be needed.

7.3.5.4 CNCP Telecommunication's Infoswitch

Infoswitch was designed as an integrated CS/PS network to offer data communication services in competition with Datapac's services in Canada. The original emphasis was to capture all the existing nonintelligent synchronous and asynchronous terminals and then to grow to adapt to needs as they emerge. Infoswitch is now a fully connected four-node network employing 19.2- and

56-KBPS trunks. CNCP plans to add additional smaller nodes and concentrators as traffic patterns demand. PDP 11/40 minicomputers provide the processing power to the major nodes. Infoswitch provides both a hybrid circuit and packet switching mode and a pure packet switching mode. The routes are fixed on a call-by-call basis.

Infoswitch offers basically three services: (1) Infoexchange Service (IES), which is a digital, circuit switched service; (2) Infocall service (ICS), which provides virtual circuit connections using either character mode asynchronous terminals or block mode synchronous terminals; and (3) Infogram service (IGS), which provides a PS service analogous to Datapac 3000 service, but involving Infogram network access protocol (INAP). INAP is a simpler protocol than X.25. CNCP has not rejected X.25 and other CCITT recommendations, but has simply postponed their implementations until the time is right.

In comparison, Infoswitch has many similarities with the Pacuit network discussed in 7.3.4.

7.3.5.5 European Informatic Network (EIN)

This multinational PS network was established to provide information exchange among several research centers, facilitate discussion and comparison of national networks, promote European standards, and provide potential models for future networks.

The EIN consists of five primary switching centers—London, Paris, Zurich, Milan, and Ispra—and seven secondary centers. The five major nodes are connected by six 9600-BPS trunks. An NCC also is provided at the United Kingdom's NPL facilities. Some recently designated centers can also access the network through the PTT networks.

The EIN is essentially a datagram network, following France's Cyclades and the United States's Arpanet, although the network has facilities to provide end-to-end packet ordering and flow control if desired. EIN also employs a distributed dynamic routing method similar to that used in Arpanet.

EIN has always been engaged in the development of high-level protocols, such as (1) transport station (TS) for end-to-end distribution of related packets, (2) virtual terminal protocol (VTP) for incompatible terminals, (3) file transfer protocol (FTP), and (4) remote-job-entry protocol (RJEP). EIN offers many interesting facilities, such as delivery confirmation to a destination major node and trace data for studying the routes and diagnostic data in case of nondeliveries.

7.3.5.6 Euronet

Euronet was designed to provide access to data bases within the nine European Economic Community (EEC) countries and thus develop a common market for scientific and technical information. Euronet is jointly owned by the nine PTT's and the Commission for European Communities (CEC).

Euronet is a PS network based largely on the French PTT's Transpac. It consists of four PS nodes—in Frankfurt, London, Paris, and Rome—and five remote access nodes—in Amsterdam, Brussels, Copenhagen, Dublin, and Luxembourg: 48 KBPS trunks will connect PS nodes, and 9600-BPS trunks will connect the remote access nodes with the PS nodes. Euronet will start with one NCC, but its design allows multiple NCCs.

Euronet is based on the CCITT recommendations X.25, X.3, X.28, and X.29, just as Transpac is. Consequently, it will support packet-mode, synchronous, block-mode, synchronous, and character-mode, asynchronous terminals.

An interesting facility provided by Euronet will deal with an automatic translation system, called Systran, for technical and scientific texts accessed from data bases.

The network is designed to handle about 2.5 million DB enquiries or about 1 million session hours in 1985. The network response time should range between 1 and 3 seconds. The design goal for MTBF is 200 hours.

7.3.5.7 SITA (Societe Internationale de Telecommunications Aeronautique) Network

SITA manages a worldwide network to handle type A (reservation) and type B (administrative MS) traffic for about 220 airlines. The SITA network is a two-level network. The backbone network consists of nine high level centers (HLCs), and it is based upon the packet switching concept to handle interairline type B traffic. Each of the low-level subnetworks handles its own type A and type B traffic through its own host-FE node, which also acts as a concentration point for the type B interairline traffic. SITA is now showing signs of overloading, and a new PS network based on CCITT recommendations is planned.

7.3.5.8 EPSS (Experimental Packet Switching Service)

EPSS was first offered in 1977 by the British Post Office to users in the United Kingdom. It consists of three PS exchanges (PSEs)—in London, Manchester, and Glasgow. The network is based on a virtual-call concept, but does not follow other CCITT recommendations. EPSS employs a fixed alternate routing technique at each node, whereby if both the primary and the alternate routes have failed, the information packet is sent back to the originator.

Because EPSS did not conform to international standards, most of the original customer base has disappeared. Some of them, e.g., British Steel Corp., are developing their own private PS networks. A new PSS based on CCITT recommendations is being developed and will be operational soon.

7.3.5.9 IPSS (International PS Service)

IPSS was the first international PS service offered outside North America. It was first offered in 1978, and it replaced the one-way data base access (DBA) service, which began in 1977 in conjunction with WUI. In contrast, IPSS is a two-way service offered with the cooperation of International Record Carriers (IRCs), Telenet, and Tymnet. The service will support both character-mode, asynchronous (at 110 to 300 and 1200 BPS) and block-mode, synchronous (at 2.4, 4.8, or 9.6 KBPS) terminals. All the U.K. subscribers will access the IPSS-PSE at London. PSE hardware was supplied by Telenet Corp. and has all the capabilities described in 7.3.2.

7.3.5.10 Cyclades of France

Cyclades is identical to Arpanet, because it was also developed for resource sharing among universities and government computer centers. The network, sometimes also called "Cigale," employs the purest form of Datagram concept, whereby the network is a black box that transports individual packets to destination hosts, also called *transport stations,* without any knowledge of messages and without any flow control. The network employs a two-level, distributed dynamic routing technique, whereby the packet is first sent to a region and later to subregions. Cyclades has had a profound influence on PS technology, and CCITT is considering a Datagram facility within X.25. The customer base of Cyclades will eventually transfer to Transpac, when the latter becomes fully operational.

7.3.5.11 RCP Network of France

RCP is also an experimental PS network set up by the French PTT in the same way EPSS was set up in the United Kingdom. Its operation began in 1975. RCP is based upon the virtual-circuit concept to minimize host modifications—a commendable goal for a public network. Currently, the network consists of 5 nodes, 40 synchronous ports, and 300 asynchronous ports. Nodes are connected via 9600-BPS trunks, and multiplexer access nodes are connected to main nodes via 4800-BPS trunks. RCP will continue to aid in the development of new protocols after Transpac begins to offer PS service throughout France.

7.3.5.12 Transpac of France

Transpac is a public PS service in France. The network consists of 12 PS nodes and 13 concentrator nodes. Each PS node will be connected to the network by at least two 72-KBPS trunks. An NMC at Rennes manages the entire network. Transpac employs a virtual-circuit concept through all network levels—once the full connection is made for a call, all the related packets are sent sequentially on the established path. A four-level protocol, including a multiplexing level, is employed. Three levels are identical to that for X.25. Transpac was designed to serve about 30,000 terminals in 1985. Transit time through the network is expected to be 200 milliseconds 90% of the time. Transpac was designed to provide a call setup time of 1.5 seconds or less. Duplication of all critical hardware should provide high availability.

7.3.5.13 RETD of Spain

RETD is perhaps the first public data network that offered PS service in 1971, before PS standards were available. Consequently, it does not employ X.25 protocols. Currently, it consists of 3 PS nodes and 30 concentrator nodes. PS nodes are connected by 9600-BPS trunks. Protocols are based upon virtual-call concepts. Maximum length of a packet is 270 bytes, with 255 bytes of user data. It serves about 4000 terminals. There is a plan to implement a six-node PS network based on CCITT recommendations. Concentrators, multiplexer nodes, 48-KBPS trunks, and adaptive routing are also planned.

7.3.5.14 D-50 PS Service in Japan

D-50 is an outgrowth of the experimental DDX-2 PS network. It consists of one PS node in Tokyo and seven multiplexer nodes. The various nodes are interconnected via 48-KBPS trunks. D-50 is an X.25-based service that employs a fixed routing plan, as in Transpac. Both packet-mode and non-packet-mode terminals can be accommodated. Many interesting facilities, such as fast select, permanent virtual circuit, closed circuit group, automatic dialing, direct call, and abbreviated dialing, are offered. D-50 is designed to serve about 500 packet mode DTEs. Network transit times ranging from 150 to 500 milliseconds and call setup times ranging from .35 to 1.5 seconds are expected. On the average, 1 out of 100 million bits will be in error, and sytem availability of 99.97 percent is expected.

7.3.5.15 Some Concluding Remarks on PS Networks

Many other countries, such as Belgium, Federal Republic of Germany, The Netherlands, Nordic, and South Africa are also planning public data networks based on PS technology. These countries will be followed later by several developing nations, such as India.

Because their PTTs are actively engaged in CCITT's activities, it is natural to expect that international standards will be employed for designing their public data networks. PTTs have learned several lessons by now. Standards will allow economical interworking among various networks and will force vendors to offer standard hardware and software to fit their hosts/terminals for interfacing to the public data networks.

Public data networks may not be the panacea for all users. Several large corporations, e.g., British Steel Corp., may find that private PS networks can handle their needs more effectively and economically. Several corporations have traditionally managed their own CS networks for their voice applications. As their data requirements grow, they would like to integrate the two requirements and manage their total communication resources. No public offering exists to handle this need. In the United States, SBS (Satellite Business Systems) is prepared to offer this service, but the economics of its service has not been subjected to competitive forces yet.

7.4 MESSAGE-SWITCHED (MS) SYSTEMS

The computer-controlled MS system was born through the merger of computer technology and the need to automate the torn-tape teletypewriter message exchange operations for the U.S. airlines. A human looked at the message appearing on the paper tape of a teletypewriter, manually tore off the message, and fed the paper tape to another machine tied to the destination station. As the interairline message traffic grew, the manual exchange became a terrible scene. Several research and development projects were initiated in the United States to design a computer-controlled MS system during the early 1960s.

Collins Radio Co. developed the first commercially successful system that employed a communication processor built around a core random access memory (RAM), a read-only memory (ROM) and a large disk file storage. By 1963, this system had become extremely popular among the airlines and Aeronautical Radio Inc., which serves many small airlines.

The major user facilities offered by MS systems were complete end-to-end message assurance, extremely good utilization of expensive user links through the use of long-term queing offered within the MS node, and long-term (up to 24 hours or even longer) protected storage. Designing the system was not easy. New data structures had to be created to achieve an efficient use of core and disk storages. A real-time operating system had to be developed for better CPU utilization.

Technology dealing with data communication has progressed dramatically since the early 1960s. As shown in subsection 7.3, PS technology is replacing MS in many applications because PS is more responsive, more economical, and more flexible. Even the SITA network (see 7.3) in Europe showed how a large number of MS subnetworks could be combined through a higher-level PS network to achieve great economies of scale.

However, there are still many applications where end-to-end message assurance and long-term protected storage are necessary. Airlines still require message switching systems. Frequently, their MS requirements are combined with their reservation traffic. This requires a front-end communication processor that not only communicates with a reservation host but also manages the entire communication network. Large financial institutions and banks also deal with both store-and-forward and inquiry response messages. Some of their messages involve millions of dollars and must be protected in a centralized storage until the transaction is completed to everyone's satisfaction.

In terms of the future, MS will tend to become just another facility within a public data network (PDN). Again, when the office of tomorrow becomes a reality, MS is bound to play an even greater role in distributing a large amount of interoffice memos and mail and storing and retrieving a large amount of word processing data for later retrievals or printouts.

In the following paragraphs, we will briefly describe two modern MS systems. The choice was difficult, for there are at least several hundred distinct MS systems operating in the world. Our objective was to highlight all the features of MS systems that justify their existence.

7.4.1 Pan American (Pan Am) Airline's Information Exchange and Distribution (IED) System

7.4.1.1 An Application Summary

In 1977, Pan Am integrated several separate networks that performed such applications as load control, operational control, crew and equipment assignments, material supply, cargo operation, and airline operations. The result was IED.

7.4.1.2 Network Topology

Figure 7.20 illustrates IED network topology and IED interfaces to two other network systems, namely Pan Am's Reservation and Arinc's MS network that handles other airlines' and interairline traffic. IED obeys the SCMD topology defined in Chapter 2. IED serves about 150 dedicated, multidrop lines and about 1200 terminals scattered throughout the world at Pan Am's facilities. One of the low-speed line provides an interface to the SITA network (see 7.3), providing Pan Am access to the world's airlines. Two 2400-BPS lines interface IES to the Chicago Arinc's MS center, giving Pan Am access to all the U.S. airlines. Integration became complete with the addition of a communication interface between IES and the PANAMAC II reservation host.

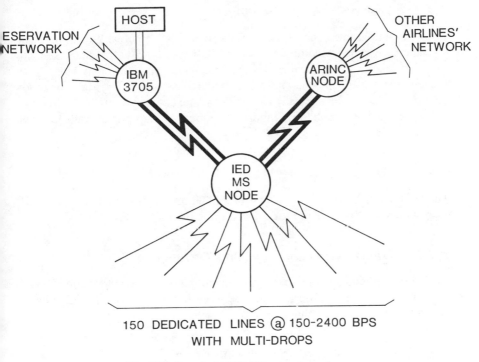

Fig. 7.20. Pam Am's IED MS network topology.

7.4.1.3 Identification Scheme

IED employs the ATA/IATA addressing structures within a message header. The American Transportation Association (ATA) and the International Airline Transportation Association (IATA) employ the alphanumeric addressing code "CCCSSAL," where CCC is the city name code, SS is the numerical station code, and AL is the airline name.

7.4.1.4 User Interfaces

A typical user enters a message with the proper format and address and waits for the terminal to be polled. When the message is fully received by the IED node, the user gets an acknowledgment. Facilities such as group codes, specified period of protected/long-term storage, and up to four levels of message priorities are available.

7.4.1.5 Traffic Flows and Routing

IED is a simple one-node network, thus requiring no network routing. Each message is switched according to the first-in-first-out (FIFO) scheme as modified by the allowable priorities. As the IED node obeys the delay model with random arrivals and exponentially distributed message lengths, high utilization of output links can be realized. The polling cycle can be optimally designed by taking into account each link's input and output loadings and average message holding times.

7.4.1.6 Traffic Statistics

The IED MS node handles in excess of 20,000 messages per peak day. A bell-shaped curve defines the message distribution within the day.

7.4.1.7 Transmission and Signaling Techniques

Analog transmission and inband signaling techniques are employed on 150 user lines. The synchronous interface link between IED and PANAMAC is based on digital transmission techniques.

7.4.1.8 Iterative Modeling of the MS Node

Figure 5.5 illustrates the main resources of the IED or any other modern MS node. A dual disk file storage is needed to provide a long-term protected storage to every message that enters the MS node. The disk file is also used for storing the entire software system and checkpoint data. Availability of the software system on disk enables quick initial program load (IPL) at the start of operation or after each recovery. The checkpoint tables are updated every few seconds because they record critical data regarding messages in process and active buffers. In case the on-line processor fails, the standby processor is automatically activated, checkpoint data is read from the disk file, and recovery takes place. Some messages may be marked "Possible Duplicate" when outputted. Great care is taken not to lose a single message that has been acknowledged by the MS node.

The magnetic tapes provide long-term journaling of either the entire traffic or just high-level logs. In rare cases, when both disk files are down, an IPL can occur from a magnetic tape.

The MS node employs the C-System multicomputer architecture (see Ref. 11 and subsection 7.5 for details) for interconnecting several minicomputer-based programmable channel termination groups (PCTGs) and peripheral devices to achieve high nodal throughput. An input message is first divided into 120-byte segments by a PCTG. which adds 8 bytes for chaining and other logical functions. These segments are then sent to the C-8561 message processor, which then edits the message, decodes the addresses, the routing function, from the header, stores the message on the disk file in the form of chained segments with addresses determined according to a preassignment scheme (see Ref. 10), and then queues the message for transmission on a proper link.

The disk write/read requests are batched, ordered according to the rotational latency, and then serviced for achieving high throughput. As a dual disk file subsystem is essential for providing an economical, long-term, protected storage for all messages, there is no alternative to this technique. Section II discusses analytical tools for computing the throughput of a disk file subsystem using batching and ordering. Message segmentation also results in efficient utilization of core buffers and disk file storage. This case is also discussed in Section II.

Programmable PCTGs accommodate a wide variety of terminals and line protocols associated with older but separate networks.

The MS node employs two C-8561 processors, one on-line and the other standby. The standby computer is constantly monitoring the on-line processor. When the on-line processor fails, the standby processor reads the checkpoint tables and assumes control of the network.

Several administrative, traffic, and resource utilization reports are available for the management of the IED network.

7.4.1.9 Performance Parameters

The throughput capacity is about 165,000 store-and-forward messages per day.

Response time is not critical for most of the IED applications.

MS node availability is in excess of 99.9 percent.

7.4.2 Interbank MS Networks

An increasing number of financial institutions are discovering the benefits of MS technology to automate their funds transfer and administrative communication with other banks. Two interbank networks are operational at present. The SWIFT (Society for Worldwide Interbank Financial Telecommunications) network became operational in late 1976. It serves about 369 banks in 15 countries of Western Europe, Canada, and the United States (see Ref. 31). A similar network, called the "Bankwire II," became operational in early 1978. It serves about 270 member banks in the United States. Both these networks handle similar applications.

7.4.2.1 An Application Summary

The main applications are those of funds transfer, asset settlement, and administrative exchange. Interbank messages dealing with confirmation of funds transfer, confirmation of federal funds borrowing or lending, advice on loan participation renewals or repayments, notifications of prime rate change, customer account balances, letter of credit information, and confirmation of collection can be sent to other banks with end-to-end assurance. Furthermore, both networks are designed to achieve a high degree of availability through the use of two MS nodes in the network, each MS node characterized by a redundant computer configuration. The users of these networks are banks that subscribe to the service for a fee. Both these networks represent "leading edge" MS technology.

7.4.2.3 Network Topology

Both the SWIFT and Bankwire II networks are hierarchical networks, as shown in Figs. 7.21 and 7.22. Both networks consist of two MS nodes each and several concentrators. Each concentrator serves a group of dumb/intelligent terminals located on the premises of member banks. An interesting aspect of both networks is that each concentrator has an alternate path to the second center. This results in enhanced survivability in case of a total center failure. Whereas SWIFT shows a two-center, multidrop topology, the Bankwire II represents a pure two-center, two-star topology.

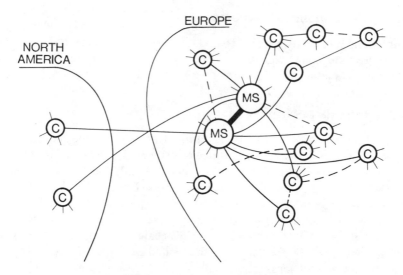

Fig. 7.21. SWIFT network topology.

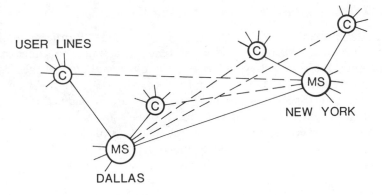

Fig. 7.22. Bankwire II network topology.

The concentrators are connected to the centers in the two networks via 9600- or 4800-BPS trunks, and the two centers are connected to one another by two 9600-BPS trunks (Bankwire II).

7.4.2.3 Identification Scheme

Each terminal is assigned a unique address. A member bank may have more than one terminal, and each terminal may receive only certain types of messages. A message may have more than one address, or one may use certain group codes (Bankwire II) to address multiple terminals. Message headers have been standardized for easier message processing.

7.4.2.4 User Interfaces

Both networks handle asynchronous and synchronous terminals, such as Telex, teletypewriters, and CRTs. Bankwire II also handles TWX terminals.

Interbank MS networks provide end-to-end assurance by sending IMA (input-message-acknowledgment) and delivered message acknowledgements whenever required by an application. In some implementations, if the message gets delayed beyond a certain limit, typically 20 minutes, then a DLA (delayed acknowledgment) will be sent.

In some cases, if the message cannot be sent to the destination, a designated alternate terminal may receive the traffic, or it may be stored at an MS node for delivery at a later date when the trouble is fixed. In some other cases, reject message notifications may be sent to the originators.

The users (bank employees) who enter data prefer the intelligent terminal because it prompts the operator to enter the message correctly.

7.4.2.5 Traffic Flows and Routing Control

Most of the interbank networks consist of one or two nodes. Furthermore, there is only one primary MS node at any one time. As a result, no sophisticated routing technique is needed. All messages flow to the primary node, get logged in the primary data base (DB), then in the secondary DB, and finally are sent to the destination. Special queues and checkpoints are maintained for all processes, so that if any failure occurs, no information is lost during an intranodal recovery period or during an internodal recovery procedure. This application thus employs the distributed DBM system concept.

7.4.2.6 Traffic Statistics

A typical interbank network handles about 20,000 to 60,000 messages a day. Message length generally ranges from 250 to 400 characters. Internal overheads are added to ensure data integrity. Stringent requirements for data integrity generate a good deal of service messages that travel from one subsystem to another and from one node to another.

7.4.2.7 Transmission and Signaling Techniques

Existing systems employ analog transmission techniques for exchange of digital data between network nodes. Some short user lines employ baseband transmission techniques.

In-band signaling is employed on all types of links.

7.4.2.8 Iterative Modeling of Network Nodes

Most of the MS nodes can be modeled as shown in Fig. 5.5. Many different brands of processors are used depending on the type of a node. To illustrate, the SWIFT network employs the Burroughs B3700 computer for message switching, the Burroughs B774 as a communication controller in an MS node, and a Burroughs B775 computer to synthesize a concentrator. Similarly, the Bankwire II network uses a C-System architecture to synthesize a local multicomputer network (see subsection 7.5 for details) for a MS node and employs a DEC PDP-11 minicomputer to synthesize a concentrator. One could synthesize a minicomputer-based, interbank network with modest capabilities.

7.4.2.9 Performance Parameters

Interbank MS networks owe their existence to basic economics. On an average day, some member banks process over $1 billion of fund transfers for a wide client base of correspondent banks. Labor and time cost money to member banks. These networks provide a unit cost of about $.20 to $.30 per message, which, when we consider an average delivery time of 1 to 5 minutes, beats all other alternatives, such as ordinary mail, certified mail, TWX/Telex, telephone, facsimile, and mailgram. Furthermore, the user bank derives many side benefits such as audit trails, later message retrievals, positive IMAs, DLAs, DMAs, data integrity, and high network availability.

Because these networks attract more customers with time, the network architecture must allow growth.

Due to the nature of business, utmost system availability (in excess of 99.5 percent) must be guaranteed without compromising data integrity. Protection against general blackouts or other disasters must be provided through the availability of redundant DBs and switching centers.

7.4.2.10 Concluding Remarks

Interbank networks will continue to be separate networks managed by consortiums of banks. Public data networks are incapable of providing all the facilities provided by either the SWIFT or Bankwire II system.

With the advent of home terminals and new user services, daily bank transactions are bound to increase rapidly. This will give rise to additional networks.

7.4.3 Summary Models of Some Other MS Systems

We described a pure MS system for an airline in 7.4.1. Arinc also employs a large MS node to switch interairline administrative traffic. Its network is a single level, in terms of switching nodes, network unlike the SITA network.

There are other airlines that combine MS and inquiry/response transactions into a single system. Air Canada employs a front-end (FE) node that provides an interface between a large network of over 2000 low or medium-speed terminals and a set of Univac 1100 host processors that produce responses to inquiries. The FE node not only switches inquiry/response type transactions, but also provides MS facility to administrative traffic. The FE also provides low-speed interfaces to the SITA, CNT, and Arinc MS networks.

The Air Canada FE employs the C-System multicomputer architecture (see 7.5 for details) to synthesize the switching node. Sufficient hardware redundancy is provided to achieve FE availability of 99.95 percent or better. Because the FE stores the inquiry/response traffic during the period the host subsystem, generally without backup, is down, the system availability is enhanced.

Many other airlines, such as Scandinavian Airlines, Braniff, and American Airlines, employs similar FEs. In some cases (e.g., British Airways system), large hosts handle both MS and inquiry/response traffic.

Two interesting applications have recently emerged to provide integrated networks for large banks.

The Credit Lyonnais's Refonte System employs three FEs (each using the C-System architecture) to interconnect dispersed host processors and over 6000 bank teller positions and back office terminals to offer a highly reliable inquiry/response system with a response time of about 1.5 seconds. All three nodes must fail to result in a total system failure.

The Barclay Bank's BINS (Barclay's Integrated Network System) also employs several FEs (using CDC's Cyber 1000 architecture) to integrate three original but separate networks. Each of these old networks served about 600 to 900 branches.

Both networks above also employ concentrators to achieve significant savings in communication costs. Since cutover, these two networks have added many other functions to achieve greater economies of scale.

Large MS nodes emphasize the features that justify the MS technology. However, small MS nodes far outnumber the large MS nodes. The advent of low-cost minicomputers gave rise to low-cost, programmable communication processors for synthesizing MS nodes, FEs, and concentrators. These communication processors replaced quite a few hardwired controllers that managed a small number of communication lines under the direct supervision of a host. Several papers (e.g., Ref. 32) can be consulted for studying both small and large communication processors.

7.5 DISTRIBUTED DATA PROCESSING (DDP) SYSTEMS

Human civilization is in the throes of a fourth major revolution—previous revolutions being the wheel, steam engine (or the industrial revolutions), and the computer. Distributed data processing (DDP) represents the new revolution.

At present, there is a good deal of controversy regarding the true definition of DDP. According to Enslow (Ref. 33), a DDP system must have physical dispersion of shared DP resources, communication/control functions, and shared data elements throughout the network system. The dispersed DP resources must be transparent to the users, and the DDP service must continue to be provided despite unit failures in the network. There is no existing system that satisfies all the prerequisites of DDP as defined by Enslow. A great deal of hardware and software development is required before a truly dispersed DDP system becomes a reality.

There are quite a few computer networks and DP network architectures that allow only the physical dispersion of computers in the network. Such computer networks provide faster response times, higher throughputs, higher availabilities, and lower costs than a computer network with only a single DP node. Availability of cheap minicomputers and microcomputers is accelerating this trend. Such computer networks are bound to eventually evolve into true DDP networks as defined by Enslow.

The merging of computer and communication technologies has provided the designer new challenges in the design of computer network architectures. (See Ref. 35 for a detailed discussion.) Actually, DDP demands detailed trade-off analyses involving distribution of the various functions throughout the network. Suddenly, the solution space becomes too large for any designer. A blind immersion into the DDP world is bound to cause disappointments and grief.

In the limit, a computer network system may require only the dispersion of stand-alone DP equipment at every desk—a solution that may increase the productivity of a company manyfold. One might say that, because there are no communication channels connecting the various DP nodes, this is not a computer network. In this case, the network is replaced by the human communication channels available within the organizational structure. Such a system, although representing an extreme case, should be folded into the definition of a computer network, as it differs from a centralized DP system involving a huge, impersonal, batch-oriented DP center enclosed within a fortlike building. Similarly, there may be a myriad of solutions based on network control philosophies—from autonomous control of DP nodes to a centralized control of all DP nodes. Furthermore, there may be a single DB facility or many DB facilities (identical/distinct/mixed) scattered through the network. In any case, a computer network system must not be separated from the user's needs (Ref. 36).

Some recent experiences (e.g., see Ref. 34) have shown that a computer network system must be designed to fit the multilevel, hierarchical structure of an organization to achieve such benefits as high throughput, fast response times, high productivity, high availability, reduced communication costs, reduced costs through resource sharing, and good adaptability to traffic growth or new applications. There are many sad stories of cases when the organizational structures were dictated by the centralized DP operations.

In the following pages, we will attempt to model several well-known computer network systems classified according to the following criteria:

1. local networks
2. geographically dispersed networks

The local networks involve several cooperating processing elements interconnected via wideband digital facilities to solve one or more applications as desired by the user. The extreme example of a computer network involving unconnected, autonomous DP resources is too straightforward for modeling. Consequently, such cases are ignored. (See Ref. 40 for a general introduction to local computer networks.)

A geographically dispersed computer network system implies several DP/switching nodes interconnected via long-haul transmission facilities. Such a network allows resource sharing to a community of users scattered over a vast area.

Both types of networks may be characterized by unique architectures.

Several of the network systems considered for modeling here could have appeared as PS networks. However, a subjective decision was made to include these in the DDP subsection, because they derive their existence from DP capabilities.

7.5.1 C-System Architecture

About 25 local networks employing this novel architecture have been implemented. Applications include inquiry/response, MS, and software development. The idea behind C-System was conceived in 1968, and it took three years to develop it. References 11 and 37 describe the multicomputer architecture and related performance issues in detail. We will highlight the main ideas in the following paragraphs.

7.5.1.1 An Application Summary

This architecture is mainly used to synthesize complex nodes for MS, inquiry/response, and front-ending (FE) applications requiring high throughputs, fast response times, and extremely high availabilities. As a result, large airlines and banking institutions have been the major users.

7.5.1.2 Network Topology

Figure 7.23 illustrates the network topology within the framework of C-System architecture. The local multicomputer network consists of several 32-bit communication processors (C-8500s), host processors, and minicomputer-based PCTGs (programmable channel termination groups). The interconnection between the C-8500 computers, host processors, and the peripherals, e.g., disk files, magnetic tapes, and high-speed printers, is realized through a 32-MBPS time-division-exchange (TDX) loop.

The interconnection between a given C-8500 communication processor and the associated PCTGs is achieved through a 1.288-MBPS time division multiplexed (TDM) loop. Although there is no restriction in the number of C-8500 processors in a local network, most nodal realizations consist of only two and sometimes three such processors. Up to 16 PCTGs can be connected to each C-8500, and each PCTG can serve up to 64 low-speed or 16 medium-speed or

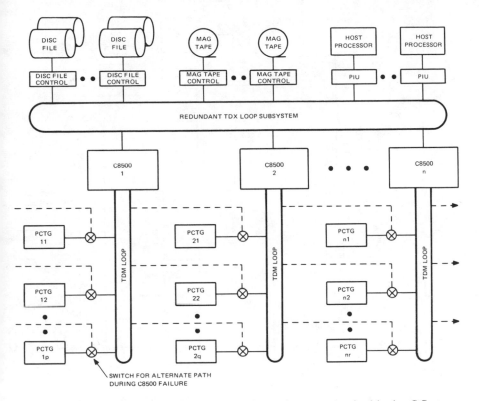

Fig. 7.23. A generalized multicomputer network topology associated with the C-System architecture.

a few high-speed links. Consequently, a local network can provide a good deal of computer-to-computer or terminal-to-computer communication.

Even the four core modules of each C-8500 and the various users of its ALU (arithmetic logic unit) time are organized in the form of a network, as illustrated in Fig. 7.24. The three transfer links provide CS paths between the device controllers and memory modules on a direct memory access (DMA) basis. Transfers follow a priority hierarchy assigned to memory users, PSU, MSU, (DC0, DC1), (DC2, DC3), DC4, and ALU. The MSU and DCUs are hardwired queue servers for the respective users.

7.5.1.3 Identification Scheme

Time slots on the TDX and TDM loops are assigned at IPL time to the various devices on a permanent basis for allowing communication between them and

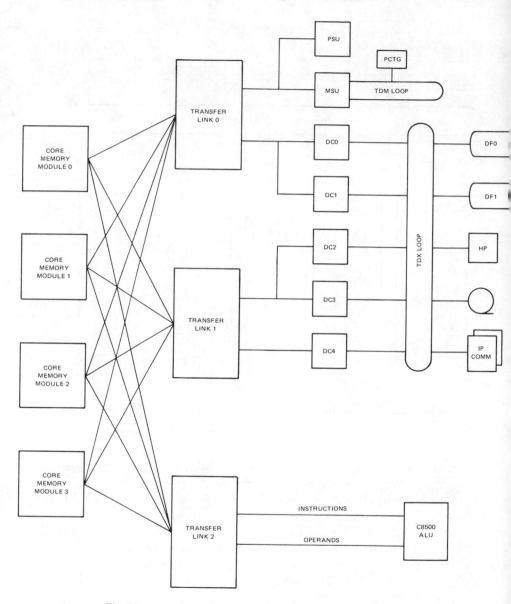

Fig. 7.24. Topology of an internal network within a C-8500 processor.

C-8500. All the communication links and associated terminals as served by PCTGs are assigned addresses that are maintained in the primary memory of each C-8500.

7.5.1.4 User Interfaces

A control console is provided at each C-8500 and PCTG minicomputer for allowing initialization, software development or management, and manual switchovers. Capability also exists for the generation of resource utilization reports upon request.

7.5.1.5 Traffic Flows and Routing Control

The major flows are between C-8500 memory and disk files, between C-8500 memory and the PCTGs, between C-8500 memory and host processors, and between C-8500 memory and magnetic tapes. Data from the various devices on the TDX devices is multiplexed on a bit-by-bit basis. Data from the various TDM devices is multiplexed on a word-by-word (32 bits each) basis. The various flows between C-8500 and TDX/TDM devices are implemented on permanent TDM circuits. Data flows between C-8500 and terminals are implemented using store-and-forward techniques.

The data flow among C-8500 memory and the various TDX/TDM devices are generally in block form. To illustrate, data may be written and read from the disk file in the form of 128-byte segments. Time gaps between segment writes/reads are caused by arm-positioning time or disk latency. Similarly, data may be written and read from the magnetic tapes in the form of 2048-byte records to minimize the overhead caused by starts and stops.

Contention among the various C-8500 processors for the shared peripheral devices will tend to slow the data flows.

Traffic flows among the C-8500 processors and the TDX loop devices are determined by assignment of the 16 TDX channels (2 MBPS each) to each of the shared devices.

Each disk file controller is assigned two TDX channels. Because most MS applications require two redundant disk files, one fourth of TDX bandwidth is utilized for C-8500 to disk file flows.

Each host processor is generally assigned a single TDX channel. This bandwidth is generally enough to overload the host in terms of transactions to be processed.

A magnetic tape controller is also assigned a single TDX channel. A single TDX channel can be subdivided into several channels. One such channel, rated at 125 KBPS, is reserved for processor-to-processor communication.

Similarly, the flows between a C-8500 and the associated PCTGs can be influenced by assigning to each PCTG a certain number out of the available 256 TDM channels, each rated at 4800 BPS. Allowable combinations are 1, 8, 16, and 32 TDM channels, resulting in effective capacities of 4.8, 38.4, 76.8, or 153.6 KBPS, respectively.

From the previous discussion, it should be clear that any flow between C-8500 and a TDX/TDM device can be influenced simply by varying the number of TDX/TDM channels assigned to that device. The flows between the C-8500 and the various memory modules can be evened through interleaving of program instructions.

7.5.1.6 Traffic Statistics

A given application will determine the traffic statistics. However, a survey of many C-System-based nodal installations provides the following basic data.

The disk file subsystem handles anywhere from 50 to 200 disk accesses per second.

The host processor handles anywhere from 10 to 100 inquiries per second.

In regard to the C-8500 ALU, about 46 percent of the instructions require no operand fetches, 54 percent of instructions require one operand, and 12 percent of instructions require read-modify-writes.

7.5.1.7 Transmission and Signaling Techniques

The C-System architecture employs the principle of time division multiplexing for communication among the various computers in a local network. Two types of loops are employed for interconnections.

As most channels are of the dedicated type, simple signaling procedures are employed for alerting, error control, and buffering.

7.5.1.8 Iterative Modeling of the Network Nodes

The C-8500 node has been modeled to a sufficient degree in 7.5.1.2.

A PCTG terminates user communication lines, provides buffering, concentration, line management, and communication with the C-8500 via MSU (multiplex service unit), using packet switching techniques. The basic unit includes a minicomputer (designated CCM in Fig. 7.25) with core storage of up to 64 kbytes.

A user communication line is terminated into a PCTG via a line termination unit (LTU), which handles the character assembly and distribution functions. A line concentrator module (LCM) provides the interconnection between the LTU and the PCTG data bus. One LCM can handle up to 16 LTUs, and a

PCTG can handle up to 4 LCMs, resulting in a PCTG line termination capacity of 64 lines. Other line termination units (not shown in Fig. 7.25) that operate in a DMA mode and microprogrammable LCMs are available for terminating a wide variety of user lines/terminals.

A single PCTG can connect to more than one C-8500 processor to allow shared load operation and higher availability through better connectivity.

A few words on the C-8500 and PCTG operating systems are in order. Called *communication operating system* (COS) and *message multiplexer operating system* (MMOS) respectively, these are flexible, modular, hierarchical, software structures needed for real-time MS and inquiry/response applications. An interesting feature of these OSs is an interruptable timer that allocates ALU time to software modules at each level in a cyclic manner. As all modules are of the reentrant type, multiprogramming is achieved.

COS also allows batching and ordering of disk accesses for optimizing the disk file subsystem.

A trunk interface handler (TIH) is a part of MMOS providing a capability to connect a remote PCTG/concentrator to a C-System node via a trunk.

7.5.1.9 Performance Parameters

Two types of C-8500 processors have been employed—C-8561 and C-8562. The new C-8562 processor is about three times faster than the C-8561 processor, and it has proven itself to be an appropriate resource for most modern applications. For this reason, performance parameters described below apply only to a node with a C-8562 processor.

Considering most real-time applications, in which a branch instruction occurs once every 5.1 instructions, 46 percent of instructions require no operand fetches, and 54 percent of instructions require 1 operand, a C-8562 can perform about 550,000 instructions per second.

A shared disk file subsystem can perform 200 to 300 disk reads/writes per second. The higher limit corresponds to a case with normal queuing on output circuits. Abnormally long queues on output circuits increase the number of disk cylinders over which the arm-positioning mechanism must traverse for outputting.

Each PCTG can handle from 12,800 to 60,000 BPS, depending upon the configuration.

A C-System node can handle about 100 typical inquiry-response transactions per second or about 30 typical airline store-and-forward messages per second.

A typical response time associated with a C-System node ranges from 0.5 to 1 second, depending upon the application and loading.

The cost of a transaction attributable to a C-System node can be computed as based on the total costs incurred during the seven-year life cycle. The results show that an inquiry/response transaction should cost about 0.2 cents, and a MS transaction should cost about 0.6 cents.

The observed availability of installed C-System nodes is in excess of 0.995. This results from (1) redundant TDX loop subsystem, (2) multiple C-8500 processors employed in either shared-load or standby modes, (3) dual disk file controllers, and (4) multiple connectivity for each PCTG.

If a C-8500 fails in the shared-load mode, the switchover to the functioning processor(s) is almost instantaneous. A C-8500 failure in the standby mode demands a switchover time of about 10 seconds spent on initialization and reading of checkpoint tables from one of the two disk files.

When a PCTG fails, the subnetwork it serves remains isolated until a spare PCTG replaces the failed unit and it is downline loaded, taking about a few minutes.

7.5.1.10 Concluding Remarks

The C-System node has been particularly useful in real-time airline and banking applications characterized by centralized data bases, high throughputs, and fast response times. Its major limitation for some of the newer applications has been in the area of limited core storage. However, an enhancement of C-8562 will soon allow an addressable storage of at least 2 mbytes.

7.5.2 Network Systems Corp.'s Local Network Architecture

Network Systems Corp. (NSC) was founded in 1974 and developed a local network architecture employing a wide-band coaxial cable called HYPERchannel®.

7.5.2.1 An Application Summary

It provides DDP capabilities in a network of heterogeneous processing elements and storage controllers. Front-ending, sharing of secondary storage elements, and load sharing are some of its many applications.

Over 20 local network nodes based on this architecture have been implemented thus far.

7.5.2.2 Network Topology

HYPERchannel® employs a bus topology, as shown in Fig. 7.25. A shared, wideband (50-MBPS) COAX cable is employed for intercommunications

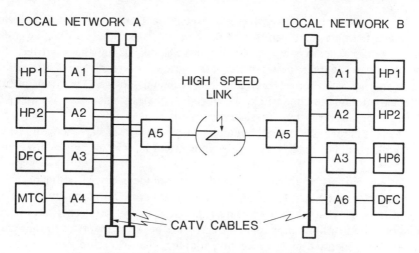

Fig. 7.25. Network Systems Corp. local network architecture.

based on a broadcast principle. The bus can be shared by CPUs and I/O devices of different manufacturers. This is achieved through the use of adapters. Special adapters are available to interface with long-haul links for interconnecting two or more local networks. Up to 64 adapters can be connected to each bus, and an adapter can serve up to four independent buses or cables. The cable length can be 1000 feet or even higher using special designs.

7.5.2.3 Identification Scheme

Each adapter is assigned an 8-bit identification code. Each adapter is also assigned a 16-bit physical access code to achieve special user groups within a local network.

7.5.2.4 User Interfaces

The local network is transparent to all users through the use of a common interface. Such an architecture enables a combination of advantages, such as lower costs, higher throughputs, and higher availability.

7.5.2.5 Traffic Flows and Routing

A network message consists of two sections—the message proper and, optionally, associated data. The message proper may be up to 64 bytes, and the length of the associated data is not limited.

After a preliminary handshake between the transmitting and receiving adapters, the data is transmitted in the form of 1024 byte packets. An alternating buffer scheme is employed that enables concurrent flows between the device and its adapter, between the transmitting and receiving adapters, and between the receiving adapter and the receiving device. The transmitting adapter employs the same trunk, access code, and destination code as employed during the initial transmit message operation.

The asynchronous TDM technique is employed for sharing the cable bandwidth. Accordingly, each message is transmitted at the full bandwidth of the cable.

The carrier-sense-multiaccess (CSMA) technique is employed for resolving contention on the cable. If carrier is sensed just before initiating transmission, the operation is postponed. Two or more adapters can initiate concurrent transmissions due to a finite propagation delay time between adapters. In that case, no ACK is generated by the receiving adapter, due to garbled messages.

To get out of this state (concurrent transmissions), an n-delay mechanism is employed for allowing each adapter to begin transmitting only after a unique delay has occurred after detecting a no-carrier-sensed state. Each adapter is assigned a unique delay time.

7.5.2.6 Traffic Statistics

These will depend upon the application.

7.5.2.7 Transmission and Signaling Techniques

The data trunks employ a baseband, phase modulation technique for transmission.

In-band signaling is employed for transmission of control information. A 24-bit sync pattern is transmitted on the front end of the message to synchronize the receiving adapter, and a 56-bit sync pattern is used as a pad in the trailing end of the message to supply the clock to the receiver.

7.5.2.8 Iterative Modeling of Network Nodes

Special adapters are available for interfacing all well-known computers and peripheral device controllers. Each adapter has a standard trunk interface on one side and a specialized interface to the connected device. Up to 12 circuit boards constitute an adapter. Each adapter is microprocessor-controlled and generally consists of 4096 bytes of buffer storage.

Special adapters are also available for implementing long-haul links at 44 MBPS (T3 carrier), 1.5 MBPS (T1 carrier), 250 KBPS, and 50 KBPS.

7.5.2.9 Performance Parameters

Actual performance data on existing systems is unavailable. However, it can be surmised that its commercial success is attributable to (1) higher reliability than star-type local networks, (2) high transfer rates between processors and peripheral devices on a shared communication facility, and (3) load sharing capabilities through the use of shared peripheral devices among several front-end processors.

An interesting comparison can be made between the hierarchical C-System and NSC's single-level network architectures. The C-System employs two TDM loops with dedicated time slots to achieve zero response time delays for intercommunication. NSC employs the asynchronous TDM technique for efficient sharing of a wideband cable.

7.5.2.10 Concluding Remarks

NSC has been quite responsive to meeting needs of many groups of users. Investigations into the use of long-haul satellite links is being conducted.

NSC's architecture should be quite useful in providing a high-speed distribution mechanism at each satellite ground station for communication between diverse computers belonging to the site. Ideas being addressed are: (1) providing additional buffering for the link adapter to handle long propagation times, and (2) developing a demand multiplexing scheme for a satellite link.

7.5.3 Xerox's Ethernet Architecture for Local Networks

Ethernet was developed in the mid-1970s at Xerox's Palo Alto Research Center (see Ref. 42). It also employs a coaxial cable for connecting processors and peripheral devices. Its topology is identical to that shown in Fig. 7.25.

The major difference between the Ethernet and the Network Systems Corp.'s (NSC's) architectures is related to the manner of handling trunk contention.

The adapter in NSC's network employs a carrier-sensing technique; it does not detect collision during transmission. Collision detection is achieved through the nonreceipt of ACKs from receiving adapters.

Ethernet employs a carrier-sense-multiple-access scheme with collision detection (CSMA/CD). Transmission in Ethernet is permitted only when an idle trunk (no carrier) is sensed. However, two or more adapters may sense the idle trunk simultaneously and begin transmitting. Because the transmission time of messages exceeds the propagation time between the two adapters, collision will be experienced. Each adapter is capable of detecting a collision dur-

ing transmission, however, and will stop transmitting, resulting in a higher utilization of the shared cable bandwidth.

Another local network that employs the above control technique has been
developed at Ford Motor Co. (see Ref. 43 for a description of Ford's LNA
network).

7.5.4 Ring Topology for Local Networks

The bus as employed in the previous subsections is a passive medium with each
node listening. In other words, each adapter on the bus does not regenerate the
messages. A node can fail without disrupting the bus.

However, several local networks, notably the Distributed Computing System
(DCS) of the University of California at Irvine, employ the ring topology,
which requires that each ring interface be able to selectively remove a message
from the ring or to pass it on to the next node. This requires an active repeater
at each node.

Several control strategies suitable for the ring topology are based on the idea
that permission to use the shared facility is passed sequentially around the ring
from node to node. The DCS employs an 8-bit control token that is passed
sequentially around the ring. A node that receives the token may remove it,
send a message, and then pass another token. A slight variation of this is to
continuously transmit around the ring's message slots sequences of bits sufficient to hold a full message. A slot may be full or empty. A node receiving an
empty slot may mark the slot as full and insert a message in it. This technique
was originally described by Pierce (Ref. 45) and employed in ring networks at
Cambridge University and at NBS.

In other regards, a ring topology can yield capabilities similar to those
achieved through a bus topology, as described in 7.5.2 and 7.5.3.

7.5.5 Summary Models of Other Local Networks

In previous subsections, we described some local network architectures and
their properties or capabilities. There was no intent to ignore other local network architectures. See Ref. 46 to study many other ways to implement computer interconnections for achieving local networks. The proceedings of data
communications and computer networking symposia are also rich sources of
local network architectures (see Refs. 47, 48, and 49).

An example of a local network that comes closest to a DDPS is the Carnegie
Mellon University's experimental multi-mini system, C.mmp. It connects 16
processors to 16 shared memory modules through a fast switch. No processor
is a master, but the kernel of an operating system, called *Hydra,* may reside in
any one processor or any number of them simultaneously.

The Cablenet architecture developed at Mitre uses packet switching and a layered protocol. Local networks employing double loop architectures have been implemented at Ohio State University and by Science Applications Inc. of La Jolla. See Ref. 49 for more details.

A local computer network called HMINET (see Ref. 49) has been developed by the Hahn-Meitner-Institut of Berlin, Germany. This network employs message switching techniques and a star topology. Future plans are to implement the ISO's open architecture (see the appendix) with all seven layers of networking.

Two local networks that also employ the ring topology are known as TECH-NEC and SPIDER. The TECHNEC was developed at the Illinois Institute of Technology, and the SPIDER was developed at Bell Laboratories. Whereas DCS and SPIDER employ minicomputers as elements, the TECHNEC employs only microcomputers (LSI-11s as CPUs and RCA's COSMAC as ring interface units). Whereas DCS and SPIDER are designed as information utilities, the TECHNEC is used as a computing system for a distributed system.

No discussion of local networks can be complete without mentioning the use of packet radio to achieve local computer networking. A broadcast technique can be used by a set of computing resources, fixed or mobile, to provide either an information or a DP utility to scattered users. A great deal of research has been directed by ARPA and Xerox, resulting in ALOHA and XTEN architectures, respectively.

The ALOHA employs the unslotted and the slotted techniques with or without CSMA for handling contention on the shared wideband facility. Nonpersistent (transmission is delayed after collision detection followed by no carrier) or 1-persistent (transmission is achieved immediately after detection of no carrier following collision) schemes can be used to control the utilization of the shared transmission facility.

The XTEN employs the cellular radio microwave broadcast channel and TDMA technique for local (6-mile radius) networking.

The previous paragraphs dealt with the lower layers of local network designs. Topics related to topology, link control, and transport control were emphasized. The higher layers, dealing with the network service functions and user application functions, were not dealt with.

Each useful computer network must implement the higher layers of functions in some fashion. The trend is toward the ISO's open system architecture (see the appendix).

In the following paragraphs, we will model some extended (geographically distributed) computer network architectures, describing the various layers that characterize each. Such network architectures as AT&T's ACS will not be included, for such architectures handle only the first three layers of communication protocols, namely physical/electrical, link control, and packet/message control.

Although the Arpanet is a resource sharing computer network, it is not included in the discussion here for two reasons: it was described in detail as a packet transport facility in 7.3, and a description of its higher-level DP protocols is readily available in the literature.

7.5.6 DECNET/DNA Architecture

DECNET is a collection of hardware and software products that fit the digital network architecture (DNA) developed by the Digital Equipment Corp. (DEC) in 1975.

7.5.6.1 An Application Summary

DNA is designed to achieve the following specific goals: (1) to permit a variety of DEC computers (16-, 32-, and 36-bit words) running a variety of DEC operating systems (real-time, timesharing, and transaction processing) to be connected in a computer network supported by DECNET components, (2) to support any combination of HDX and FDX, synchronous or asynchronous, point-to-point or multipoint, serial or parallel communication facilities, (3) to offer program-to-program communication, remote file access, and remote system loading in the form of network functions, (4) to offer cost-effective alternatives to custom-designed computer networks, (5) to allow network configurations to fit user's organizational needs, and (6) to allow for orderly growth or upgrading.

The scope and complexity of DNA has caused a phased development of DECNET components. The first phase, as announced in 1976, was limited mainly to real-time data acquisition and control. By the end of 1977, about 1700 DECNET nodes had been installed. The second phase, as released in 1978, is reflected in about 1000 DECNET nodes. X.25 and SNA interfaces are available. The third phase is now underway to achieve most of the DNA objectives.

7.5.6.2 Network Topology

The DNA allows for a fully distributed network topology. This capability allows the designer to achieve any topology that will fit the user organization's needs. Such topologies as single level, hierarchical, SCSS, MCMS, and MCMD, can be constructed. In a fully distributed topology, any nodal failure will not cause the failure of the network, if enough connectivity is provided in the network.

7.5.6.3 Identification Scheme

Sixteen bits identify each network node and 8 bits identify each station attached to a node in a multidrop configuration.

7.5.6.4 User Interfaces

There are four types of user interfaces: (1) to execute certain jobs in scattered resources through program-to-program communication, (2) to create, transfer, delete, and rename files and directories in local and remote nodes as limited by access, (3) downline loading of a local or remote node, and (4) virtual terminal access employing both DEC and many non-DEC protocols.

These user interfaces provide the capabilities of networkwide resource sharing, distributed data base management (DDBM), and centralized network management or control.

7.5.6.5 Traffic Flows and Routing

Each DECNET node has its own routing tables that can be periodically updated to reflect the best routes to any other network node. The dynamic routing capability can be employed to achieve high system availability.

Because DECNET is a multilayered design (discussed later), each layer adds a certain amount of overhead to the user data before sending it to the next layer of the same node. This goes on until it reaches the last layer. The data link layer adds its own overhead before transmitting to another node.

7.5.6.6 Traffic Statistics

The traffic statistics vary according to the nodal characteristics and the number of nodes employed in the network.

7.5.6.7 Transmission and Signaling Techniques

At present, DECNET is capable of handling EIA RS-232-C or the CCITT V.24 transmission protocols that involve analog signals carrying digital information. Interfaces to digital transmission facilities, such as DDS/DSDS, X.21, are being developed. Similarly, other protocols, such as X.25, will also be handled in the future.

Transmission of control information from node to node and from layer to layer is done through in-band signaling. Each packet carries the control information and user data, whenever applicable.

7.5.6.8 Iterative Modeling of Network Nodes

Each network node within the DNA can be constructed with DEC hardware and software modules.

The hardware modules can be any DEC computer, such as 16-bit PDP-11, 32-bit VAX-11, or 36-bit PDP-10/20, with any attached DEC peripheral equipment.

There is a large choice of operating systems, such as RSX series, RSTS/E, RT11, VAX/VMS, and TOPS-20, depending upon the processor employed and the application (real-time, transaction processing, or timesharing).

To support DNA, five layers of protocols have been developed: (1) physical link protocol, (2) data link protocol, digital data communication message protocol (DDCMP), (3) transport protocol, (4) network service protocol (NSP), and (5) device access protocol (DAP). Of course, there is the user layer that always belongs to the user at the highest level of all protocols.

The physical link layer provides the physical/electrical interfaces. The data link layer provides a transport protocol for an error-free communication with a neighboring node. The transport layer provides an end-to-end routing within the network. The NSP layer provides a location-independent communication mechanism for both the user layer and the network application layer. The DAP provides the user interface to the network functions and services. See Fig. 7.26 for an illustration of DECNET modules and their relationships to DNA layers and non-DEC modules.

Each DNA layer at a given node may include one or more DECNET modules that will provide the desired network services at that node. Some networks will have identical modules at each node to yield high availability and throughput. Cooperation between two modules that are in separate nodes can occur only if these modules belong to the same layer.

7.5.6.9 Performance Parameters

It is difficult to compare DECNET with other architectures without identical applications. However, a DECNET implementation should, in general, be cheaper than any custom-designed system. It would be desirable to obtain costs for each transaction handled by the network in a manner illustrated in 7.5.1.9.

Because each DECNET node segments messages if they exceed 576 bytes, and about 32 bytes are used as packet overhead, overall transmission efficiency as high as 95 percent can be achieved.

Network throughput and response times will depend upon the choice of hardware and software modules selected.

DDCMP is quite effective on earth satellite links, as it permits as many as 255 outstanding packets, as compared with 7 for SDLC, before waiting for a response from the other side.

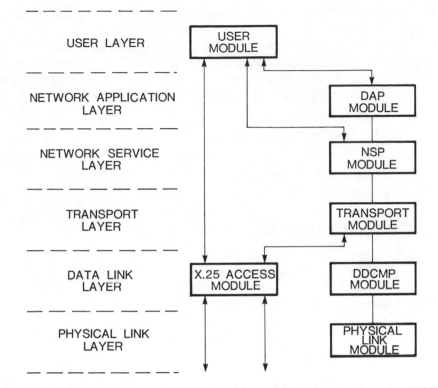

Fig. 7.26. Relationship between DECNET modules and DNA layers and non-DECNET modules.

Two 16-bit, cyclic redundancy check (CRC) codes are employed for the header and the data to achieve excellent error detection.

7.5.6.10 Concluding Remarks

Planning for Phase III of DECNET enhancements is underway. One important goal is to achieve compatibility between Phase II and Phase III products. Some new functions, such as auto-dial, and multipoint mode operation/routing, will be added to the available functions. See Refs. 50 and 51 for additional information on DECNET and DNA.

7.5.7 IBM's System Network Architecture (SNA)

SNA was announced by IBM in September 1974. SNA is a collection of hardware and software modules required for implementing a distributed computer network to meet the user's needs economically, systematically, and quickly. Just like the DECNET/DNA discussed earlier, SNA has also been constantly evolving. Some of the new improvements are reflected by SNA 2, SNA 3, SNA 4.1, and SNA 4.2 packages. The number of installations that are operational with SNA is not exactly known despite several efforts, but is assumed to range between 500 and 1000. See Refs. 52, 53, and 54 for a detailed study of SNA.

7.5.7.1 An Application Summary

The major applications for SNA have been in the areas of inquiry/response, sales order entry, and inventory control. With the new improvements, DDBM application is bound to grow in the future.

7.5.7.2 Network Topology

Each SNA node consists of a physical unit (PU). Some physical units are assigned the responsibility of a system service control point (SSCP). Each node also consists of a logical unit (LU) through which an operator or an application program accesses the network. Each LU is associated with a network address and contains a services manager and one or more half-sessions. One half-session of an LU can be connected to another half-session of another LU in another node through the network to form a full session.

On a logical level, the SNA network consists of interconnected LUs, resulting in a purely distributed network. As a consequence, an SNA-based network may consist of very simple nodes, e.g., intelligent terminals, and a very complicated node, e.g., a large host, that controls a large domain.

Whereas DECNET is a fully distributed network, SNA is primarily a hierarchical network. As a result, hierarchical multicenter, multidrop topologies are easily obtained.

7.5.7.3 Identification Scheme

An SNA-based network consists of three kinds of network addressable units (NAUs): logic unit, physical unit, and system service control point.

A network is divided into domains, where each domain consists of an SSCP and all the PUs, LUs, links, and link stations controlled by an SSCP in the form of activations or deactivations.

A subdivision of a domain is called an *addressable subarea*.

PUs are further divided into several types implying nodal complexities. Type 1 and 2 PUs are the terminals and cluster controllers, respectively, and Type 4 and 5 PUs are the communication controllers and host processors, respectively.

Similarly, the LUs are also divided into several types. An LU implemented in a host is called a *primary* LU (PLU).

Each SSCP contains the centralized data about the current state of its domain. Each PU (one in each node) works with the associated SSCP to control the elements of its subarea.

7.5.7.4 User Interfaces

When the operator wants to call in a program situated in a host or SSCP, a LOGON request unit (RU) is created and sent to the SSCP, where a syntax scan converts the LOGON message into a formatted INITIATE request.

The INITIATE request contains the name of the LU with which the session is desired, the mode of operation, e.g., batch or interactive, and user data. The SSCP transforms the LU name into a network address (16 bits), uses this address and the mode to create a control initiate (CINIT) command and sends it along with user data to the PLU, the primary logic unit at the SSCP that controls the session. The PLU may accept or reject the session request. If the request is accepted, the PLU transforms the CINIT into a BIND and sends it to the secondary LU at the terminal. The BIND establishes the session.

When the session is finished, the PLU sends a CLEAR, followed by an UNBIND.

If any PU or a link en route fails during the session, the session must be reestablished to finish the job.

7.5.7.5 Traffic Flows and Routing

User messages are handled as request units (RUs). As a message passes through the various layers, headers are appended until the link control component adds a header and a trailer to create a basic link unit (BLU). When the BLU travels to the next physical unit (PU), the headers and trailers are stripped and added again before traveling to another PU.

SNA allows up to eight routes between any two network nodes. When the session is initiated, a list of virtual routes is specified. The session is assigned the first available route from the list. Each route is checked for loops at this time. Should a session be disrupted, due to failure of node or link in this route, a new session must be initiated on another route. Thus, a modified static routing strategy is employed. SNA performs the routing functions within the path control layer (discussed later).

SNA also provides a mechanism for traffic flow control to prevent congestion within the network. This mechanism can operate on a local or a global basis.

A recent enhancement called the *advanced communication function* (ACF) can allow a network configuration with multiple SSCPs sharing the control of

PUs, LUs, links, and link stations within a domain. This capability can be utilized to (1) smooth out the congestion within the network and (2) achieve sharing of critical resources.

7.5.7.6 Traffic Statistics

Not available.

7.5.7.7 Transmission and Signaling Techniques

SNA supports synchronous data link control (SDLC), which is a subset of ISO's high-level data link control (HDLC). SNA products currently implement CCITT recommendation V.24, which requires conventional modems. Therefore, SNA can employ both analog and digital transmission techniques.

An inband signaling scheme is used. All the control information is appended to the basic information units during interlayer or inter-PU communication.

7.5.7.8 Iterative Modeling of Network Nodes

Like DECNET/DNA, SNA is also a multilayered design. Six control levels characterize SNA: (1) physical control, (2) data link control, (3) path control, (4) transmission and data flow control, (5) presentation services, and (6) end user. The physical layer is the mechanical/electrical interface between the DTE and DCE. The data link control layer transfers packets error-free across any noisy link. The path control layer routes incoming packets to the appropriate outgoing link toward the final destination. The transmission and data flow control layer manages each session. The presentation services layer defines the end user's port into the network in terms of code, format, etc. See Fig. 7.27 for an illustration of control layers in a fully developed SNA node.

In comparison to the seven control layers of the ISO open system architecture, as discussed in the appendix, SNA shows many similarities.

Basic SNA nodes are SSCP-hosts, 370X-type communication controllers, cluster controllers, and intelligent terminals. Conversion to SNA requires replacing the existing software modules with new versions, but does not require changing the interfaces between these modules and application programs (or end users).

See Fig. 7.28 for generalized representations of SNA nodes.

7.5.7.9 Performance Parameters

It is difficult to discuss all the performance parameters in the absence of an actual SNA implementation. However, several observations have been made in Refs. 53 and 54 that may be studied to get a deeper insight into SNA.

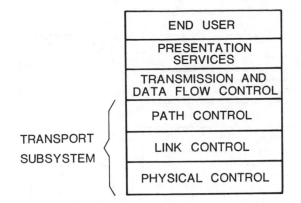

Fig. 7.27. SNA control layers within an SSCP node.

Multihost network configurations that are possible through ACF have eliminated most of the criticisms levied at the original version of SNA. Higher reliability, higher throughputs, and higher resource sharing can now be achieved.

In general, a migration to SNA will require more memory (approximately 1 mbytes) in the host node. Some SNA migrations have also experienced slightly lower host throughputs. However, these shortcomings are generally offset by the savings achieved through network sharing by many applications.

The SDLC protocol in SNA is still hampered by the limitation of only seven outstanding frames when working with satellite systems. Most designs require up to 32 outstanding frames before requiring a response from the other end to offset the long delays in satellite communication.

ACF enables high network availabilities through multiple routes and resource sharing. However, the biggest concern with all computer network architectures is a lack of integrated/centralized control and diagnostic capabilities as available in voice communication systems.

7.5.7.10 Concluding Remarks

Like all other computer network architectures, SNA has been evolving since the first day of its announcement in 1974. Pressures of the marketplace, technology, and users will continue to shape changes in SNA.

In the coming years, the biggest enhancements to SNA will come from increased availabilities of interfaces to other public networks. IBM has already announced its commitment to provide X.21/X.25 interface products in several countries. The control layers of SNA are general enough to allow such an evolution. Corr and Neal (Ref. 52) deal with these issues in detail.

SNA enables the distribution of DP resources in a network to meet the needs

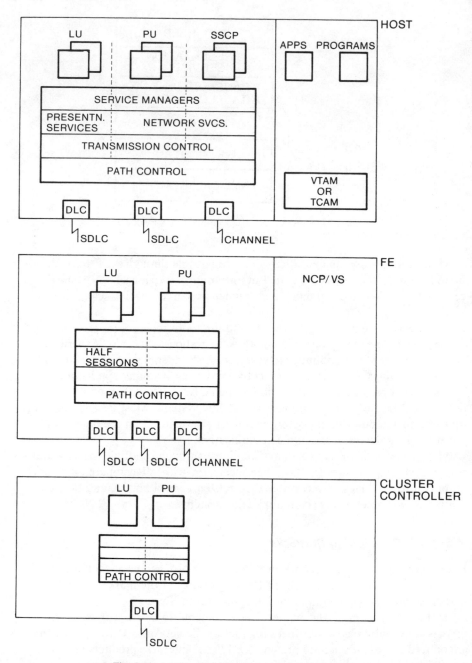

Fig. 7.28. A generalized representation of SNA nodes.

of any organization. Further reductions in hardware and memory costs will accelerate this capability of SNA. The recent announcement of the 8100 distributed processing system provides a glimpse at a future IBM networking strategy.

7.5.8 Summary Models of Other Well-Known Computer Architectures

In the previous pages, we described two popular computer architectures. Their choice was dictated by the way DP resources are distributed. DECNET is based on the nonhierarchical topology and dynamic routing, and SNA favors the hierarchical topology and a modified static routing technique.

Many other computer vendors have announced multilayered computer architectures. A summary of their architectures follows.

7.5.8.1 Univac's Distributed Communication Architecture (DCA)

DCA is a layered architecture, just as SNA and DECNET are. DCA is a set of control concepts and interfaces within which hardware and software modules can be designed. See Fig. 7.29 for a general representation of DCA.

Network control is distributed as in DECNET. Such hierarchical concepts as PLUs, SLUs, and LUs are missing. Terminals and application programs are simply communication system users (CSUs). A transparent transport network (TN) is achieved through trunk control, route control, and data unit control (DUC) layers. The TN functions are generally implemented in each distributed communications processor (DCP).

The termination system is a layered telecommunication access method (host resident) for session control, flow control, and presentation services. The CSU and TS functions will exist in terminal systems in the form of firmware.

Dynamic routing is employed in DCA. Univac intends to employ the UDLC, a superset of HDLC, link control protocol for private leased lines and channel-oriented protocol for host-DCP communication. Univac has made commitments to support X.25 for interfacing with public data networks.

7.5.8.2 NCR's Distributed Network Architecture (DNA)

The fully developed DNA consists of a new telecommunication access method called NCR/TAM and the data transporting network called NCR/DTN. The host resident NCR/TAM acts as a boundary between application programs and the communication system and performs the presentation services, address translations, and session control. The NCR/DTN is composed of communication facilities and communication processors of all sizes. The various layers

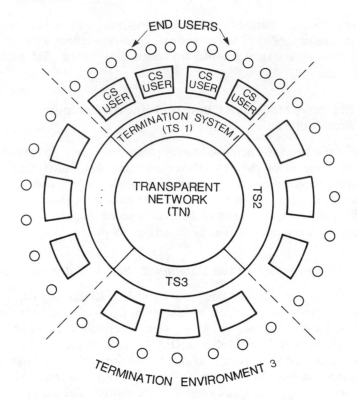

Fig. 7.29. A generalized representation of DCA network architecture.

of NCR/DTN software are: NCR/DLC is the link control layer; the route management layer is a dynamic path control layer; and the communication system services layer controls the end-to-end protocols. The end users are called the *correspondents* in DNA.

Both the Datagram and virtual circuits can be supported through the handling of unnumbered, one-packet-long messages or multipacket messages, respectively.

NCR is committed to provide compatibility between DEC's ADCCP, CCITT's X.25, ISO's HDLC, and IBM's SDLC wherever required in the network.

7.5.8.3 Concluding Remarks

We have described only four types of computer network architectures for extended areas. The reader must not get the idea that there are no other possible architectures. In fact, all the local network architectures described earlier can be converted into extended network architectures through linking of several local networks. Of course, one must develop an extended transport control mechanism to complete the architecture. Consequently, there exist an unlimited number of computer network architectures. Several factors determine the eventual success of a particular computer network architecture. The existing base of hardware and software modules is definitely a factor. Cost is another important parameter. But the most important factor, which is ignored frequently, is how the solution fits the user's needs.

The success of a computer network is closely linked to a user's ability to see a relationship between the solution and his organizational needs. The days of mysterious, fenced in, giant DP centers are vanishing. A good computer network architecture must be simple enough for a corporate executive to comprehend it. Unfortunately, we are not there yet.

Several innovating companies, e.g., Datapoint, are developing new architectures for offices and homes of tomorrow. Some of these new architectures will eventually evolve into a true DDP system that satisfies Enslow's definition (Ref. 33).

7.6 DISTRIBUTED-DATA-BASE-MANAGEMENT SYSTEMS (DDBMS)

DBM involves searches, retrievals, and updates of data elements within a single data base and, hence, should be a part of the data processing (DP) technology. The computer networks, as discussed in 7.5, provide a natural foundation for the introduction of DDBM concepts. We could have combined these two fields in 7.5, although that would have become difficult when we emphasized only the DP functions.

There are several aspects of DDBM that need special attention from the modeling point of view. These views have to do with the distribution of data bases within the framework of a shared communication network and the problems that creates for the system analyst and the system designer. Such aspects must be modeled and analyzed for their effects on system performance.

Before we model some existing DDBM systems, a discussion of some unique properties of DDBM are in order. Consult Refs. 55 to 59 for further studies of DDBM if desired.

7.6.1 Properties of DDBM

Although technology is helping the introduction of DDBMSs through reduction of: (1) cost per bit of primary, secondary, and tertiary storages; and (2) cost of computation, it has no direct effect on the problems related to modeling.

The areas that do influence modeling are as follows: (1) user interfaces, (2) methods of DB distribution, and (3) DBM computers.

7.6.1.1 User Interfaces

User interfaces deal with data models or DB structures and common DB architectures.

There are two types of data models: (1) the generalized hierarchical or network data model, and (2) the relational data model. The generalized hierarchical data model requires the user to specify storage structures, access paths, and data structures in considerable detail. The result is treelike structures, generally constructed of pointers to linked lists. These tend to be quite complex and inflexible. Most of the experience in DBM, however, is related to the generalized hierarchical data models. In contrast, the relational data model generally shields the user from the complexity of storage structures, data structures, and access paths. The resulting model is in the form of tables or relations, with each entry in the relation called a *tuple,* or a record. Most of the current research is in relational data models that, although they result in lower performance, yield a good deal of flexibility. With costs of hardware going down, the future is with relational data models.

Recent advances in the high-level languages are prompting the development of a common DBM architecture that will support the existing and new DBM systems dealing with both the generalized hierarchical and the relational data models. This approach will support multiple views of data, that is, subschemas (users' definitions of data formats) and schemas (union of subschemas at a system level).

It is generally known (see Ref. 58) that very little effort is spent on defining a subschema for each application or end user and modeling the schema. Without this effort, the task of developing the common DBM architecture will be quite expensive, if not impossible.

7.6.1.2 Methods of DB Distribution

The need to distribute DB within the corporate network should be dictated by the user's grade of service requirements and cost constraints. Distribution of DB can be achieved through either partitioning or replication or both. *Partitioning* is achieved when disjoint sets of data are placed at distant nodes in the corporate network. *Replication* is achieved when two or more copies of the same data set are placed at different nodes of the corporate network.

Partitioning is generally recommended when a region generates most of the DB queries from the partitioned data subset and when fast response times are desired. Partitioning results in "misses," however, when the query has to be sent to another node for service. If the "miss" rate is high in a large DDB, a centralized DBMS may become preferable.

Replication is generally recommended when high performance, with emphasis on reliability and constant tunability, is desired. Nonetheless, these benefits must be weighed against the additional communication costs and software complexities required for synchronized updates to maintain a desired level of data coherence, a measure of difference among the various DB copies at any time.

Many applications require batched updates during nighttime only. For that case, there is no penalty for replication. But there are applications, e.g., airline reservations, where real-time updates are required. For that case, it is impossible to achieve a fully coherent and a fully prompt DDBMS. It is interesting to note that even in the case of a centralized DBMS of an airline, "no show" passengers force a certain amount of overbooking and cause legal problems for the air carrier. It is possible that full coherence may not be needed in most cases. What we need is a DDBMS that converges to full coherence quickly after updates cease to occur (weak consistency).

Several techniques exist for synchronized updates of replicated data sets within the network. In centralized DBMS, such mechanisms as "locks" on data elements can be set to effect serialization of updates, which in turn ensures consistency of data. Serialization of updates to all copies must occur in the same order to achieve consistency.

Several recently developed techniques for achieving synchronized updates require some form of preanalysis of all DB queries and updates to achieve either strong consistency (when all copies of data are updated simultaneously) or weak consistency. In some designs "time stamps," or sequence numbers are assigned by a master node before sending DB queries/updates to other nodes to achieve weak consistency throughout the network.

7.6.1.3 DBM Processor

The recently generated interest in the common DBM architecture is closely related to the need for a DBM processor that is capable of supporting several data models (both the generalized hierarchical and relational) and associative storage devices. Such a DBM processor can then be incorporated in each network node to provide an integrated DDBMS whose configuration is totally transparent to users.

Some of the host functions can also be divided into application and DB functions and fitted into two minicomputers. The latter arrangement is sometimes called the *back-end DBM computer*—a solution that has already been found useful in several applications (see Ref. 60). Furthermore, the back-end computer may or may not be assisted by an intelligent associative processor.

In a DDBMS, some other important functions need to be implemented. These deal with supporting the communication port, for linking one node with other nodes, and a network data directory, for guiding "misses" and update requests to appropriate nodes.

There is a great deal of work needed to make local network architectures perform DBM functions locally. The DCS system developed at the University of Irvine (see 7.5) is an attempt in that direction. DDBM is a very complex field, and it should demand full respect from designers. Even a simple task, such as recovery of a DDBMS, can be taxing.

7.6.2 Summary Models of Some DDBM Systems

Every PS and DDP system considered earlier can be a basis for DDBMS topology, although all considerations of DDBM were overridden by other properties of network systems.

DDBMSs have always experienced extremely high start-up costs, and consequently the literature on DDBM is still very sparse. The decreasing cost of hardware and an increasing need for DDBM systems is now spurring a great deal of interest in such systems for solving the needs of large corporations.

Despite the difficulties involved with obtaining in-depth articles on DDBM systems, Refs. 56 and 59 did provide a glimpse into some systems, which are described in the following paragraphs.

7.6.2.1 SITA

SITA (see 7.3.5.7 for additional description) should be considered as a super-position of many individual airline networks, each designed for an inquiry-response application employing a centralized passenger-name-record data base. When a "miss" occurs, requiring a query from another airline's DBMS, an exception message is sent to another node via a higher-level backbone network. Therefore, SITA employs the concepts of partitioning and "miss" messages to accomplish DDBM.

7.6.2.2 Arinc

Arinc is an American equivalent of SITA. It also uses the concepts of partitioning and "miss" messages to accomplish DDBM.

There are many large airlines in some developing countries that would like to implement economical DDBM systems. They can employ the SITA or Arinc models with one exception—use minicomputers to handle subnetworks (based on flights, regions, or days of flight) and a backbone network.

7.6.2.3 Celanese

The Celanese system employs two major DBM nodes and uses the concept of weak consistency achieved through periodic updates. The corporate network also consists of minor nodes that maintain their own unique data.

Therefore, the Celanese system employs the concepts of limited replication and networkwide partitioning to achieve DDBM.

7.6.2.4 Bank of America

The bank employs two large, partitioned DBM nodes and the concept of exception messages for handling inquiry-response applications.

7.6.2.5 Arpanet

It employs a unique operating system called RSEXEC (Resource Sharing Executive System), developed by Bolt, Beranek and Newman, to achieve networkwide resource sharing in the form of file accessing and automatic maintenance of duplicated files.

7.6.2.6 Lowes COs. Inc.

Each of the 140 stores maintains its own partitioned data base. Each DBMS serves about 16 terminals and handles on-line inventory and customer invoicing applications.

The 140 sites are connected through a network used during nights for (1) updating the central DB with summary data, and (2) downline loading of site DBs with the latest pricing data.

7.6.2.7 Aeroquip Corp.

The company had been using a centralized DBM system at the corporate city for inventory control and order processing for several years when they wished to extend the service to all cities. They chose to implement a partitioned DBM node in each city and use nighttime updates of the centralized DB and refreshes of the partitioned DBs. All exception transactions are batched for 5 minutes and serviced by the central site via a WATS line.

7.6.2.8 DARPA's SDD-1 DDBMS

This system is being developed by Computer Corp. of America under contract to the Defense Advanced Research Project Agency (DARPA). A prototype already exists, and it reflects many emerging new concepts related to DDBM.

The relational data model is employed throughout the network. A high-level language is used to access data from a data base that is distributed over a number of nodes interconnected via Arpanet. Both replication and partitioning are employed. Each node consists of a transaction module (TM) and a data module. TM adheres to a protocol, as defined by the preanalysis, to ensure DB consistency. See Ref. 59 for more details.

7.7 FUTURE TRENDS

In this chapter, we have tried to classify and model some well-known network systems according to the switching technique (CS, PS, or MS) or the application (DP or DBM). Some of the trends should have become apparent when studying the existing computer networks and DDBM systems. Several of the emerging computer networks are in the process of implementing multilayered protocols around a transparent, switched communication network. Such a trend is also getting an assist from the proposed ISO's open system architecture (see the appendix).

The future revolution, as we see it, will take place in achieving a "truly" distributed DP system, as defined earlier. But meanwhile, a pseudorevolution will occur in the area of "offices of tomorrow" and/or integrated networks designed to handle all forms of applications, such as voice, interactive data, batch data transfers, message switching, host sharing, and distributed DBM. With the proliferation of home computers and terminals, an unprecedented rise of user needs will also take place. A combination of corporate and ordinary citizen's needs will give rise to what Martin (Ref. 61) calls a "wired society" with a myriad of interconnected networks.

The modeling complexity of such integrated network systems is thus bound to grow. The top-down modeling methodology, as based on successive decompositions and as described in this book, should be useful.

REFERENCES

1. Schwartz, Mischa. (1959) *Information, Transmission, Modulation and Noise.* New York: McGraw-Hill Book Co., Inc.
2. BTL Staff. (1977) *Engineering and Operations in the Bell Systems.* Bell Telephone Laboratories, Inc.
3. Collins Radio Technical Staff. (1971) *General Purpose Communication Networks.* Collins Radio Co., unpublished report.
4. Kimbleton, S. R., and G. M. Schneider. Computer communication networks: Approaches, objectives and performance considerations. *ACM Computing Surveys,* September 1975.
5. Anderson, G. A. and E. D. Jenson. Computer interconnection structures: Taxonomy, characteristics and examples. *ACM Computing Survey,* March 1977.

6. Reddi, S. S., and E. A. Fenstel. A conceptual framework for computer architectures. *ACM Computing Surveys,* June 1976.

7. Enslow, P. H., Jr. Multiprocessor organization—A survey. *ACM Computing Surveys,* March 1977.

8. Gosslau, K. (1966) *Special Systems or Computer Control for Message Switching.* Proc. IFIP Congress, New York, 1965. Washington: Spartan Books.

9. Sharma, R. L. An approach toward evaluating digital computer-controlled message switching systems. IFIP Congress, New York, 1965.

10. Sharma, R. L. Analysis of a scheme for information organization and retrieval from a disc file. IFIP Congress, Edinburgh, Scotland, 1968.

11. Sharma, R. L., et al. C-System multiprocessor network architecture. IFIP Congress, Stockholm, Sweden, 1974.

12. Zurcher, W. F. Iterative, multilevel modeling. IFIP Congress, Edinburgh, Scotland, 1968.

13. Medina, M. Report on grade-of-service recommendation. CCITT Temporary Document 79-E, April 1977.

14. Martin, J. (1975) *Telecommunications Systems Analysis.* New York: John Wiley & Sons.

15. Collins, A. A., and R. D. Pederson (1973) *Telecommunications: A Time for Innovation.* Dallas: Merle Collins Foundation.

16. Clos, C. A study of non-blocking switching networks. *Bell Syst. Tech. J.* Vol. 32, March 1953.

17. Jacobeous, C. A study of congestion in link systems. *Erickson Tech.* No. 48, 1950.

18. Lee, C. Y. Analysis of switching networks. *Bell Syst. Tech. J.* Vol. 34, November 1955.

19. Duffy, F. P., and T. W. Thatcher. 1969–1970 connection survey: Analog transmission performance on the switched telecommunication network. *Bell Syst. Tech. J.* Vol. 50, No. 4, April 1971, 1311–1347.

20. Balkovic, M. D., et al. 1969–1971 connection survey: high speed voice band data transmission performance on the switched telecommunication network. *Bell Syst. Tech. J.* Vol. 50, No. 4, April 1971, 1349–1384.

21. McNamara, J. E. (1978) *Technical Aspects of Data Communication.* Bedford, Mass.: Digital Equipment Corp.

22. Baran, P., et al. On distributed communication, Vols. 1–9. Rand Corporation Research Documents, August 1964.

23. Davies, D. W., et al. A digital communication network for computers giving rapid response times at remote terminals. ACM symp. Operating System Problems, October 1967.

24. Roberts, L. G., and B. D. Wessler. Computer network development to achieve resouce sharing. *Proc. SJCC* 1970.

25. Logica Limited. *Packet Switching Report.* September 1978.

26. Kleinrock, L. Principles and lessons learnt in packet switching. *Proc.* IEEE Vol. 66, No. 11, 1978.

27. Online Conferences Ltd. *Data Communication Networks.* Conference proceedings, May 1977.

28. Anonymous. (1977) *Computer Transmission Corp.: M3200 PACUIT (TM) Network Switching and Management System: A Computer Technology Report.* Philadelphia: Auerbach Publishers, Inc.
29. Keyes, N., and M. Gerla. Hybrid packet and circuit switching. *Telecommunications,* July 1978.
30. Leger, G. L. LSI ready to make a mark on packet switching networks. *Electronics,* December 20, 1979.
31. Lapidus, G. Swift network. Data Communication, September/October 1976.
32. DATAPRO. *All About Communication Processors.* A periodic report.
33. Enslow, P. H., Jr. What is a distributed data processing system? *Computer,* January 1978.
34. IDC. Distributed processing. *Fortune,* a special advertisement, June 4, 1979.
35. Sharma, R. L. Computers and Communication: Challenges, risks and opportunities. *Signal,* September 1977.
36. Sharma, R. L. Network: A show that must fit the audience. *Data Management,* March 1978.
37. Sharma, R. L., A. D. Inglé, and P. T. de Sousa. Performance of some C-system configurations. Proc. Computer Networking Symposium, December 12, 1979.
38. Wolf, J. J., et al. Analysis and simulation of the distributed double loop computer network (DDLCN). Proc. Computer Networking Symposium, December 12, 1979.
39. Christensen, G. S. Links between computer-room networks. *Telecommunications,* February 1979.
40. Clark, D. D., K. K. Pogran, and D. P. Reed. An introduction to local area networks. *Proc. IEEE* Vol. 66, No. 11, November 1978.
41. Network Systems Corp. Publication No. A01-000-02.
42. Boggs, D. R., and R. M. Metcalfe. Ethernet: Distributed packet switching for local computer networks. *Commun. ACM* Vol. 19, No. 7, July 1976.
43. Sherman, R. H., M. G. Gable, and G. McClure. Concepts, strategies for local data network architectures. *Data Communications,* July 1978.
44. Farber, D. J., et al. The distributed computer system. Proc. COMPCON 73, February 1973.
45. Pierce, J. R. Networks for block switching of data. *Bell Syst. Tech. J.* Vol. 51, July/August 1972.
46. Anderson, G. A., and E. D. Jensen. Computer interconnection structures: Taxonomy, characteristics, and examples. *ACM Computing Surveys* Vol. 7, No. 4, December 1975.
47. Liebowitz, B. H., and J. H. Carson (eds.). TUTORIAL: distributed processing. Proc. COMPCON 77, September 1977.
48. ACM/IEEE, Proc. 6th Data Commun. Symp., November 1979.
49. IEEE, Proc. Computer Networking Symp., December 12, 1979.
50. Loveland, R. A. Putting DECNET into perspective. *Datamation,* March 1979.
51. Digital Equipment Corp. (1976) DECNET. Also reproduced in Ref. 47.
52. Gray, J. P., and T. B. McNeill. SNA multiple-system networking; V. Ahuja. Routing and flow control in system network architecture; F. P. Corr and D. H.

Neal. SNA and emerging international standards. *IBM Systems J.* Vol. 18, No. 2, 1979.

53. Berglund, R. G. Comparing network architectures. *Datamation,* February 1978.
54. Yasaki, E. K. IBM's offering of SNA: Some find it a success. *Datamation,* February 1978.
55. Champine, G. A. Current trends in data base systems. *Computer,* May 1979.
56. Champine, G. A. Six approaches to distributed data bases. *Datamation,* May 1977.
57. Champine, G. A. Four approaches to a data base computer. *Datamation,* December 1978.
58. Holland, R. H. DBMS: Developing user views. *Datamation,* February 1980.
59. Rothnie, J. B., Jr. Distributed DBMS no longer just a concept. *Data Communications,* January 1980.
60. Canaday, R. H., et al. A back-end computer for data base management. *Management/Data Base Systems* (an ACM publication), October 1974.
61. Martin, J. (1978) *Wired Society.* Englewood Cliffs, N.J.: Prentice-Hall.
62. Snow, N. E., and N. Knapp, Jr. System overview. *Bell Syst. Tech. J.* Vol. 54, No. 5, 1975, 811.
63. Mahoney, J. J., Jr. J. J. Mansell, and R. C. Matlack. User's view of the network. *Bell Syst. Tech. J.,* Vol. 54, No. 5, 1975, 833.

Section II
Network System Analysis

Chapter 8
Introduction to Network System Analysis

When designing or acquiring a new system or product, one must determine if it will do what it is meant to do. If we need a ladder to climb up to a second-story window, we must measure the ladder to make sure it is long enough. In addition, we must ensure that it has enough rungs at proper intervals and that the rungs are strong enough. So also should we know if the frame of the ladder is strong enough. Answers to some of these questions may depend on who is to use the ladder. The requirements of a 6-foot football player are likely to be quite different from those of a five-year-old child. And we must be able to afford either to buy or to build such a ladder. In short, we must analyze the ladder. More accurately, we must analyze a system called a ladder. When we have accomplished an analysis, we can brand a specific ladder under consideration as "suitable" or "unsuitable" for our purpose. Thus, the analysis of a system plays an important and integral part in the process of design or procurement of a system.

This section deals with analysis of network systems. It discusses a variety of issues related to network systems. The importance of some of the discussion will be obvious, whereas some issues might seem irrelevant. The latter relate to the design of networks, a topic dealt with in detail in Section III.

In large systems, which most network systems are, it is necessary to tackle an analysis in a number of stages. If analysis of an entire system is attempted at once, one fears an uncontrollable explosion of parameters to be analyzed. The possibility of overlooking some important issue must be considered as well. It is prudent, therefore, to treat a system at various levels, from the outermost, macroscopic, network level to the innermost, microscopic, component level. In this section, network systems are treated at two major levels—the network level, in which networks are collections of nodes and connecting links, and the node level, in which the focus is on a single node in the network. Both these levels will be further divided into sublevels as required.

Network systems must be analyzed with respect to several attributes. Identification of important attributes is itself a part of analysis. System attributes can generally be grouped into four classes: (1) temporal attributes, (2) throughput, (3) capacity, and (4) cost attributes. The list of attributes is by no means exhaustive, nor is the order in which they are listed any indication of their relative importance. Different system requirements can render different attributes more critical than others.

Temporal attributes cover such requirements as those on response times and delays. In some network functions, establishing a connection in a voice switching network, for example, end-to-end delay is a critical factor. Throughput, the total amount of traffic handled by a system in a fixed time period, for example, is a significant attribute of nearly all network systems. In such systems as message switching network nodes, in which a message may be stored for some significant amount of time, storage capacity becomes a critical attribute. There is no system in which the cost is not a factor. It should be noted that these atributes are not totally independent of each other. In some examples to follow, it will be obvious how changes in one attribute may affect the others. Nevertheless, in analyzing the effects of one set of attributes, it is often convenient to hold all other attributes invariant.

Several techniques are being practiced for network system analysis. *Analytical modeling* has been the most common technique used over the years. It derives its popularity from the fact that if the initial model of a system is accurate and mathematically solvable, then all questions relating to the system's performance can be answered with relative ease. For small systems or for systems that are well understood, accurate analytical modeling is quite feasible. For large systems, an attempt may be made to divide them into small subsystems. When the behavior of a subsystem is statistically independent of the behavior of other subsystems, the subsystem can be modeled independently.

Analytical modeling proves inadequate when a large or complex system cannot be conveniently dissected into statistically independent subdivisions. As the complexity of a model increases, solvability of mathematical equations decreases, sometimes drastically. Complex models are often solved using numerical techniques, i.e., using computational methods. The advantage of easy answers to all questions no longer exists. Computational models are also potentially expensive.

An alternative to analytical modeling is *simulation*. It may be possible to simulate each component of a system in detail, resulting in an *emulation* of the system. Alternatively, simulation of the statistical behavior of a component or a group of components may be preferred, resulting in a *statistical simulation* of the system. The particular choice will depend upon the system application and upon the desired degree of detail. Simulation, to mean either emulation or statistical simulation, can be performed in hardware, firmware, or software.

Another set of techniques used in analysis is not really an alternative, but a complement to the aforementioned techniques. This set can be collectively called the *technique of measurement*. By the "seeing-is-believing" paradigm, the importance of measurements is obvious to all, but just what to measure and how to interpret the measurements are issues often overlooked.

Chapter 9 develops and discusses the techniques for network system analysis. Chapters 10 and 11 exhibit uses of the techniques in network level and node level analyses, respectively.

Chapter 9
Techniques for Analysis

9.1 FUNDAMENTALS OF QUEUING THEORY

Queuing theory deals with the random behavior of a queuing process within a network node. The links are assumed to be memoryless and to act as servers only. Queuing theory can be studied in terms of probability distributions and queuing processes.

9.1.1 Probability Distributions

The concept of *probability* needs to be invoked whenever an experiment is repeated a large number of times under essentially the same conditions and yet the outcomes vary in an irregular fashion that defies all attempts at an exact prediction.

The outcome of a random experiment is termed an *event*. The event E consists of any outcome with the property E. Associated with a long sequence of random experiments will be a number $P(E)$, termed a *probability*, which gives the relative frequency of the occurrence of E. The frequency interpretation of probability is replaced by an axiomatic definition below.

An indivisible outcome of a random experiment is called an *elementary event* or a *sample point*. The aggregate of all the sample points defines a *sample space*, denoted by S. A probability function, P, may be defined to obey the following axioms:

1. $0 <= P(E) <= 1.0$. This implies that the probability of an event is always nonnegative and can never exceed 1.0.
2. If E_0 is an event that cannot occur in the sample space, then $P(E_0) = 0$.
3. $P(S) = 1$ when the event is the entire sample space (S).
4. If E_1 and E_2 are disjoint (mutually exclusive) events in (S), then $P(E_1 + E_2) = P(E_1) + P(E_2)$, where ($E_1 + E_2$) is the event of E_1 or E_2.

In addition to the above axioms, the probility functions also use the following concepts:

5. A *random variable* is a variable whose value depends upon the outcome of an experiment. For example, in a coin tossing experiment, the random variable X can be defined as follows:

$$X = (1 \text{ if the coin shows a head, 0 if it shows a tail})$$

The numbers obtained by direct observation of natural processes are often regarded as observed values of random variables.

6. Associated with any one-dimensional random variable X is a unique distribution function (d.f.) $F(x)$ defined as follows:

$$F(x) = P(X <= x)$$

where $P(X <= x)$ signifies, for $-00 < x < + 00$, the probability of the event "$X <= x$." The probability that X takes on a value within the interval "$a < X < b$" is given by the following relation:

$$P(a < X <= b) = F(b) - F(a)$$

Some useful discrete probability distributions are *binomial* and *Poisson*, defined as follows:

$$P(X = k) = ((n!)/(k!(n - k)!)) * (p^k) * (1 - p)^{(n-k)} \text{binomial}$$
$$P(X = k) = \lambda^k * \exp(-\lambda)/k! \text{ Poisson}$$

where
  p is a constant between 1 and 0
  n is any integer
  k is a positive integer less than n
  λ is a positive constant representing the parameter of the distribution and

Some useful continuous probability distributions are the *exponential* and the *normal* distributions. Their density functions (the derivative of the d.f.) are expressed as follows:

$$f(y) = (1/t) * (\exp(-y/t)) \text{ for } y >= 0$$
$$= 0 \qquad\qquad\qquad \text{ for } y < 0 \quad \bigg\} \text{ exponential}$$
$$f(y) = (1/\sigma * \mathrm{sqr}(2\pi))) * \exp(-(y - m)^2/(2*\sigma^2)) \text{ normal}$$

where
  t is any positive constant
  m is any constant and
  σ is positive

9.1.2 Simple Queuing Process

A queuing process can be illustrated as shown in Fig. 9.1. Information units requiring service are generated over time by an input source. These information units enter the queuing system and join a queue. At certain points in time, a member of the queue is selected for service by the service mechanism according to some rules known as *service discipline*. The required service is then performed by the service mechanism, after which the information unit leaves the queuing system.

We need to define all the components involved in the queuing process.

9.1.2.1 Input Source

One characteristic of the input source is its population size. The *population size* is the total number of information units that might require service from time to time. In a CS system, it might mean the number of subscribers. The size may be assumed to be either infinite or finite. The infinite case simplifies computations. The finite case creates analytical difficulties, because the number of units in the queuing system affects the number of potential calling units outside the system at any given time.

The second characteristic of the input source deals with the *distribution function,* which defines the way the information units arrive at the queuing

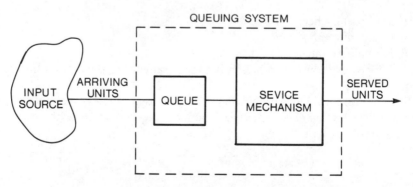

Fig. 9.1. The basic queuing process.

system. The most common assumption is that the number of units generated until any specific time has a Poisson distribution. This is the case where arrivals to the queuing system occur at random and at a certain average rate.

This is also analogous to the assumption that the probability distribution of the time between consecutive arrivals (= interarrival time) is an exponential distribution.

9.1.2.2 Queue

A *queue* is characterized by the maximum permissible number of information units that can be stored in the queue. A queue is called *infinite* or *finite* according to its capacity. Again, the finite queue creates a good deal of analytical difficulty.

9.1.2.3 Service Discipline

The *service discipline* in a queuing process defines the order in which members of the queue are chosen for service. To illustrate, one may use the first-in-first-out (FIFO) or the last-in-first-out (LIFO) scheme. In some systems, a purely *random* scheme may be employed. In special designs, the order of service may be determined by a *priority* procedure. Unless otherwise specified, the FIFO approach is implicitly assumed by queuing models.

9.1.2.4 Service Mechanism

The service mechanism consists of one or more service vehicles, each of which contains one or more *servers,* each of which can serve an information unit in parallel with other servers. Each server is assumed to complete the service of one unit before attempting to serve another. The number of service vehicles and the number of servers per vehicle must be defined. Usually, there is only one vehicle per service mechanism, and usually there is one or a finite number of servers per service vehicle.

The time spent on service by each server is known as the *service time,* or *holding time.* The queuing process is not completely defined until the service time distribution for each server is known. In most practical cases, an identical service time distribution is associated with all servers. The Erlangian distribution or one of its special cases, the exponential distribution, is generally assumed. The degenerate distribution, or the *constant service time,* is also assumed for some systems.

The attributes described above define the queuing process. Other attributes are needed to describe the performance of a queuing system.

9.1.3 Performance Attributes of a Queuing System

9.1.3.1

$P(n)$ = probability that exactly n units are in the queuing system. The units in the system may be either waiting to get serviced or being serviced.

9.1.3.2

L = expected number of units in the system. L includes units in the queue and those being served.

9.1.3.3

$L(q)$ = expected queue length, $L(q)$ implies only those units that are waiting in the queue.

9.1.3.4

W = expected waiting time in the system as experienced by each unit. W includes both the waiting time and the service time.

9.1.3.5

$W(q)$ = expected waiting time in the queue as experienced by each unit. $W(q)$ excludes the service time.

The above concepts can now be applied to describe the behavior of some well-known queuing systems.

9.1.4 Queuing Systems

There are two types of queuing systems employed in switched communication systems:

1. loss system
2. delay system

A *loss* system is a queuing system that throws out the unit from the system if there is no free server at the time the unit is taken out of the queue for service. There may be some variations, such as retaining the unit in the system for a certain specified time before throwing it out due to the lack of a free server. The performance of a loss system is generally measured in terms of the probability of loss or simply blocking probability.

The *delay* system is a queuing system in which the unit remains in the queue until it is serviced. The performance of a delay system is generally determined by the probability distribution for the time spent in the system. The first two moments are particularly important in the design of switching nodes. In some cases, the queue length distribution is also useful in designing the nodal buffer space.

We will apply the above notions in describing the behavior of some useful queuing systems. Only the final results will be described. No attempt is made to derive the results. See Refs. 1 to 4 for a more thorough treatment of the subject.

9.1.4.1 Loss System/Full Availability/Infinite Source/Random Arrivals/Exponential Service Times

The probability of blocking ($= B$) in a steady-state condition can be expressed in terms of the number of servers ($= N$) and offered traffic in erlangs ($= A$ = product of arrival rate and average service time) as follows:

$$B = (A^N/A!) \left/ \sum_{i=0}^{N} (A^i/i!) \right. \qquad 9.1.1$$

where $X!$ denotes X factorial $= 1*2*3* \ldots X$. Equation 9.1.1 is often called the Erlang's B formula, which assumes that the blocked calls are cleared from the system, never to return as retrial attempts. Equation 9.1.1 is difficult to evaluate numerically for large values of N. A recursion relationship is often employed to obtain easy solutions:

$$B(N + 1) = \frac{A*B(N)}{N = 1 + B(N)} \qquad 9.1.2$$

Equation 9.1.2 can thus be used to compute all values of B for any N, starting with 0.

If all the blocked called are allowed to return, it can be shown that the offered traffic will be increased to the following value during statistical equilibrium:

$$A(\text{new}) = A(1 + B + B^2 + \ldots) = A/(1 - B) \qquad 9.1.3$$

The new value of offered traffic can then be used to compute the altered value of blocking, using Eq. 9.1.2. The above technique can be used to handle other values of retrials.

If the total time a unit spends in the system equals the sum of waiting time in the queue and the average service time, two results are of interest:

$$P(n) = (A^n)*(\exp(-A))/n! \qquad\qquad 9.1.4$$
$$B = 1 - P(n) \qquad\qquad 9.1.5$$

Because Eq. 9.1.4 represents the Poisson distribution as described in paragraph 9.1.1, Eq. 9.1.5 is called *Poisson's blocking formula*. Sometimes, a distinction is made in representing the GOS in a system: B.XX represents XX percent of blocking computed according to the Erlang B formula, and P.XX represents XX percent of blocking computed according to Poisson's formula.

A comparison between the two variations of the same system (i.e., lost units cleared versus lost calls held) will show that the Poisson formula results in higher blocking than that given by the Erlang B formula for a given traffic load, A, and number of servers, N.

The Erlang B and Poisson formulas are commonly used in computing the blocking probabilities of queuing systems encountered in a CS node, where the arriving call requests first vie for service from a pool of common control equipment and later vie for service from N servers in the form of voice-grade circuits. Calls may be blocked at either of the two queuing systems.

In some CS systems, the overflow traffic is presented to another loss system. For this case, the average load of overflow traffic and variance of the overflow traffic are of interest to the analysts and designers.

These values are given by Eqs. 9.1.6 and 9.1.7:

$$R = A*B = \text{overflow traffic} \qquad\qquad 9.1.6$$
$$D = R*((A/(N + 1 - A + R)) - R = \text{variance} \qquad\qquad 9.1.7$$

9.1.4.2 Loss System/Full Availability/Finite Source/Random Arrivals/Exponential Service Times

In this system, the finite source can generate a maximum of M units at any time. In practical systems, $M >= N$, where N is the number of servers. For a given arrival rate, λ, and average service time, TH, the blocking probability can be expressed in the form of a recursion formula as follows:

$$B(N) = \frac{(M - N)*\lambda*TH*B(N - 1)}{N + (M - N)*\lambda*TH*B(N - 1)} \qquad\qquad 9.1.8$$

Comparing the two loss systems described above may be difficult due to the absence of an expression for A (offered traffic) in Eq. 9.1.8. Due to the finite source, the offered load, A, takes on a new expression:

$$A = (M*\lambda*TH)/(1 + \lambda*TH*(1 - B(n)))$$ 9.1.9

The blocking probability is always less for this system than for a similar system with an infinite source.

9.1.4.3 Delay System/Full Availability/Infinite Source/Random Arrivals/Exponential Service Times

There are two variations of this system:

1. single server $(M/M/1)$ queue
2. S servers $(M/M/S)$ queue

Using the arrival rate (λ), average service rate (μ), and the average utilization of the $M/M/1$ queue $(\rho = \lambda/\mu)$, performance of the queuing system can be expressed as follows:

$$L = \rho/(1 - \rho)$$ 9.1.10
$$L(q) = \rho*L$$ 9.1.11
$$W = 1/(\mu - \lambda)$$ 9.1.12
$$W(q) = (\lambda/\mu)/(\mu - \lambda)$$ 9.1.13

The probability of system delay, T, exceeding a value t, can be expressed as:

$$P(T > t) = \exp(-\mu*(1 - \rho)*t)$$ 9.1.14

with standard deviation of T as:

$$\sigma(T) = (1/\mu)/(1 - \rho) = 1/(\mu - \lambda)$$ 9.1.15

To obtain similar expressions for the $M/M/S$ queue with identical S servers, one needs the following relations:

$$P(0) = 1 \left/ \left[\sum_{n=0}^{s-1} \frac{(\lambda/\mu)^n}{n!} + \frac{(\lambda/\mu)^s}{s!} * \frac{1}{(1 - \lambda/\mu s)} \right] \right.$$
$$\rho = \lambda/(\mu*s)$$

Using these expressions, we can express the performance of the $M/M/S$ queue as follows:

$$L(q) = \frac{P(0)*(\lambda/\mu)^s*\rho}{s!(1-\rho)^2}$$ 9.1.16

$$L = L(q) + (\lambda/\mu)$$ 9.1.17

$$W(q) = L(q)/\lambda$$ 9.1.18

$$W = W(q) + 1/\mu$$ 9.1.19

$$P(T > t) = e^{-\mu t}*\left[\frac{P(0)*(\lambda/\mu)^s}{s!(1-\rho)}*\left(\frac{1 - e^{-\mu t(s-1-\lambda/\mu)}}{s-1-\lambda/\mu}\right)\right]$$ 9.1.20

9.1.4.4 Delay System/Full Availability/Infinite Source/Random Arrivals/Constant Service Times (M/D/S)

The performance of an $M/D/1$ queue can be expressed as follows:

$$L(q) = \rho^2/(1-\rho)^2$$ 9.1.21

$$L = [\rho^2/(2*(1-\rho))] + \rho$$ 9.1.22

$$W(q) = (\rho/\mu)/(2*(1-\rho)) + \rho$$ 9.1.23

$$W = (2-\rho)*(1/\mu)/(2*(1-\rho))$$ 9.1.24

$$\sigma(T) = [(1/\mu)/(1-\rho)]*\sqrt{(\rho/3) - \rho^2/12}$$ 9.1.25

Similar expressions for the $M/D/S$ queue are too complicated to describe here.

See Refs. 1, 2, and 5 for a discussion of other special queuing systems. See Ref. 6 for useful tables dealing with $M/M/S$ queues for the case of a finite source. Queues with priorities have also been described in the above references. Such queues will become more prevalent with the advent of new nodal designs and complex user's requirements.

The analysis becomes complicated when two or more queuing systems are combined to form a network of queues. Two or more queuing systems can be combined in tandem or in parallel. The queues may have finite or infinite space. The arrival statistics will exhibit complicated distributions. Many research papers treating special cases are published each year. Their usefulness to practical cases is in direct proportion to the accuracy demanded in analysis. In most cases, the analysis can be simplified by assuming stochastic independence among all queuing systems and random arrivals for each system.

9.2 FUNDAMENTALS OF NETWORK ANALYSIS

There are several aspects of an existing network that need to be analyzed. Such an analysis is mandatory for a trade-off study in which several network solutions may be modeled and evaluated prior to a final selection. Three properties of a network are generally of interest:

1. connectivity
2. traffic flows
3. network capacity

9.2.1 Network Connectivity

Connectivity of an n-node network can be expressed in terms of a connection matrix, $C(n)$, as defined below:

$$C(n) = \begin{bmatrix} c_{11} & c_{12} & . & . & . & c_{1n} \\ c_{21} & c_{22} & . & . & . & c_{2n} \\ .. & & .. & & & .. \\ c_{n1} & c_{n2} & . & . & . & c_{nn} \end{bmatrix} \begin{bmatrix} 0 & 1 & . & . & . & 1 \\ 1 & 1 & . & . & . & 0 \\ . & . & . & . & . & . \\ 1 & 0 & . & . & . & 1 \end{bmatrix} \qquad 9.2.1$$

where 1 for $c(i,j)$ element represents a direct connection between node i and node j, and a 0 for a $c(i,j)$ element implies an absence of a direct connection between node i and node j. Equation 9.2.1 represents a directed graph, for each matrix element, $c(i,j)$ implies a direction. To illustrate, a fully connected connection matrix for a 5-node, $C(5)$, is expressed as follows:

$$C(5) = \begin{bmatrix} 1 & 1 & 1 & 1 & 1 \\ 1 & 1 & 1 & 1 & 1 \\ 1 & 1 & 1 & 1 & 1 \\ 1 & 1 & 1 & 1 & 1 \\ 1 & 1 & 1 & 1 & 1 \end{bmatrix} \qquad 9.2.2$$

The connections, $c(i,j) = 1$ should be considered with care, because they represent looping within a node.

A measure of network connectivity can be defined as follows

$$K = \sum_{i=1}^{n} \sum_{j=1}^{n} c(i,j) <= n^2 \qquad 9.2.3$$

9.2.2 Network Flows

To study the various network flows, one needs first to introduce the concept of a path that a call or a transaction follows between a node i and a node j. A path can be represented by a directed vector whose elements are the branches encountered en route. A path can be illustrated as follows:

$$P(i,j) = (c(i,k), \ldots, c(l,j)) \qquad\qquad 9.2.4$$

The length of a path can be defined as the number of branches traversed en route. To illustrate, let us study the 5-node network graph of Fig. 9.2 and the corresponding connection matrix.

Using simple visual inspection, one can enumerate paths of lengths 1, 2, and 3 as follows:

1. $c(1,2)$, $c(1,3)$, $c(1,5)$; $c(2,1)$, $c(2,3)$, $c(3,1)$, $c(3,2)$, $c(3,4)$; $c(4,3)$, $c(4,5)$; $c(5,4)$, $c(5,1)$
2. $(c(1,2)c(2,3))$, $(c(1,3)c(3,4) + c(1,5)c(5,4))$,
   $(c(2,3)c(3,4))$, $(c(2,1)c(1,5))$,
   $(c(3,1)c(1,5) + c(3,4)c(4,5))$, $(c(4,3)c(3,2))$,
   $(c(4,3)c(3,1) + c(5,4)c(4,1))$
3. $(c(1,2)c(2,3)c(3,4))$, $(c(1,5)c(5,4)c(4,3))$,
   $(c(2,1)c(1,5)c(5,4) + c(2,1)c(1,3)c(3,4))$,
   $(c(3,2)c(2,1)c(1,5))$, $(c(3,1)c(1,5)c(5,4))$,
   $(c(3,4)c(4,5)c(5,1))$,
   $(c(4,5)c(5,1)c(1,2) + c(4,3)c(3,1)c(1,2))$,
   $(c(4,3)c(3,2)c(2,1))$, $(c(5,1)c(1,3)c(3,4))$,
   $(c(5,1)c(1,2)c(2,3))$, $(c(5,4)c(4,3)c(3,2))$

The above approach gets extremely complicated as the network becomes larger than shown in Fig. 9.2.

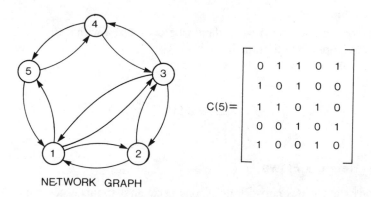

NETWORK GRAPH

$$C(5) = \begin{bmatrix} 0 & 1 & 1 & 0 & 1 \\ 1 & 0 & 1 & 0 & 0 \\ 1 & 1 & 0 & 1 & 0 \\ 0 & 0 & 1 & 0 & 1 \\ 1 & 0 & 0 & 1 & 0 \end{bmatrix}$$

Fig. 9.2. Graph of a 5-node network and its connection matrix.

One can enumerate all the paths of length q or less between any two nodes in the network using the following steps:

1. Obtain a connection matrix consisting of directed branches, as shown in Fig. 9.2.
2. Compute the *path matrix* $P(q)$ whose elements represent all proper paths of length q, using the following steps:
   a. Let $P(1) = C(n)$.
   b. Obtain $P(q)$ using the relation $P(q) = (C(n)*P(q-1))$.
   c. Reject all items, as they appear, in which any subscript appears more than twice. This eliminates all redundant paths and keeps only the proper paths.

By means of the above procedure, the above-mentioned paths for the 5-node network of Fig. 9.2 can be automatically enumerated.

Enumeration of paths between any two nodes can be a useful analytical tool in computing the loads on all trunks of a network. The following steps must be executed:

1. Enumerate paths of lengths q or less between any two nodes.
2. Choose the best path based on certain criteria, such as minimum path length in terms of hops or mileage, cost, etc.
3. Add the from-to traffic load on all the branches of the path.
4. Repeat steps 1, 2, and 3 for all pairs of network nodes.

The from-to traffic loads as required in step 3 can be obtained from a 100 percent sampled call log of a system. In case the traffic logs record only the customer vehicles (e.g., PABX, concentrator, etc.), homing data specifying which customer vehicle is connected to which network node is required. See Ref. 7 for additional insight into this very interesting subject.

9.2.3 Network Capacity

In some cases, computation of a given network capacity is required. The *capacity* of a network can be defined as the total number of calls or packets or transactions that can be sustained during an average second of a busy hour (see Section III for a definition of busy hour).

The capacity of a network is directly related to the capacity of each node to handle traffic, the capacity of each trunk bundle connecting two nodes, and the path lengths followed by transactions.

Let us assume that all traffic is of the intranodal type, implying that traffic entering each node from a customer vehicle (CV) goes to another CV connected to the same node. In this extreme case, the network trunks are not required. The capacity of this hypothetical network is simply the summation of all intranodal erlangs.

Let us now assume a fully connected network. This results in all paths of lengths 1, with longer paths disallowed. In this case, the total capacity of this network in erlangs can be expressed as follows:

$$E = \sum_{i=1}^{N} E(i,i) + \sum_{i,j}^{N} E(i,j)$$

A network that exhibits varying lengths of paths or alternate paths with varying lengths, an average path length q can be computed for the internodal traffic, using the procedure described earlier. In this case, the network capacity in erlangs can be stated as follows:

$$E = \sum_{i=1}^{N} E(i,i) + (1/q)*\sum_{i,j}^{N} E(i,j)$$

If there is only one source node and one sink node in a multinode network, computer algorithms exist (using either linear programming or max-flow-min-cut techniques), that provide all the paths to achieve maximal capacity. The algorithm requires the specification of all link capacities (in erlangs) and a connection matrix. Because every node in a switched communication network acts as both a source and a sink, the problem gets out of hand. Consult Refs. 8, 9, and 10 for excellent treatises on these techniques.

9.3 SIMULATION TECHNIQUE

Statistical simulation using large, data processing computers has been a popular technique for studying complex systems. Simulation offers an alternative to the analytical approach when the complexity of a system prohibits exact solutions. Simulation also offers a means to evaluate and compare new systems before they are actually built.

A simulation model describes events, their effects on system components and on other events, and their occurrence, based on the underlying statistical behavior. When driven by a proper statistical input stream, a simulation model imitates the system being simulated and generates data equivalent to measurement in a real system experiment.

Simulation of a system undergoes three phases: (1) building of a simulation model, (2) design of simulation experiments, and (3) analysis of data generated in simulation experiments. All three phases are equally important in successful usage of the simulation technique.

9.3.1 Simulation Model

It is hardly surprising that the formulation of simulation is critical; it is not obvious, however, that essential to proper formulation is the choice of the level at which a system is simulated. A microscopic level of detail will increase costs in the development of the model and in the execution of simulation experiments. On the other hand, some of the questions may remain unanswered if the level of detail does not reach a certain depth. A judicious trade-off is often required. The level of detail should be fine enough to answer the questions posed and yet be so macroscopic as to ignore details not essential to the results sought.

9.3.2 Simulators

A *simulator* is a tool that allows an analyst to define and execute a simulation model. A simulator may be written explicitly by the analyst in software, using such languages as FORTRAN or PASCAL. Alternatively, languages specifically designed for simulation, for example GPSS or SIMULA, may be used. The choice will depend upon the system to be simulated.

Fundamental to all simulators are the notions of simulated time and statistically controllable events. Any action that alters the state of a simulated system is an event. A simulator predicts, either deterministically or statistically, the time at which an event is to occur. This information is maintained in a data structure called the *event list*. This list may often be sorted in increasing time order. A simulator also maintains a simulated clock that holds the "current" time. A simulator operates as follows (see Fig. 9.3) The event list is scanned to find the next event. The time value associated with the event found is the new value for the clock. The effects of the event are simulated, causing the system state to change. Statistics are updated. The event just simulated may cause future events. Where necessary, new events and corresponding time are predicted, and the event list is updated. Unless certain predefined conditions are met, the simulation cycle is repeated as long as the event list is not empty.

Implementation of the event list requires deletion and addition of entries, namely events and times, and, on occasion, requires reordering of entries. A data structure, known as a linked list, is appropriate for these requirements. Figure 9.4 shows an implementation of the event list as a linked list. Two pointers, FIRST and LAST, indicate, respectively, the beginning and the final elements in the list. Additionally, associated with each entry is a pointer or a link to the next entry in the list. This allows both additions and deletions of entries while maintaining the list in a sorted order.

A simulator is designed to imitate some stochastic behavior of the components of a system. If arrival of messages in a system is modeled as a stochastic

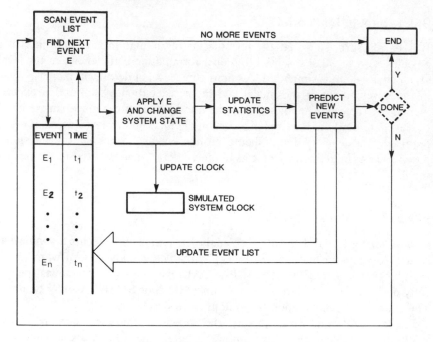

Fig. 9.3. Actions of a simulator.

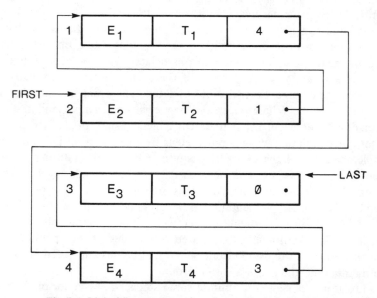

Fig. 9.4. Linked list representation of event list in a simulator.

process, then the time interval between two messages should behave like a random variable drawn from the process. A simulator generates sequences of numbers that follow the rules of the underlying stochastic process. In most simulators, the sequences are not truly random in that they can be exactly duplicated if the same starting value, called *seed,* is used. Such sequences are known as *pseudorandom sequences.*

A considerable amount of research has been carried out in the generation of random numbers. Several techniques have been devised and are available through the literature. A popular approach has been to generate uniform random sequences of integers, i.e., probabilities of occurrence of any two integers, m and n, in some range (a,b) are exactly equal, and to derive other random distributions from such a sequence.

Perhaps the simplest of the uniform pseudorandom sequence generators uses the multiplicative congruence method. In this method, R_i, the ith number in the sequence, obeys the relation:

$$R_i = a * R_{i-1} \, (mod \; m)$$

where *mod* implies the modulo operation. Because pseudorandom sequences are repeated when given the same seed, if a random number in the sequence is repeated, so will be the numbers that follow. That is, if $R_i = R_j$, then $R_{i+1} = R_{j+1}$, $R_{i+2} = R_{j+2}$ and so on. Furthermore, if the seed, R_0, is repeated after k numbers, then it will be repeated every k numbers; the number k is called the *period* of the pseudorandom sequence. It has been shown (Ref. 38) that if m and a are so chosen that they satisfy the following:

$$m = p^c$$
$$p = \text{prime number} > 2$$
$$c = \text{positive integer and}$$
$$a^{(m-1)} = 1 \, (mod \; m)$$

and if R_0 is relatively prime to m, then the pseudorandom sequence has a period of $(m - 1)$. Without the derivation, it may be simply stated that the values

$$m = 2^{31} - 1 = 2147483647$$
$$a = 7^5 = 16807$$

and the relation

$$R_i = a * R_{i-1} \, (mod \; m)$$

meet the criteria. These values are the most useful for the IBM System/360, in which registers are 32-bits wide with 31-bit integer arithmetic (1 bit for the sign). It can also be shown that if

$$m = 2^b$$
$$b = \text{positive integer and}$$
$$a = 3 \ (mod \ 8) \ \text{or} \ a = 5 \ (mod \ 8)$$

then the pseudorandom sequence generated by the recursive relation above has a period of $(m/4)$. This particular method is quite popular, for choice of width of a machine word for b simplifies the *mod* operation to mere truncation of high-order bits. A more detailed discussion can be found in Ref. 38.

A general technique called *transformation method* is used to generate pseudorandom sequences of distributions other than uniform. A uniform pseudorandom sequence is generated and the values are translated using simple arithmetic transformation. Two most commonly used distributions are obtained from a uniform pseudorandom sequence $\{R_i\}$ as follows:

a. Exponential distribution with parameter λ:

$$X_i = - \ (1/\lambda) \ln (1 - R_i)$$

b. Normal distribution with mean zero and variance unity

$$Y = (-2 \log R_{i-1})^{(1/2)} * \sin (2\pi R_i)$$

To obtain mean u and variance v^2:

$$Z_i = u + v * Y_i$$

For systems that exhibit a very particular behavior, it may be necessary to write a simulator using a high-level programming language, or even an assembly language. For most systems, however, simulation languages are quite adequate. They might result in somewhat inefficient experimentation or in the generation of myriad unwanted statistics, but the reduction in the development period for the simulation model often justifies their use.

9.4 MEASUREMENT TECHNIQUE

Measurement is perhaps the most obviously appealing technique in that it shows what is and not what should be. When certain inputs are applied to a given system and the outputs measured, they represent the exact mapping from inputs to outputs as performed by the system transfer function. And yet, measurement serves only a complementary function to other analysis techniques. Several reasons can be cited for the inadequacy of measurement as a stand-alone technique.

Measurement techniques often treat a system or a subsystem as a "black box." Responses of the black box to a set of inputs can be recorded accurately. If the system is in the same state and if the same inputs are applied, then the response can be accurately predicted. The experiment by itself, however, gives little information about responses in a different system state or to a different set of inputs. Insight into the system's working, which is essential to accurate prediction, is lacking. Only a finite subset of mapping between the inputs and outputs is known. A complete definition of the transfer function, and therefore, complete understanding of the system, can be achieved only if the entire input variable space and the entire system state space are exhaustively tested in the measurement experiment. A large input space will reduce practicability of such an experiment. In fact, the experiment may be impossible; because the system is assumed to be a black box, there may be no way to determine the state the system is in.

It is also the case, in the shrinking semiconductor technology, that not all parameters one would like to observe can be measured, because not all parts of a system or circuit are accessible for measurement. When an entire processor is on a single LSI chip, it is quite likely that certain signals appearing at the output of some internal gates (for example, a "carry" flip-flop in one of its registers) may not be directly accessible. If a signal in question is observable, then an experiment involving several measurements for a sequence of inputs can be devised. From the results, the value of the signal at the gate would be deduced. Such a procedure is undesirable when the value of the signal is to be observed without disturbing the state of the system. Furthermore, the signal may not be observable at all; there would be no way to determine the value of the signal.

Measurements serve admirably in conjunction with other methods. In analytical modeling, measurements can be used to validate a model. They can also be used to construct the initial model itself. While measurement techniques are applied to real systems, simulations provide measurements on simulated systems.

The measurement problem is that of determining: (1) what information is needed, (2) which measurements will provide the information. (3) how to obtain the measurements, and (4) how to interpret the measurements. The first two of these subproblems are the most difficult ones; in fact, they are a form of a more basic question, namely, "what should constitute the results of analysis?" This entire section is an attempt to answer the question. The following discussion concentrates on data analysis, i.e., interpretation of measurements. Although the discussion refers to measurements, it is equally applicable to the analysis of data gathered from a simulation experiment.

9.4.1 Measurement Tools

Methods used in measurement can generally be classified into hardware tools and software tools. They perform functions of sampling, collection, storage, and reporting of statistical data.

A representative block diagram of a hardware monitor is shown in Fig. 9.5. The probes into the measured system detect signals that are to be monitored. The hardware monitor simply counts the number of events, or electrical signals, and the time between events. The definition of an event varies substantially from system to system. In one system, an event may be merely the appearance of a certain logic value (0 or 1) at a flip-flop, though in another event may mean that the value of a certain signal or register is between some predetermined limits.

Software tools are based on adding instructions, either in a continuous stream of system instructions or in an interruptlike (trap) manner. Measurements vary from the counting of the number of times an instruction or a memory location is accessed to the timing of an entire program or a sequence of instructions.

Hardware tools are popular because they can be used in such an independent manner that they do not alter the system performance. Software tools tend to interfere with the stream of system instructions. Hardware tools operate at a microscopic level and have the ability to monitor electrical signals. Software

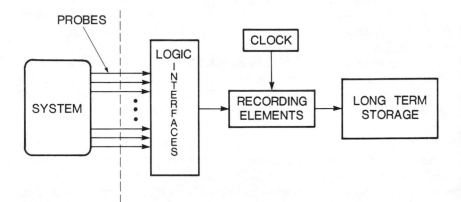

Fig. 9.5. Hardware performance monitor.

tools are more applicable to a higher level of programs or subprograms. Software tools draw their popularity from their flexibility, ease of use, and, generally, low cost.

9.4.2 Design of an Experiment

The discussion in this and the following subsection is presented with a view of application to measurement experiments, but it is equally applicable to simulation experiments.

An experiment consists of many session, or runs. The first step in the design of an experiment is the identification of important factors, or parameters. Often, this turns out to be an extremely difficult task. These factors can be grouped into two classes, controllable factors and observable factors. An experiment is designed to manipulate the controllable factors in such a fashion that by measuring the observable factors certain inferences can be drawn about the system performance. The feasibility of such inferences and their accuracy is a function of the controllability of the independent factors, interdependence among the observable factors, length of a session, and many such aspects of the experiment.

The length of a session is an important parameter of the experiments. The longer the session, the greater the number of data samples, the smaller the variation in sampled statistics, and the tighter the confidence interval around the estimates. The importance of large sample size will become clearer in the next subsection.

Several theoretical approaches to select levels of controllable factors have been proposed. Although a large number of levels is desirable to study the complete variability, a small number of levels is more economical. Because complete randomization under the principle of randomization is impractical, the observations may be grouped into *blocks*. Experimental units within a block exhibit homogeneity under some criterion. The levels within blocks are arranged in random order to yield a *randomized block design*. Such experiments fall into the general category of *factorial designs*, i.e., designs in which a number of factors are controlled at various levels. After some experience with a system, it may become possible to eliminate some randomization by discarding information with low interrelationships. Known as the *fractional factorial design*, the techniques still demands a large number of experiments.

9.4.3 Analysis of Experimental Data

The final important phase in a measurement or a simulation experiment is that of data analysis. A large amount of data is usually gathered, and it is necessary to reduce it in order to evaluate its significance.

Corresponding to a sample, i.e., a set of observations, for some observable factor is an underlying probability distribution. For every parameter of this probability distribution, there is a counterpart in its sample. For example, the counterpart of the population mean is the sample variance. A sample statistic may be used as an estimator of its corresponding population parameter. If sample statistic G is used as an estimator for a population parameter y, and if

$$E(G) = y$$

i.e., the expected value of G is y, then G is said to be an unbiased estimator of y. In other words, if a large number of samples are gathered and if values of G calculated for each sample are averaged, this average tends to the value y as the number of samples tend to infinity.

With this definition, it is clear that an unbiased estimator is desirable because, as the number of samples increases, the estimate moves closer to the actual value of the parameter, and prediction of the same statistic for future samples becomes more accurate. Suppose there exists a sample $\{X_1, X_2, \ldots X_n\}$ of an observable factor X. For the factor X, let the population mean be u and the population variance by $v^2 \to$. The goal of an experiment and the subsequent data analysis is to estimate u and v from observed samples. Define:

$$\text{sample mean} = M = \left(\sum_i X_i \right) \Big/ N \quad \text{and} \quad \text{sample variance}$$

$$= s^2 = \left(\sum_i X_i^2 \right) \Big/ N - M^2$$

It can be shown that

$$E(M) = E(X) = u$$

That is, the sample mean M is an unbiased estimator of u. Nevertheless,

$$E(s^2 \to) = ((N - 1)/N)\, v^2$$

and therefore, the sample variance s^2 is not an unbiased estimator of the population variance v^2. Now, if $V = (N/(N - 1)) \cdot s^2$ then

$$E(V) = v^2$$

In other words, the modified sample variance V is an unbiased estimator of v^2.

Using an unbiased estimator is only one of the approaches taken. Among the other methods used to determine estimators are the principle of maximum likelihood and estimates on pooled samples.

Population mean and population variance are two parameters that are often sought. A measure of how close the sample average is to the population mean is found in a confidence interval. A confidence interval is an estimated range in which the true population mean will lie with a given probability. If N samples are drawn for an observable factor X with mean u and variance v^2, then, according to the central limit theorem, the distribution of M, the sample average, approaches normal distribution for large N. This normal distribution has a mean u and a variance v^2/N. If

$$Z = \frac{M - u}{v/\sqrt{N}}$$

then, as N increases, the distribution of Z approaches the normal distribution with mean zero and variance unity. Using standard tables for the normal distribution, we can determine the interval probability,

$$p = P(-b <= Z <= b)$$

for a given b. Conversely, given a probability figure, it is possible to establish b. Note that,

$$P\left(M - b*\frac{v}{\sqrt{N}} < u < M + b*\frac{v}{\sqrt{N}}\right) - P$$

Therefore,

$$M \pm b*\frac{v}{\sqrt{N}}$$

is called the $p*100$ percent confidence interval for u. In other words, with a probability p, the population mean u will lie in this interval.

Conducting experiments on a previously unknown system, it is quite likely that the population variance v^2 is not known. To handle this case, instead of Z, a new variable is defined:

$$T = \frac{M - u}{s/\sqrt{N - 1}}$$

The distribution of T is called Student's t distribution. Standard tables for Student's distribution are available, and they can be used to determine the confidence interval as before.

Weh two factors X and Y are under investigation in the same sample, their interrelationship should be established. A sample correlation coefficient, called the *Pearson product-moment correlation coefficient,* is defined as

$$r_{xy} = \frac{\sum_i (x_i - M_x)*(Y_i - M_y)}{N*S_x*S_y}$$

where M_x, M_y = sample means of X and Y, respectively, and s_x^2, s_y^2 = sample variances of X and Y, respectively. The value of r_{xy} is an indication of the linearity of the relationship between X and Y. If they are totally unrelated in the sample, then $r_{xy} = 0$. If the relationship is perfectly linear, and if Y increases as X increases, then $r_{xy} = +1$. Furthermore, if the relationship is perfectly linear, and if Y decreases as X increases, then $r_{xy} = -1$.

Several other data analysis techniques are used. It is not the intent of this section to list all possible techniques, but only a selection. The references at the end of Section II should adequately serve those desiring additional details.

Chapter 10
Network System Level Analysis

Chapter 9 discussed many useful tools that can be employed for network system analysis, which can be divided into two categories:

1. network system level analysis
2. network nodal level analysis

In this chapter, we shall deal with the first type of analysis. The nodal level analysis will be discussed in Chapter 11.

Network system level analysis techniques differ for each type of network system. Circuit switching, packet switching, message switching, DDP, and DDBM present unique network level problems that must be solved using the techniques discussed earlier.

10.1 CIRCUIT-SWITCHED SYSTEMS

Quite frequently, the user is interested in analyzing the end-to-end GOS of a CS network. This requirement involves the computation of the following GOS parameters:

1. total call connect time, measured as the time elapsed between the moment all digits are dialed and the moment the destination terminal is made "busy"
2. end-to-end blocking probability experienced by a call request

The total connect time can be expressed as the sum of (1) processing time delays experienced by each network node and (2) transmission delays experienced by the signaling data on each link of the path.

Because the delay encountered in each network node is a random quantity, characterized by an average and a variance, and because most networks exhibit different path lengths, as caused by congestion, the connect time will also exhibit a random variation characterized by a probability distribution.

The techniques for computing the delays in network nodes will be described in Chapter 11.

To compute the delays due to signaling on each trunk in the path, the problem must be divided into two subproblems.

First, the delays due to signaling digits must be computed. The number of dialed digits will vary depending on the call types. Seven digits may be involved for the on-net calls. Ten digits may be involved for off-net calls. In some systems, if congestion is experienced for an on-net call, the 7 digits may be converted to 10 digits to reach the destination via off-net access lines, e.g., watts or FX lines. Some systems allow abbreviated dialing. Some additional digits are appended to the control message as required by the particular protocol. Knowing the link speeds, one can now compute the delay distribution for each link.

Next, the effect of path length variation on the total transmission delay must be computed. Using the path enumeration scheme described earlier and the paths allowed for each call type, one can derive a path length distribution and hence the total connect time distribution. The first two moments are generally necessary.

Let us represent the nodal delay by $T(nd)$, link delay by $I(ld)$, and the first two moments (average and variance) of a distribution involving a random variable X by $AVG(X)$ and $VAR(X)$, respectively. We can derive the average and variance of the system connect time (T_c) by invoking the central limit, which shows that in the limit, sums of random variables give rise to a normal distribution. The $AVG(T_c)$ can, accordingly, be defined as follows:

$$AVG(T_c) = \sum_{i=1}^{N} AVG(T_i(nd)) + \sum_{i=1}^{L} AVG(T_i(ld)) \qquad 10.1.1$$

where N is the number of network nodes in the path of the call, and L is the number of links in the path of the call. Actually $L = N - 1$.

The variance of the connect time distribution can also be defined as:

$$VAR(T_c) = \sum_{i=1}^{N} VAR(T_i(nd)) + \sum_{i=1}^{L} VAR(T_i(ld)) \qquad 10.1.2$$

Using the above quantities, one can then derive expressions for 95 percentile, 99 percentile, and 99.9 percentile values of system connect times, expressed as follows:

$$T_c(90\%) = AVG(T_c) + 1.28*(SQR(VAR(T_c))) \qquad 10.1.3$$
$$T_c(95\%) = AVG(T_c) + 1.65*(SQR(VAR(T_c))) \qquad 10.1.4$$
$$T_c(99\%) = AVG(T_c) + 2.33*(SQR(VAR(T_c))) \qquad 10.1.5$$
$$T_c(99.9\%) = AVG(T_c) + 3.09*(SQR(VAR(T_c))) \qquad 10.1.6$$

As all nodes and links have similar behaviors, the central limit should be valid for this kind of analysis. One dominant, constituent random variable can determine the final distribution.

The end-to-end blocking probability and its distribution can be derived using a similar technique as that employed for system connect time.

Most CS networks are designed to provide a low end-to-end blocking probability for the first attempt. To illustrate, most of the corporate CS voice networks provide a GOS of about B.10. The public telephone networks, e.g., Bell's PTS, provides a GOS of about B.01. As a call traverses a path of at least two access lines and a trunk, the individual blocking factor of each link stage must be much lower than the end-to-end GOS. Due to the difficulties involved in computing the end-to-end GOS as a function of the complex routing techniques employed in the network, and the fact that the routing tables may change with time, most networks are designed by requiring a fixed blocking probability for each route. It is left to the analyst to compute the actual distribution of end-to-end GOS for an existing network, using the following method:

1. Enumerate all the paths for each call type and their probabilities of occurrence.
2. Compute the GOS of each path by adding the individual blocking factors.
3. Add the probabilities of paths with identical GOS.
4. Plot the GOS values on the abscissa and the associated probabilities on the ordinate of an $X - Y$ graph.

This method should provide a useful distribution of end-to-end GOS valid for the CS network system.

Large CS network systems also require some trade-offs among centralized, hierarchical, and distributed routing schemes. The centralized scheme requires a centralized master node to decide all the routes within the network. This scheme works well with an overlayed common channel signaling (CCS) data network.

The hierarchical routing method divides the network into clusters, each cluster being controlled by a major node of its own. Such an approach makes the routing tables in the master node less formidable, but tends to increase the connect times, due to uncertain path lengths within the clusters.

There are two versions of distributed routing—one in which each node is aware of its neighbors only, and the other requiring full information about all other nodes. Although both versions require the same amount of complexity in all nodes, the first version is simpler to design. Of course, the first version will need some minimal data regarding the destination node to prevent needless looping within the network. Distributed routing (first version) is very desirable for networks that are always growing.

To compare these routing schemes for various connectivities and traffic flows is a difficult task. Analytical models can be constructed for approximate trade-offs. Simulation of very large networks will tend to be expensive. If a great deal of optimization is needed, however, simulation may be the only way to achieve the objectives.

Bell's PTS employs a combination of the centralized master node with a CCS network and alternate routing at each node in the network (see Fig. 7.1). Most of the corporate CS networks with 3 to 16 nodes function properly with the distributed routing method, coupled with alternate routing tables provided at each node.

Some analyses may demand a cost analysis using transmisssion facilities leased from different carriers. One can develop simple computer programs that can compute the transmission costs quickly if the locations of the switching nodes and the network connectivity are input. It is a good practice to maintain (1) several subroutines, each corresponding to a tariff, and (2) a data base of all the V and H coordinates of all Class 5 COs and their attributes, such as high and low density, and available specialized services (e.g. MCI, SPC, etc.). A good deal of processing time is spent on computing distances between two nodal points. Availability of V and H coordinates (a special projection system) facilitates such computations through the use of a simple formula:

$$D = \sqrt{0.1*((V1 - V2)^2 + (H1 - H2)^2)} \text{ miles} \qquad 10.1.7$$

where $V1$ and $H1$ are the coordinates of the first node, and $V2$ and $H2$ are the coordinates of the second node.

If the network is situated in another country, longitudes and latitudes must be employed, and the following formula is used for computing the mileage:

$$D = \arccos[\sin(LAT1)*\sin(LAT2) + \cos(LAT1)*\cos(LAT2)*\cos(LNG2$$
$$- LNG1)]*6371.256 \text{ Kmeters}$$
$$10.1.8$$

where LAT1, LNG1, LAT2, and LNG2 are the latitudes and longitudes of the two locations.

Some tariffs determine the cost of an incremental circuit according to not only its length but also the total mileage of all circuits leased from a given carrier. Therefore, the analysis program must maintain a running total on circuit mileage from each carrier. Such a program is generally used as a subroutine for the network synthesis process.

Another CS system where the previously developed analytical models can be applied is called the *automatic call distribution* (ACD) system. An ACD consists of two queuing systems in tandem, one LOSS type and one DELAY type, as illustrated in Fig. 10.1

A trunk bundle is leased from each city to accept calls that are served by a common pool of agents, e.g., airline agents, rental car agents, etc. Each trunk is sized to provide a desired amount of blocking to an assumed busy hour calling intensity. All the calls are queued and later served by the agents according to a first-in-first-out (FIFO) scheme. A call will remain in queue until it is served.

Each of the trunk bundles can be sized by using Eq. 9.1.1 for a given offered traffic in Erlangs (A) and the desired blocking probability (B).

The number of agent positions can be computed by using Eq. 9.1.14 for a given handled traffic in Erlang (A), the average call holding time (H), and the desired probability (P) of delay exceeding a given delay (T). In most airline applications, $P = .15$ and $T = 20$ seconds. One may question the validity of Eq. 9.1.14 because it assumes an infinite source, and only the handled traffic is used in computations. The infinite source model results in a higher value of agent positions. The use of handled traffic, instead of offered traffic, results in a lower number of agents. These two assumptions tend to neutralize each other in most ACD systems, thus eliminating the need for a very complicated solution involving a finite source and offered traffic, some of which exits the ACD system prior to being served. The abandoned calls behave strangely for each system, strengthening the belief that the callers who hang up before being served do so for several reasons, delay being only one of them.

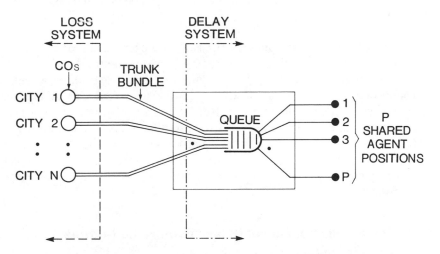

Fig. 10.1. A block diagram of an ACD system consisting of two queues in tandem.

10.2 PACKET-SWITCHED AND MESSAGE-SWITCHED NETWORKS

There are many aspects of a given PS network that must be analyzed for a specific application. Some of these problems can be described as follows:

1. average link utilization
2. distribution of packet delays through the network
3. broadcast channel analysis
4. trade-offs among different routing techniques
5. transmission cost analysis

10.2.1 Average Link Utilization

A close relationship exists between link utilization, frame length (a frame contains the packet as shown in the Appendix a), link capacity, propagation delay on the link, bit error rate over the link, and the data link control procedure (e.g., IBM's SDLC and ISO's HDLC) employed. Reference 18 develops mathematical models for analyzing the maximum achievable link utilizations in the network. The models are applicable to a link connecting two network nodes. As most systems employ identical links and packet lengths within the network, the results will apply to every link.

The results show that if 9600-BPS terrestrial trunks are employed, 1000-bit-long frames can yield link utilizations ranging between .8 to .95 for error rates lower than 10^{-5} and modulo count of 8($\cong$equal to outstanding frames waiting for acknowledgment). Longer frames (10,000 to 100,000 bits) and higher modulo counts are required to obtain the same utilization for 9600-BPS satellite circuits.

The 50-KBPS terrestrial trunks require slightly longer frames to achieve the same utilization for a modulo count of 8; 50-KBPS satellite trunks will exhibit low utilizations (about 0.2) for 1000-bit frames an a modulo count of 8. Modulo counts of 32 and longer frames will be required to achieve high utilization.

The analytical models developed in Ref. 18 can be programmed on a personal computer and employed to yield useful results for all practical designs.

Higher utilization of network links is not the only objective. It should be combined with the delays a packet experiences through the network. Long packets may yield higher link utilizations, but may create unacceptable delays through the network.

10.2.2 Distribution of Packet Delays through the Network

For a given network system, the user may require the average, 90 percentile, and 95 percentile values of packet delays. This task will first require the enumeration of all network paths and their probabilities using the approach described in 9.2. This data will yield a profile of a typical path.

The delay on each link of the typical path can then be computed using the queuing models discussed in 9.1.4.3. See Fig. 10.2 for a representation of the last queue in a network node and the link server as parts of a queuing system to be studied. Let C be the capacity of the link in bits per second, λ be the packet arrival rate per second, and B be the average packet length (exponential distribution is assumed due to all types of packets), in bits. Using Eq. 9.1.12 and the equivalence $u = C/B$, we can express the average delay (W) through the queuing system as follows:

$$W = 1/((C/B) - \lambda) \qquad 10.2.1$$

which is identical to the equation derived by Kleinrock (Ref. 13) and used for studying the delays in PS networks.

According to Eq. 9.1.15, the standard deviation of delay is also expressed by the same expression.

Knowing the actual arrival rate and capacity of each link in a typical path, one can now compute the average delay and associated standard deviation of delay for each link in the path.

To these values, we must add the delays experienced in each node in the path. See Chapter 11 for a discussion of nodal design parameters that influence delays through the various queuing systems inside the node.

The average and 90 (plus others if needed) percentile values of network delays can now be computed, using a method illustrated by Eqs. 10.1.1 and 10.1.2

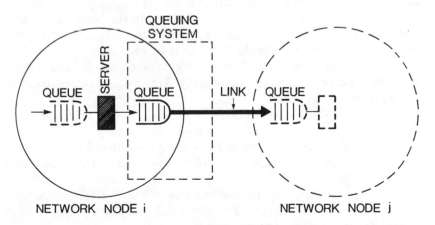

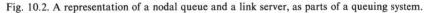

Fig. 10.2. A representation of a nodal queue and a link server, as parts of a queuing system.

10.2.3 Broadcast Channel Analysis

Many systems employ a wideband broadcast channel to switch packets among a large number of users. To illustrate, several local network architectures (see 7.4) employ a wideband bus to interchange packets among several users. A satellite system employs the now famous ALOHA protocol to switch packets among a large number of users. These are examples of *multiple access* (MA) *techniques* for sharing a communication facility.

Some common MA techniques are: frequency division multiple access (FDMA), time division multiple access (TDMA), code division multiple access (CDMA), and asynchronous TDMA (ATDMA).

FDMA, TDMA, and CDMA are traditional channel-oriented MA techniques designed for voice or batched applications. Because interactive data applications involve intermittent, or bursty, traffic from a large group of users, the old MA techniques introduce inefficiencies in the use of fixed assigned channels.

ATDMA (see Chapter 4 for a detailed discussion) became a natural choice for terrestrial, point-to-point networks. Only two nodes communicate with one another over a link, and there is no additional network level contention.

When a broadcast channel, e.g., a shared bus or a satellite circuit, is employed, however, all users are listening to a transmitted packet. Techniques must be devised to retransmit when two or more users transmit their packets concurrently in such a manner as to achieve statistical equilibrium and stable operation.

The ALOHA, slotted ALOHA, CSMA, CSMA with collision detection, and reservation protocols are some of the well-known techniques for either living with contention or avoiding contention altogether.

The ALOHA assumes no synchronization among a large number of users who transmit packets in a random, bursty fashion. In the event two or more packets collide—a state each transmitter realizes after channel propagation time—each user transmits its packet after a randomized delay.

In slotted ALOHA, the channel time is slotted, and users are restricted to transmit their packets during those slots only. This reduces contention when compared to unslotted ALOHA.

The carrier-sense-multiaccess (CSMA) technique allows a user to transmit a packet when no carrier is sensed. Such a scheme is suitable for a local network using a bus topology, because carrier sensing is easily realized. Collisions are discovered after acknowledgments are received and retransmissions are randomized, as in ALOHA.

A technique combining CSMA and real-time collision detection improves the performance, for transmissions are terminated immediately after collision detection. Retransmissions are randomized.

The reservation ATDMA techniques eliminate contention by reserving the available TDM or FDM subchannels to subscribers through the use of a shared, single-reservation subchannel. Any one of the above ATDMA techniques could be used to share the reservation subchannel.

Several researchers (Refs 16, 19, and 20) have studied the performance of the above techniques for sharing a broadcast channel for packet switching.

Performance can be studied and compared only by plotting average packet delay versus channel utilization and hardware/software costs, but that is rather difficult. Actually, there is no single protocol that is optimum for all applications, traffic models, and all sizes of user populations. At this time, only a few general statements can be made regarding maximum channel throughputs achievable and delays expected.

The slotted ALOHA is the best technique in terms of observed delays at low channel utilizations ($\simeq 0.2$ or less) for a large number (>50) of users characterized by bursty traffic. Despite that the maximum channel utilization is only 0.368.

The reservation techniques are good all around for bursty traffic and short/long messages (one or more packets per message). Channel utilizations of as high as 0.8 are achievable.

The fixed TDMA technique, which is realized by eliminating the reservation subchannels and fixed-assigning the subchannels to users, turns out to be an excellent solution for a small number of bursty or nonbursty users. High channel utilizations are achievable for only the nonbursty users.

The CSMA technique with collision detection is the best one for bus topology, as low delays and high channel utilizations (>0.8) are possible.

10.2.4 Trade-offs Among Different Routing Schemes

Only slight differences exist among the routing schemes implemented for CS and PS networks. See Ref. 22 for an analytical study of distributed and hierarchical routing schemes for packet switching. It shows that for a network with nodes exceeding 100, hierarchical routing within a network, composed of clusters, minimizes the size of routing tables, and hence nodal complexity, for fixed performance goals (throughput and delays). With fewer nodes, a distributed, dynamic routing scheme is appropriate.

Reference 25 describes a simulation study of an 8-node overconnected network topology and the 19-node ARPA topology operating with adaptive routing with or without priority traffic. The performance, which was measured in terms of throughput, average delays, and undelivered message, was shown to improve drastically in networks with high connectivity and program enhancements.

Reference 21 presents a simulation study of secure centralized and distributed networks.

10.2.5 Network Cost Analysis

The cost of an existing network can be computed using the approach defined in 10.1.3. That is the only way to characterize actual costs. Use of simplified, linear models may be adequate for comparing different switched network models, but may prove very misleading for computing the costs of communication facilities leased from several common and specialized carriers.

There is a great deal of interest in comparing CS and PS technologies for a given application or a given mix of applications. See Refs. 23 and 24 for studies dealing with throughputs, network delays, and total costs of CS and PS network systems. Reference 24 develops detailed analytical models for switching hardware/software costs valid for a mixed application (2700 Erlangs for voice, 36.15 MBPS of data traffic with 50 percent bulk and 50 percent interactive). Several voice digitization rates and types of CS are also considered. Although Gitman and Frank (Ref 24) conclude that PS technology is superior to CS technology in every respect, they do discuss problems related to migration from the large existing CS networks base.

10.3 DISTRIBUTED DATA PROCESSING SYSTEMS

Distributed data processing is a term in vogue and has been used with several meanings. As described by the purest definition, it implies distribution of data processing, control, and communication. Little is known about the analysis of such systems, and it remains an important area for continuing effort.

Some choose to call systems like Arpanet DDP systems. Here, they are treated under the category of computer networks and are covered in 10.1 and 10.2.

10.4 DISTRIBUTED-DATA-BASE-MANAGEMENT

Much as the DDP systems, distributed DBM systems imply the distribution of data base storage functions, and data base control. It is quite possible to have DBM systems that use distributed data processing with centralized data base and systems that use centralized data processing with distributed data base.

The DDBM systems potentially offer high availability and throughput; this is achieved at the cost of synchronization protocols to maintain data base consistency and communication between the distributed copies of the data base. The analysis of DDBM systems is another open, challenging area for future research. Some very early thoughts on this complex subject can be found in Refs. 26 through 29.

Chapter 11
Network Switching Node Analysis

11.1 INTRODUCTION

A network switching node performs a number of functions. The primary function of a switching node is, as the name suggests, switching. It may be switching voice for telephone calls, messages, or any digitized data. A switching node will also provide some secondary functions, such as long-term storage of data, collection of statistics, etc. A node may also serve as a composite subsystem, performing switching as well as such other functions as data processing or data base management.

A network switching node will also perform certain network-related functions. In addition to connecting a call, delivering a message, or routing a packet, it may also maintain and update user directories, maintain and update routing information, temporarily assume the role of a master in a network, monitor neighboring nodes, and so on. Functions performed by a switching node in a particular network are a combination of (or sometimes, a compromise between) the user requirements and the choice of the network switching technique.

Performance of a network switching node is to be evaluated in terms of the functions it is required to perform. Performance analysis attempts to answer two types of questions. The first deals with absolute performance, e.g., how many messages can a node handle in an hour? The other type compares the performance against a requirement, e.g., will a certain function be completed within a specified time period? Questions of both types may be posed for each of the required functions. The goal of performance analysis is to answer these questions.

11.2 IDENTIFICATION OF CRITICAL RESOURCES

Performance of any system in general, and of a network switching node in particular, depends upon the performance of the resources it uses. Communication equipment, computer (or computers), processing elements, storage units, and many such components form the set of resources of a node. The task of performance analysis of a node involves identification of critical resources, performance analysis of critical resources, and a composite analysis of node performance based on the performance of resources.

Identification of critical resources is far from trivial. It depends upon the required functions of the node. As shown in Fig. 11.1, a network switching node serves the external world consisting of user interfaces and network (internodal) interfaces. The switching node may be a simple switch module or a stored program control (SPC) switch. This discussion focuses on the latter. The SPC switch itself may consist of a simple computer system, a multicomputer system, or a multiprocessor system. For the sake of initial conceptualization, Fig. 11.2 shows an SPC switching node as a simple computer system.

Resources identified in Fig. 11.2, namely processing unit, primary storage, secondary storage, I/O controller for external interfaces, and lower-level storage, and the communication paths among these resources are the potential candidates for critical resources. The communication paths usually exist only between the processing unit and other resources, but special-purpose paths between secondary and primary storage are in common use. There is also a trend toward providing additional paths to relieve the processing units of their undue burden.

The above list of critical resources is certainly not exhaustive. As switching nodes become more powerful, they invariably become more complex, adding not only to the list of resources, but also to the ways in which they are used. It is not practical to identify all possible ways of constructing a switching node, nor is it the intent of this chapter. The rest of the subsections of this chapter include analyses of identified critical resources in conventional network systems. Where a resource is isolated and its performance easily characterized, actual analyses (results) are presented. In other cases, only representative analysis and techniques are described. A list of references at the end of Section II supplements the discussion where needed.

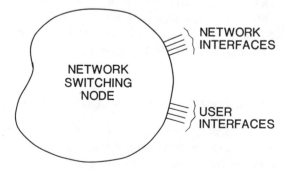

Fig. 11.1. A network switching node and its environment.

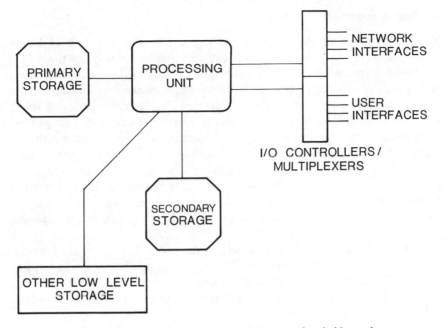

Fig. 11.2. A simple computer system as a network switching node.

11.3 BASIC LEVEL PERFORMANCE MODELS OF RESOURCES

11.3.1 External I/O Interfaces

A switching node interfaces with two external entities, the users and the other network switching nodes. Although requirements of the two interfaces might differ, the basic performance issues remain the same, namely, the loading of links, loss and retries at the links, and delays in aquiring a link.

The loading of links is estimated from the network requirements, namely, the rate at which the links are requested (i.e., request rate r) and the average time for which a link will be used (i.e., link holding time h). The expression for loading, A, (expressed in Erlangs) is:

$$A = r * h$$

For delays and loss factors, a simple M/M/S model is generally adequate. These models are fully described in paragraph 9.1 and need not be repeated here.

11.3.2 Secondary Storage

The secondary storage in switching nodes generally takes the form of disk or drum storage units. It possesses larger capacity and longer response times than the primary storage. It is a common practice today to format the secondary storage into fixed-sized portions called *cells*. In physical terms, a cell resides in a sector; the terms *cell* and *sector* are therefore used interchangeably. A larger unit, *track,* is made up of a fixed number of sectors. A secondary storage unit, thus, has a fixed number of tracks, and each track holds a fixed number of sectors of a fixed size. Each track is identified by a unique number called a *track address*. Within each track the sectors are numbered, and the sector number is called a *sector address*. Thus, track address and sector address together specify a unique cell in a secondary storage unit. The following description shows how this terminology fits disk, drum, and bubble memory units.

Disk unit: Disk units consist of physically stacked disks rotating at a constant speed (Fig. 11.3). Each physical disk has a fixed number of tracks forming concentric circles. Each track is divided into a fixed number of sectors. Each sector therefore is an arc on a disk forming a constant angle at the center. If tracks of equal circumference, i.e., having the same radius, from all the disks are visualized to be stacked on top of each other, then they are said to form a *cylinder*. A disk unit has as many cylinders as there are tracks on each disk. Components known as *read/write heads* perform the actual data transfer to and from disks. These heads are mounted on an arm.

There are two popular types of disk units. Moving-head disk units employ

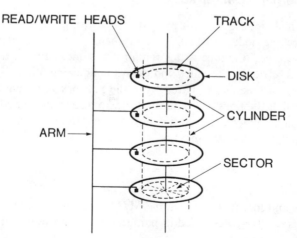

Fig. 11.3. Organization of a disk unit.

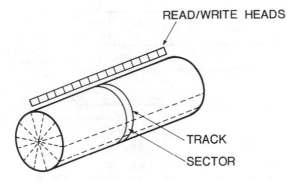

Fig. 11.4. Organization of a drum unit.

a single read/write head per disk, with the arm moving toward and away from the center to position the heads at the proper cylinder. Fixed-head disk units employ one head per track per disk, with heads permanently positioned at the tracks, thus obviating any arm movement. The time required to position a read/write head at a particular track is called the *arm-positioning time*. Clearly, the arm-positioning time for fixed-head disk units is zero.

Drum unit: Conceptually, a drum is very much like a single cylinder in a disk unit (Fig. 11.4). The read-write heads are permanently positioned at the tracks. Each track is divided into sectors of fixed size. Sectors pass under the heads as the drum rotates at a constant speed.

Bubble memory units: Bubble memory presents an entirely different technology and an unrelated structure, but with similar characteristics. Many organizations have been proposed for bubble memory storage units. The most popular is the major-minor loop organization (Fig. 11.5). The minor loops are of identical size (in number of information bits stored) and can be made to move in a synchronized manner. Minor loops can be stopped, and transfer heads can be used to copy a data bit from each minor loop into the major loop. As the minor loops move, at each instant they present a set of bits at the transfer heads. This set of bits is analogous to a sector in a drum. Once the data is copied into the major loop, the major loop can be rotated to position data under the read heads. Following the actions in reversed steps, a set of bits may be written into the minor loops.

Associated with each of the three secondary storage units mentioned above are the following time attributes that characterize their performance.

Rotation time: For disk and drum units, this is the time for one rotation of the unit. For bubble memory, this is the time required for a complete rotation of a minor loop.

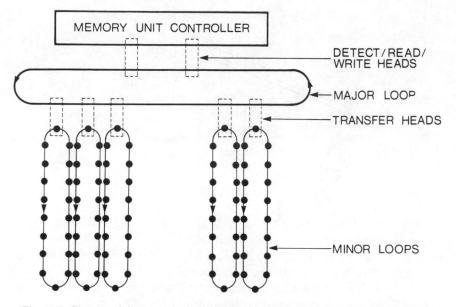

Fig. 11.5. Conceptual diagram of major-minor loop organization in bubble memory units.

Arm-positioning time: For moving-head disk units, this is the time required to position the heads at a proper cylinder. For fixed-head disk units, drums, and bubble memories, the arm-positioning time may be assumed to be zero, as arm positioning is not required.

Latency: For disk and drum units: latency is the time required for the start of the desired sector to arrive at a head after the heads have been positioned. For bubble memories, it is the time for the desired "sector" (set of bits) to arrive at the transfer heads. If a random sector is specified at an arbitrary time, the average latency is half the rotation time.

Transfer time: This is the time required to actually transfer the data after the sector is under the heads, i.e., after the latency period. For bubble memories, it is the time required to move the major loop to position the data under the read/write heads.

In the following paragraphs, performance analysis of moving-head disk units is discussed. Note that most of it can be applied to other systems by setting the arm-positioning time to zero. Two types of disk unit designs are considered. A first-in-first-out (FIFO), random accessing design in which requests are served in the order they are received. No information about the distribution of accesses is assumed. The other type of design collects a set of requests before starting to serve them. When the accesses are closely situated on the disk units, this scheme substantially improves response times.

Random Accesses. When accesses to a disk unit are so physically separated that each access lies on a separate cylinder, they are best served as they come. The service time, *ts,* is calculated as:

$$ts = tap + tl + tdt$$

where
  tap = arm-positioning time
   tl = latency
  tdt = data transfer time
      = tr/ns
   tr = rotation time and
  ns = number of sectors per track

Latency, as mentioned earlier, is half the rotation time on an average. The arm-positioning time, *tap,* is somewhat more difficult to estimate. Manufacturers of disk units usually quote the minimum *tap* (time required to move from one cylinder to an adjacent cylinder), the maximum *tap* (time required to move from the first cylinder to the last cylinder), and the average *tap.* For average response time analysis, the average *tap* is quite adequate. When more accurate analysis is required, and if an accurate access distribution is known, then the following technique may be used.

This technique involves an exhaustive testing of the disk unit. Times are measured for moves of one cylinder, two cylinders, and so on. A typical plot of data so collected might look like Fig. 11.6. If an exact analysis is desired, this data can be tabulated and used for estimating *ts* in each cell access as necessary. A more practical approach would be to use curve-fitting techniques to put the *tap* in mathematically tractable form. For example, the curve of Fig. 11.6 can be approximated by the following:

$$tap = 0.99047*(N - 1)^{10.64125} + 7 \qquad \text{for } 0 < N < 176$$
$$tap = 0.06936*(N - 175) + 33.7 \qquad \text{for } 175 < N = < 411$$

where *tap* is given in milliseconds, and N = number of cylinders moved.

Using the equations above, and given that the maximum arm movement is limited to Nz, as would be the case if the disk space were partitioned into zones and a zone size were Nz, the following equation would yield the average *tap:*

$$tap(\text{av}) = \sum_{N=1}^{Nz-1} tap(N)*2*(Nz - N)/Nz^2$$

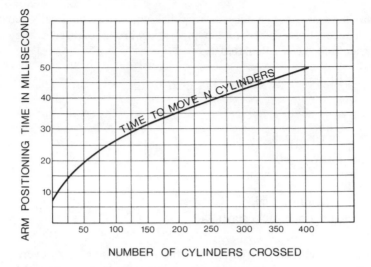

Fig. 11.6. An example of arm-positioning time as a function of number of cylinders crossed for a moving-head disk unit.

Having determined the *tap* and hence the *ts,* we can define disk loading, ρ_{disk}, as follows:

$$\rho_{\text{disk}} = ts * a_{\text{disk}}$$

where ts = service time as defined above, in seconds, and a_{disk} = disk accesses per second.

It is now possible to find the waiting time and queuing time for the disk service, using Eqs. 9.1.10 to 9.1.13. Note that this makes an implicit assumption that the disk unit may be modeled as a server to an M/M/1 queue.

Batched Accesses   When the FIFO discipline is used, the response times get increasingly longer as the disk loading attains values up to 0.7 and beyond. If the accesses are truly random, there is little choice but to partition the data into physically disjoint disk units and thus reduce the number of accesses to each unit. It is possible in some applications, however, to use locality of disk accesses to improve the average response times.

Consider a message switching application in which incoming messages are broken down into segments of equal size. The size of a segment is the same as that of a single cell on the disk unit. The incoming messages are stored exclusively on a single-disk unit. As the message processing progresses, a message is being frequently accessed, but when the processing of a message is finished, the message remains on the disk largely untouched. It is also assumed that the disk cells for a new message are allocated sequentially. Thus, during message processing, the number of cylinders being accessed is small, even if there is a large number of cells being accessed. This means that there are several accesses to each cylinder. If several access requests are collected in a batch, are recorded by cylinders, and accesses are then performed, a considerable amount of arm-positioning time could be saved.

The batching technique usually goes beyond just the saving of arm-positioning time. Once several accesses to a single cylinder are collected, an additional saving in service time can be achieved by reordering requests in a certain fashion. Consider a particular cylinder for which a batch has been collected. This cylinder has N_t tracks, and each track has N_s sectors. This cylinder can conceptually be unfolded to yield a matrix of tracks and sectors (Fig. 11.7). Because the disk unit has a single data channel, only one cell can be read at a time. This implies that cells X and Y in Fig. 11.7 must be read in different rotation. If X and Y were the only two requests in the batch, the total time to finish the batch would be

> *tap* to initially position at the cylinder
> + *tl* latency to get to X
> + *tdt* time to perform data transfer at X
> + *tr* time to go another rotation and perform data access at Y

Consider, however, the cells X and Z in Fig. 11.7. Provided there are no unforeseen delays in some other part of the system, the disk unit could perform

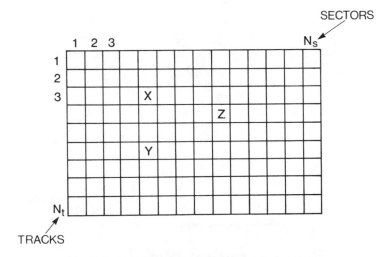

Fig. 11.7. An "unfolded" cylinder for batched accesses.

these accesses in a single rotation. If the batch were to consist of X and Z only, the time to finish the batch would be

> *tap* to initially position at the cylinder
> $+$ *tl* latency to get to X
> $+$ *tdt* time to perform data transfer at X
> $+$ *tf* time to get to Z and perform data access at Z

Note that *tf* is a fraction of time required to access Y in the other example. Thus, if there are many accesses to a cylinder distributed over the columns of the unfolded cylinder, many accesses could be performed in a single rotation. The batching on a cylinder saves not only in the arm-positioning time, but also in the latency.

The batching is implemented in simple terms as follows. When service, i.e., disk accesses, for one batch is initiated, all new incoming requests for disk access are collected in a new batch. The service for the second batch can be initiated only after the first batch has finished. Before initiating the second batch, however, the requests in the second batch are reordered, so that as many requested cells as possible are accessed in the first rotation. Then, among the remaining requests, as many as possible are accessed in the second rotation, and so on. The algorithm for such ordering can be a simple one and need not be described here. This reordering does minimize the total number of rotations required to finish the batch. Because the next batch is collected while one is being serviced, over a long period, a steady state will be reached (Fig. 11.8), where time spent in collecting a batch will be the same as time required to service it. Under these conditions, a request may be serviced in a very short

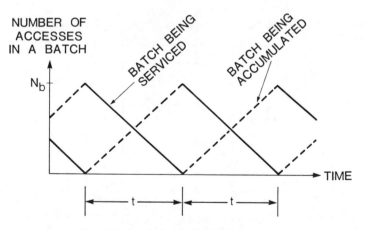

Fig. 11.8. Steady state in batched accesses.

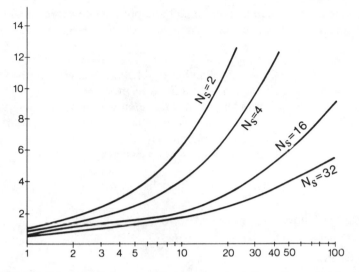

Fig. 11.9. Batched disk accesses: An example of number of rotations, R, required to service a batch of size N_b (N_t = 19, N_s = 2, 4, 16, 32).

time (if it was the last to enter the batch but the first to be serviced) or a time equal to $2*t$, if it entered the batch first and was serviced last, where t is the batch time (Fig. 11.8). The average service time, ts, is therefore $(2*t)/2$, that is t.

An exact analysis of calculating the batch service time given the batch size is lengthy and can be found in Ref. 45. Figure 11.9 is representative of its results; it shows the number of rotations required to service a batch as a function of the batch size for given numbers of N_s and N_t. The number of rotations multiplied by tr gives the batch service time t. For a certain disk request rate, R, the batch service time can be calculated by the following simple algorithm:

1. Assume an initial batch service time, t.
2. Find N_b ($= R*t$), the batch size.
3. From Fig. 11.9, find the batch service time, t_s, for N_b.
4. If $|t - t_s| < E$, where E is some small error margin, then go to step 6.
5. Set $t = t_s$. Repeat by going to step 2.
6. The solution is found. N_b is the steady-state batch size, and t is the batch service time.

This algorithm is rather limited, for step 3 requires reading a graph, which is normally done by humans. The speed with which the algorithm will converge to a solution will depend upon the choice of initial t. Given N_s and N_t, polynomial curve-fitting can be used to find an approximate expression for the service time, t_s. This will enable convergence to a solution by computational means.

Secondary Storage Capacity Another problem associated with the secondary storage is its capacity. Often encountered in message switching systems is a requirement that specifies long-term data retention on the secondary storage. It usually specifies that all messages must be stored on a secondary storage device for at least d days. This merely requires an estimate of the maximum traffic on a peak day. If this traffic is Mx messages,

$$\text{retention capacity (in cells)} = d * Mx * n_s$$

where n_s = number of segments per message.

11.3.3 Primary Storage

Primary storage in network switching nodes comes in the form of core or semiconductor memories. The primary memory is used for all processing. Its speed is a significant factor in the speed of a processing unit. The basic memory can be characterized in terms of access time (t_a), rewrite time (t_w), and cycle time (t_c). Figure 11.10 shows that the cycle time, t_c, is the sum of the access time and the rewrite time. Although the interaction with the originator of the memory access finishes at the end of t_a, the memory unit goes through an additional t_w, during which the memory unit is unavailable to the external requests. A memory unit thus spends a total time of t_c for each access. The set of data access lines coming out of memory is called a *port*. A memory unit may have one or more ports. The width of a port, i.e., the number of data lines, is usually the same as the size of a memory word. If W is the width of the port, then memory bandwidth MB of a single-ported memory is given by

$$MB = W/t_c$$

This MB is in bits per seconds. Sometimes W may be specified in bytes to yield MB in bytes per second.

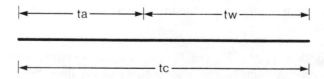

Fig. 11.10. Memory access, rewrite, and cycle times.

A closer inspection of the memory units reveals that a memory unit consists of several memory modules of equal sizes. Consequently, if there are *mm* memory modules, a memory unit could be processing *mm* requests simultaneously. This fact is used to gain higher memory bandwidths in pipelined processing units or in multiprocessor systems. An example will appear in the discussions to follow.

11.3.4 Processing Unit

In its simplest form, a processing unit is a single uniprocessor that executes its machine instructions in a sequential order. This is generally known as a *central processing unit* (CPU). A typical sequence of actions in the processing of an instruction is:

Fetch instruction from primary memory.

Decode instruction.

Fetch data (if necessary).

Execute instruction.

Write data (if necessary).

The performance of a CPU is characterized by the time it takes to complete an instruction. There are many instructions, however, and each takes a different amount of time. An average instruction time may be found by first estimating the instruction time for each type of instruction and by taking an average. Such an average is misleading because it assumes that all instructions are used equally in a sequence of instructions, and that is seldom the case. A popular method proceeds as follows. A survey is conducted over a large set of programs for the same application. The result of this survey is a frequency distribution over all instructions indicating how often each instruction is used. This frequency distribution and previously compiled instruction times are used to find the weighted average instruction time. The loading on the CPU in executing a program from that application is then found by

$$\rho_{cpu} = N * ni * ait$$

where

ρ_{cpu} = CPU loading
N = number of times the program is executed in unit time
ni = number of instructions in the program
ait = average instruction time

It must be noted here that the average instruction time, *ait,* has been estimated for a particular type of application program. It is not a characteristic parameter of the CPU alone. The *ait* can and often will change from application to application.

In some CPU designs, the approach given above is not valid. The inaccuracy arises from the fact that the instruction times of two consecutive instructions are not independent in these CPU designs. There are too many variations to describe them fully here. Figure 11.11 illustrates how fetching two instructions can take a different amount of time in two cases. In one case, both instructions are in the same memory module, and the fetches have to be performed one after the other. In the second case, the two instructions are different memory

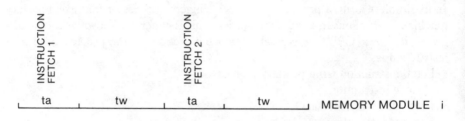

(a) TWO INSTRUCTION FETCHES TO THE SAME MEMORY MODULE

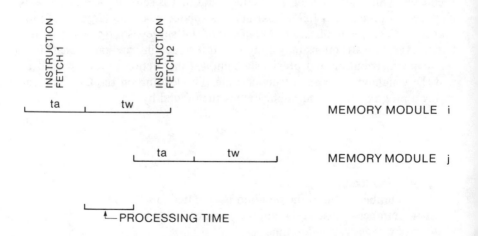

(b) TWO INSTRUCTION FETCHES TO DIFFERENT MEMORY MODULES

Fig. 11.11. Overlapping of memory accesses.

modules, thus allowing overlapping of memory accesses. This issue will be revisited in the next section.

11.4 HIGHER-LEVEL ANALYSES

11.4.1. Levels of Node Analysis

The analyses in 11.3 are necessary to understand the behavior of the basic resources, but they fall short of complete node analysis. To answer questions as to message throughput or call connect delay, higher level models are needed. In the discussion to follow, a variety of problems are presented with suggested approaches to solve them. In most of these problems, an absolute solution does not exist; that is, the method of solution itself depends upon the structure of the node and the functional requirements. The following, therefore, is not a panacea, but a sample of problems and approaches to their solutions.

11.4.2 Direct Memory Access

In Fig. 11.2, a simple computer was depicted. The figure shows a secondary storage unit or external I/O controllers connected to the processing unit, CPU. The implication is that when transferring some data in a cell in the primary storage (memory) to a sector in a disk unit, for example, the CPU reads a word at a time from the memory and transfers it to the disk unit to be written. Such operations may consume a good deal of CPU time to perform input and output.

A technique now being commonly used is called *direct memory access* (DMA). Fundamental to DMA is a direct path between I/O controllers and primary storage. To continue the example mentioned above, a direct path is provided between the disk unit controller and the primary memory (Fig. 11.12). When a piece of data is to be transferred from the memory to the disk unit, the CPU sends a message to the disk unit controller. The message includes the cell address, number of words in the data, and the disk unit track and sector addresses. The disk unit controller takes over the I/O operation, transferring the data word-by-word to the disk unit. At the same time, the CPU continues processing. Usually, the process requesting the data transfer is suspended; another process begins execution on the CPU. When the I/O data transfer is complete, the disk unit controller sends an "interrupt" signal to the CPU. At this time, the CPU interrupts the process it is executing, and invokes a special program called an *interrupt handler,* which notifies the suspended process that its request is finished. The operating system then takes control and schedules the next process to be executed, which may be the interrupted process, the process requesting the I/O data transfer, or some other process altogether.

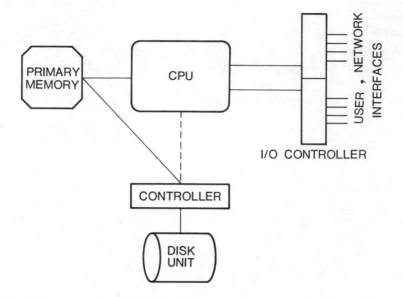

Fig. 11.12. Communication path between primary and secondary storages to facilitate direct memory access.

An alternative to a separate path between I/O controllers and the primary memory has been used in numerous structures. It is known as a *bus.* Figure 11.13 shows a representative structure, including a CPU, a primary memory, and a disk unit. Each of these "devices," and any other devices there may be, is given a unique number known as the *device address.* The device address is used to identify the device to which the data is destined. The number of data lines in the bus, known as the *bus width,* is usually the same as the memory word size. When a device wants to perform a data transfer, it first issues a request for the bus. In case of conflict among the device requests, the device with the highest priority, a preassigned number, is granted the use of the bus. Other devices must wait till the device granted the bus releases it.

Bus structures generally operate at rates faster than primary memories. The speed of the primary memory is therefore the limiting factor, and the bus loading is not excessive. Nevertheless, recalling from 11.3.3 that the effective memory bandwidth may be increased by using the possible overlap between requests to different memory modules, it is possible that the bus loading may become significant. Bus loading due to a single device is estimated to be

$$\rho_{bus} = dtr * bh$$

where

ρ_{bus} = bus loading
dtr = device transfer rate in number of words per unit time
bh = bus holding time

The last of these, the bus holding time, *bh,* will be approximately the same as *ta,* the memory access time.

11.4.3 Buffer Management

During the processing in a network switching node, information may be stored in temporary memory till that processing is finished. The temporary memory can then be used by any other process. For efficient and convenient management of memory, a portion of primary memory is partitioned off as the temporary memory. This temporary memory is further divided into smaller pieces called *buffers.* Some systems find it convenient to define all buffers to be of the same size, but others prefer to define a few standard sizes, with a buffer pool of each size.

A special process called *buffer management,* also known as memory management, acts as a monitor to the buffer pools. A process needing a buffer sends a request to the buffer management process, which allocates an available buffer to the requesting process. When finished, the requesting process releases

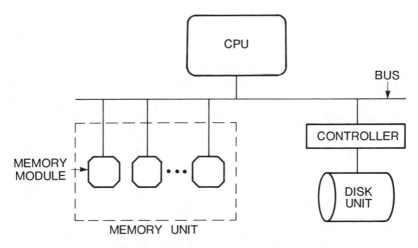

Fig. 11.13. An example of a bus structure.

the buffer so that the buffer management process can mark it available. The buffer management process is sometimes part of an operating system.

Once it is decided that the temporary memory is to be organized into fixed-size buffers, a question immediately arises. How many buffers should a system have? Clearly, the number of buffers should not be so large as to reduce the available primary memory to an insufficient size for other purposes. On the other hand, the number of buffers should be sufficiently large to ensure availability of buffers as needed. The following is an approach to answering this question.

A buffer pool may be approximately modeled as a collection of identical servers, the number of servers being infinite [48]. If the requests for buffers arrive with a Poisson distribution, with mean rate r requests per second, and if each buffer is held for an average of bh seconds, then:

$$P(k) = \text{probability that } k \text{ buffers are busy}$$
$$= \frac{(r*bh)^k}{k!} * e^{(-r*bh)}$$

The probability function for this model, Prob $(k <= N)$ for some N, is the same as the Erlang function. The value N is to be so chosen that the probability, Prob $(k <= N)$ is at least equal to some value, p. This desired value of N may be expressed as

$$N = r*bh + yp * \sqrt{r*bh}$$

where yp = a multiplier constant obtained from standard tables of Erlang function for probability p. For example, for $p = 0.99$, $yp = 2.4$, and for $p = 0.999$, $yp = 3.2$. with $yp = 3.2$, the value of N is such that the number of buffers being used is less than N 99.9 percent of the time. With the value p chosen to a desired degree of confidence, N gives the number of buffers needed.

Another problem associated with buffers is the optimum buffer size in message switching systems. Messages are of varying lengths, with an average size, M. A message is broken up into a number of segments, each of which is stored in a buffer of size, B. Each buffer also stores some linking information pointing to the next buffer of the message. If L is the size of the linking information, the optimal buffer size, B_{opt}, is given by

$$B_{opt} = L + \sqrt{2*M*L}$$

Additional discussion on this issue can be found in Ref. 51.

11.4.4 Effective Memory Performance

In 11.3.3, some basic performance issues for memory systems were discussed. It was mentioned that as a memory unit consists of a number of memory modules, a certain amount of parallelism is possible. A considerable amount of research has been directed toward analyzing the memory systems in various environments [Refs. 53 to 60]. Some of the results are presented here.

Figure 11.14 depicts the basic model. Devices $d1, d2, \ldots, dn$ make memory requests. All memory modules are assumed to be identical, and the model of a memory cycle is as before. An additional set of variables, tdi, is introduced; tdi is the time the device di spends between two of its requests to the memory unit. As expected, exact solutions in a general case are extremely difficult to achieve. Some of the solved special cases assume all devices, $d1, d2, \ldots, dn$ to be identical, or

$$td1 = td2 = \cdots = tdn = td$$

Even under this assumption, solutions are computationally complex. Some solutions, for a further restricted case, $td = tw$, are reported below.

Special Case, $td = tw$. In this case, the operations between memory and devices become synchronized. At the end of each memory cycle, each device is ready with a new request. Assuming uniform distribution of requests over the memory modules, Strecker [53] derived an approximate expression for the average number of busy memory modules, mmb, given below:

$$mmb = mm * (1 - (1 - 1/mm)^n)$$

where mm = number of memory modules and n = number of devices.

Bhandarkar [54] obtained a more exact solution by computational methods. Based on his exact solution, he proposed the following empirical approximation:

$$mmb = i * (1 - (1 - 1/i)^j)$$

where $i = \max(n,mm)$ and $j = \min(n,mm)$. Baskett and Smith [55] gave an asymptotic expression:

$$mmb = mm + n - \sqrt{(mm^2 + n^2)}$$

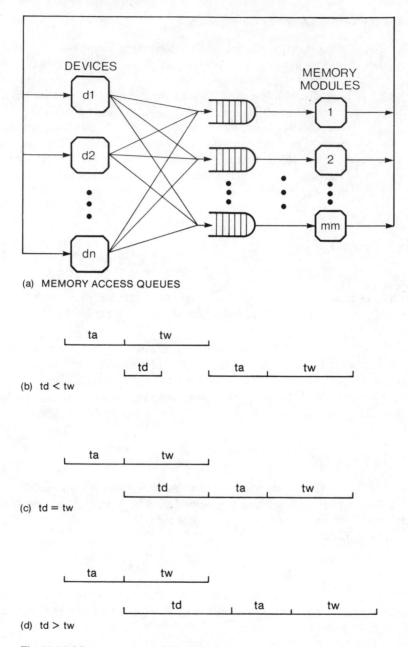

(a) MEMORY ACCESS QUEUES

(b) td < tw

(c) td = tw

(d) td > tw

Fig. 11.14. Memory access models with *n* devices accessing *mm* memory modules.

Sethi and Deo [56] developed exact expressions for a small number of devices, i.e., small n, and suggested a general approximation:

$$mmb = n - n*(n - 1)/(2*mm)$$

Noting the approximate symmetry in the numerical results, they proposed the further generalization:

$$mmb = j - j*(j - 1)/(2*i)$$

where $i = \max(n,mm)$ and $j = \min(n,mm)$.

When the assumption $td = tw$ is violated, the models become even more complicated. Often, approximate models are proposed and are substantiated by simulation results.

Note that the average number of busy memory modules, mmb, can be easily translated into the effective memory bandwidth, BW, using

$$BW = mmb/tc$$

11.4.5 Processing Time

Given such components of a switching node as a set of instructions, a program, or a software system, the processing time required to execute it is of some importance. Once the processing time is established for all components, it will then be possible to answer questions relating to the processing time for a set of components, and hence for the resultant function of the switching node, and to the loading on the processing units, and hence the throughput of the switching node.

In 11.3.4, a rudimentary approach to estimating the processing time was presented. The approach is indeed valid for a uniprocessor executing large sequential programs with few deviations, such as I/O interrupts.

A scheme to initiate DMA transfers was described in 11.4.2. At the end of a data transfer, an interrupt is posted to the CPU. This causes a process executing on the CPU to be interrupted. That the interrupted process may run correctly at a later time, some data representing the state of the process must be "remembered," i.e., saved in memory. The state is restored when the process is ready to run again. The time spent in saving and restoring the state of a process is called the *context switching time*. It represents an overhead, for it would not be necessary if the process had not been interrupted. The total overhead due to interrupts in processing of a program is a function of the number of interrupts that occur before the program finishes. In general, estimating the number of interrupts is a near impossible task, because the interrupts are caused by processes other than the one under consideration. The context switching time itself depends upon the program and its complexity, that is, it depends upon the size of data (state) that must be saved. Some processor structures use multiple sets of registers to reduce the amount of data that must be explicitly saved, thus reducing the context switching time.

In a switching node, a number of processes may share tables or data base or some data structure. To ensure data integrity, a process may "lock" a certain piece of data while it is being used. This delays any other process trying to use the same piece of data. Although the situation is similar to a multiserver queuing model, assumptions of uniform distribution over all "servers," or lockable pieces of data, may not be valid.

The structure of processing units also plays an important role. Special features employed to enhance processing speed, pipelined processing, or array processing for example, further complicate the analysis. Multiprocessing or multicomputer systems have also been used in switching nodes. The variety in systems renders it impossible to establish a common approach; each computer system structure may need a different approach.

As the systems (switching nodes) and their software become increasingly complex, analytical models are often unavailable. Approximate analytical models and simulation are the alternatives commonly employed in these cases.

11.4.6 Delays in a Switching Node

One of the questions posed in switching node performance analysis deals with delays in the system. Delay is the total time spent in performing a certain node function. When possible, a simple queuing model with a number of queues in series is used.

If a node function requires the execution of tasks $t1$, $t2$, ... , tn, in that order, a queuing model, shown in Fig. 11.15, is applicable. A first-level approximation is obtained by assuming the queues to be independent, $M/M/1$ queues. As it has been shown that the output of an $M/M/1$ queue obeys the Poisson distribution, the assumption of Poisson input at the next queue is valid. The total delay is the sum of delays in each queue. Analysis of such a queue is presented in Chapter 9.

Analysis becomes significantly more difficult if queues are not independent,

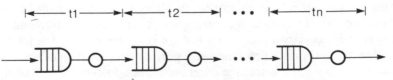

Fig. 11.15. A series queuing model for n tasks within a node.

if each queue is not $M/M/1$, or if the task cannot be identified as a simple series of actions. Markov chain models with computational solutions is a technique feasible in some cases. If interdependent tasks execute concurrently on a multitasking processor structure, perhaps the only recourse is to use statistical simulation.

11.4.7 Throughput

Throughput is the amount of work performed by a switching node in unit time. It may be expressed in calls processed per second, messages or packets received and delivered in an hour, number of data base functions performed per minute, and so on. This discussion uses the example of message switching and the number of messages processed per hour as a throughput metric, but the discussion is, in general terms, applicable to all forms of switching nodes. The throughput is assumed to mean the maximum possible throughput, thus providing a measure of node capacity.

The first step toward determining throughput is to model the processing flow in the switching function involved. In message switching, for example, a message is received, stored, and decoded, resultant output messages and their destinations are determined, and the outgoing messages are delivered. The actions of such a message switching node are tabulated below:

Incoming message processing

INPUT (receive)	Outgoing message processing
EDIT (decode)	DEQUEUE (get from queue)
ROUTE (generate outgoing message)	OUTPUT (send to destination)
QUEUE (for output)	

The QUEUE function enters messages in a queue. The messages are retrieved using the DEQUEUE function and then are transmitted to the destination.

Having identified the basic functions, the next step is to determine the loading implied by the functions on various resources. In the example above, for each of the functions (INPUT, EDIT, etc.), the following must be determined:

external I/O interface loading

number of disk accesses

buffer requirements (how many, for how long)

processing time and CPU loading

If there are several types of messages, this procedure may have to be repeated many times. Moreover, not all messages may follow the same functions in the same order. A composite processing model must be established using the results of the exercise above and the distribution of messages over all the types. The latter should be a part of system (user) specifications.

A complete processing flow model enables the calculation of loading on the critical resources for each type of message. The resource loading for an "average message" can then be determined. The term *average message* is used to imply that the loading is a weighted average of loading calculated for each type of message.

The final step is the identification of the limiting resource, the resource that supports the minimum throughput. Any one of the critical resources may be the limiting resource. In the message switching example, processing time (or CPU loading), disk unit loading, buffer usage, and external I/O interface are all candidates for the limiting factor. Once the limiting resource is identified, its limit on throughput is the maximum throughput of the switching node.

It is not unusual, while identifying the limiting resource, to discover certain bottlenecks causing the resource to be inefficient. When possible, corrective action is taken, and the performance analysis process begins again.

REFERENCES

1. Saaty, T. L. (1961) *Elements of Queuing Theory.* New York: McGraw-Hill Book Co.
2. Syski, R. (1960) *Introduction to Congestion Theory in Telephone Systems.* Edinburgh and London: Oliver and Boyd.
3. Hillier, E. S. and G. J. Lieberman. (1967) *Introduction to Operations Research.* San Francisco: Holden-Day, Inc.
4. Collins, A. A. and R. D. Pederson. (1973) *Telecommunications: A Time for Innovation. Dallas: Merle Collins Foundation.*
5. Martin, J. (1972) *Systems Analysis for Data Transmission.* Englewood Cliffs, N.J.: Prentice-Hall, Inc.
6. Peck, L. G. and R. N. Hazelwood. (1958) *Finite Queuing Tables.* New York: John Wiley and Sons.
7. Seshu, S. and M. B. Reed. (1961) *Linear Graphs and Electrical Networks.* Reading, Mass.: Addison-Wesley Publishing Co.
8. Dantzig, G. B. (1963) *Linear Programming and Extensions.* Princeton: Princeton University Press.
9. Ford, L. R. and D. R. Fulkerson (1962) *Flows in Networks.* Princeton: Princeton University Press.
10. Hadley, G. (1962) *Linear Programming.* Reading, Mass.: Addison-Wesley.
11. Anthony, A. L. and H. K. Watson. Techniques for developing analytical models. *IBM Syst. J.* Vol. 11, No. 4, 1972.
12. Jackson, J. R. Networks of waiting lines. Oper. Res. Vol. 5, 1957.
13. Kleinrock, L. On communications and networks. *IEEE Trans. Computers* Vol. C.25, No. 12, 1976. Also, Analytical and simulation methods in computer network design. *Proc. SJCC,* 1970.
14. Minoli, D. Optimal packet length for packet voice communication. *IEEE Trans. Commun.* Vol. Com 27, 1979.
15. Kleinrock, L. Principles and lessons learnt in packet communications. *Proc. IEEE* Vol. 66, No. 11, 1978.
16. Lam, S. L. Satellite packet communication-multiple access protocols and performance. *IEEE Trans. Commun.* Vol. Com. 27, 1979.

17. Kummerle, K., and H. Rudin. Packet and circuit switching: cost/performance boundaries. *Comput. Netw.* Vol. 2, 1978.
18. Kaul, A. K. Performance of high-level data link control in satellite communications. *COMSAT Tech. Rev.* Vol. 8, No. 1, Spring 1978.
19. Roberts, L. Dynamic allocation of satellite capacity. *Proc. NCC,* 1973.
20. Ng, S. F. and J. W. Mark. Multi access model for packet switching with a satellite having processing power. *IEEE Trans. Commun.* Vol. Com 26, No. 2, 1978.
21. Lientz, B. P. Trade-offs of secure processing in centralized versus distributed networks. *Comput. Netw.* Vol. 2, 1978.
22. Kleinrock, L., and F. Kamoun. Hierarchical routing for large networks. *Comput. Netw.* Vol. 1, 1977.
23. Mihayara, H. et al. Delay and throughput evaluation of switching methods in computer communication networks. *IEEE Trans. Commun.* Vol. Com 26, No. 3, 1978.
24. Gitman, I., and H. Frank. *Economic Analysis of Integrated DOD Voice and Data Networks.* Final Report, ARPA Contract: DAHC-15-73-CO135.
25. Pickholtz, R. L. and C. L. McCoy. Effects of priority discipline in routing for packet switching networks. *IEEE Trans. Commun.* Vol. Com 14, No. 5, 1976.
26. Loomis, M. S., and G. J. Popek. A model for data base distribution. IEEE tutorial: *Distributed Processing,* 1977.
27. Chu, W. W. Performance of file directory systems for data bases in star and distributed networks. AFIPS Conf. Proc., 1976.
28. Chu, W. W. Avoiding deadlocks in distributed data bases. Proc. ACM National Symposium, 1974.
29. Casey, R. G. Allocation of copies of a file in an information network. *SJCC 1972* Vol. 40, 1972.
30. Davies, D. W. and D. L. A. Barber. (1973) *Communication Networks for Computers.* New York: John Wiley and Sons.
31. Ferrari, D. (1978) *Computer Systems Performance Evaluation.* Englewood Cliffs, N.J.: Prentice-Hall.
32. Denning, P. J. and J. P. Buzen. The operational analysis of queueing network models. *ACM Computing Surveys* Vol. 10, No. 3, September 1978.
33. Wong, J. W. Queueing network modeling of computer communication networks. *ACM Computing Surveys* Vol. 10, No. 3, September 1978, 343–351.
34. Stone, H. S. (1972) *Introduction to Computer Organization and Data Structures.* New York: McGraw-Hill.
35. Fishman, G. S. (1978) *Principles of Discrete Event Simulation.* New York: John Wiley.
36. Gordon, G. (1969) *System Simulation.* Englewood Cliffs, N.J.: Prentice-Hall.
37. Knuth, D. E. (1968) *The Art of Computer Programming,* Vol. 1: *Fundamental Algorithms.* Reading, Mass.: Addison-Wesley.
38. Kobayashi, H. (1978) *Modeling and Analysis: An Introduction to System Performance Evaluation Methodology.* Reading, Mass.: Addison-Wesley.
39. Svobodova, L. (1976) *Computer Performance Measurement and Evaluation Methods: Analysis and Applications.* New York: Elsevier North-Holland.

40. Wagner, H. M. (1969) *Principles of Operations Research*. Englewood Cliffs, N.J.: Prentice-Hall.
41. Hays, W. L. and R. L. Winkler. (1971) *Statistics: Probability, Inference, and Decision*. New York: Holt, Rinehart, and Winston.
42. Anderson, R. R., G. J. Foschini, and B. Gopinath. A queuing model for a hybrid data multiplexer. *Bell Syst. Tech. J.* Vol. 58, No. 2, February 1979, 279–300.
43. Fuller, S. H. and F. Baskett. An analysis of drum storage units. *J. ACM* Vol. 22, No. 1, January, 1975, 83–105.
44. Bhandarkar, D. P. and J. E. Juliussen, Computer system advantages of magnetic bubble memories. *Computer* Vol. 8, No. 11, November 1975, 35–40.
45. Sharma, R. L. (1969) Analysis of a scheme for information organization and retrieval from a disc file. *Information Processing 68*. Amsterdam: North-Holland Publishing.
46. Bell, C. G. and A. Newell (1971) *Computer Structures: Readings and Examples*. New York: McGraw-Hill.
47. Rege, S. L. Cost, performance, and size tradeoffs for different levels in a memory hierarchy. *Computer* Vol. 9, No. 4, April 1976., 43–51.
48. IBM (1971) *Analysis of Some Queueing Models in Real-Time Systems*. IBM Publication No. GF20-0007-1. White Plains, N.Y.: IBM.
49. Knuth, D. E. (1969) *The Art of Computer Programming*, Vol. 2 *Seminumerical Algorithms*. Reading, Mass.: Addison-Wesley.
50. Coffman, E. G., and P. J. Denning. (1973) *Operating Systems Theory*. Englewood Cliffs, N.J.: Prentice-Hall.
51. Gaver, D. P. and P. A. W. Lewis. Probability models for buffer storage allocation problems. J. ACM Vol. 18, No. 2, April 1971, 186–198.
52. Chow, W. M. and L. Woo. Buffer performance analysis of communication processor during slowdown of network control. IBM J. Res. Deve., May 1977, 264–272.
53. Strecker, W. D. Analysis of the instruction execution rate in certain computer structures. Ph.D. dissertation, Carnegie-Mellon University, Pittsburgh, Pa., 1970.
54. Bhandarkar, D. P. Analysis of memory interference in multiprocessors. *IEEE Trans. Computers* Vol. C24, September 1975, 897–908.
55. Baskett, F., and A. J. Smith. Interference in multiprocessor computer systems with interleaved memory. *Commun. ACM* Vol. 19, No. 6, June 1976, 327–334.
56. Sethi, A. S. and N. Deo. Interference in multiprocessor systems with varying memory access probabilities. *Computer Science Report*. Kanpur, India: I.I.T. 1977. (Also in IEEE Computer Repository, Report No. R77-220.)
57. Skinner, C. E. and J. R. Asher. Effects of storage contention of system performance. *IBM Syst. J.* Vol. 8, No. 4, 1969, 319–333.
58. Hoogendoorn, C. H. A general model for memory interference in multiprocessors. *IEEE Trans. Computers*, October 1977, 998–1005.
59. Wulf, W. A. and C. G. Bell. C.mmp: A multi-mini-processor. *Fall Joint Computer Conference*, 1972, 765–777.
60. Bell, J., D. Casasent, and C. G. Bell. An investigation of alternative cache organization. *IEEE Trans. Computers* Vol. C-23, March 1974, 346.

Section III
Network System Design

Chapter 12
Introduction to Network Design

There are two distinct network system design tasks:

1. topological design
2. nodal design

The topological design process consists of defining the topology and geography of a network to satisfy a set of user requirements. Similarly, the nodal design process involves specifying the network nodes that can handle all the functions desired by the user.

Topological design is the subject of Section III; nodal design techniques are discussed throughout the book and in particular in Chapter 5. Both these tasks can be successfully completed only if meaningful input data is available. Furthermore, one needs to carefully control the presentation of output results. Without this control, one is apt to become flooded with useless data. The relationship among the input data, design control parameters, and output results is shown in Fig. 12.1.

12.1 INPUT DATA COLLECTION

Pertinent information on the following items is needed:

1. Network Elements—description of (a) end-of-service nodes (EOSNs), such as private branch exchanges, telephone terminals, data terminals, (b) network center nodes (switching machines or concentrators or processors), and (c) various link types that interconnect the nodes
2. Network Flows—definition of traffic flows between all end-of-service node pairs
3. Set of Requirements—specification of grade of service, quality of service, optimization criteria, and mix of tariffs to be considered.

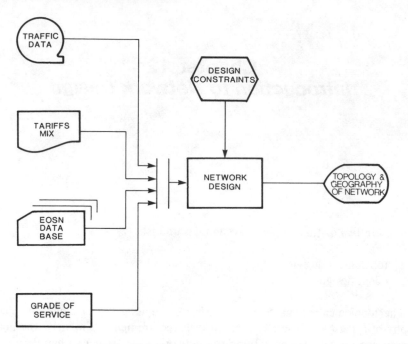

Fig. 12.1. The network planning process.

12.2 OUTPUT DATA PRESENTATION

The output at the end of the design process is described as follows:

1. Network Topology—the layout of links and network nodes best suited to meet the user's requirements
2. Network Routing—traffic flow routes or paths to be followed to meet the design goals
3. Network Geography—the dimensioning and pricing of the links and network nodes that satisfy the input data according to the chosen topology.

12.3 DESIGN METHOD

The design process has an active and a passive side.

The passive side relates to the background provided by experience and available technology. Such questions as "what types and combinations of input data are likely to be encountered?" and "what topologies and routing strategies are available and feasible?" are answered. This passive side is part of network system modeling, which was discussed in Section I.

The active side of configuration design will be divided into two subtasks:

1. transformation of input data into a form useful for the network system design (traffic data synthesis)
2. iterative processes that lead to an optimum network configuration (network synthesis)

Chapters 13 and 14 will employ and elaborate on the network system modeling methodology introduced in Section I. Whereas Chapter 13 will cover the input data (network elements, network flows, and requirements), Chapter 14 will cover the output control subjects (connectivity, functionality, traffic routing, and resource sharing). Chapter 15 will discuss some useful techniques for traffic data synthesis and network synthesis. Finally, Chapter 16 will introduce additional network planning considerations, such as cutover planning, testing, customer feedbacks into the design, and on-line network management and control.

All the tasks that will be elaborated in Chapters 13 through 16 deal with the so-called *network planning* process. The planning of even a simple network is a highly involved process. The reader should never get the idea that network planning is an automatic process requiring only a single run on a high-speed computer. Instead, the reader should consider this process as one involving an unpredictable sequence of computer runs, human observations, and judicious interpretations of the output results at every juncture of the effort.

Chapter 13
Network Components

Whereas network modeling is a top-down process, network synthesis is a bottom-up process. Synthesis usually involves multilevel network structures. At a low level, the end-of-service nodes are telephone stations or user terminals or data terminal equipment, and the network centers are private automatic branch exchanges (PABXs) or concentrators or multiplexers. Higher-level networks can then be synthesized with PABXs or concentrators as EOSNs, and tandem switching nodes as network centers. The process can go on until the multilevel network is fully synthesized. The design process for each two-level network is the same, however. This design methodology is generally employed to keep the already complicated design tools tractable.

13.1 NETWORK ELEMENTS

A generalized model of a two-level network to be designed is shown in Fig. 13.1. There are three types of network elements: (1) end-of-service nodes (EOSNs), (2) network centers (e.g., concentrators, tandem switches, processors, etc.), and (3) links (e.g., user links, lower or higher level trunks).

13.1.1 End-Of-Service Nodes (EOSNs)

EOSNs are the end devices or service vehicles where the traffic originates or terminates for the two-level network as shown in Fig. 13.1. There may be two types of EOSNs: (1) private EOSNs belonging to the customer only, and (2) public EOSNs that belong to a public network.

Customer service vehicles (CSVs) are privately owned end-of-service nodes. A CSV may be a telephone instrument, a data terminal (DTE), a private automatic branch exchange (PABX), a Centrex station, an automatic call distributor (ACD), a data concentrator, or a data multiplexer.

Public service vehicles (PSVs) are nodes of a public or foreign network. A PSV is equivalent to a gateway switch of a public network. In the United States, a central office (CO) is an example of a PSV. In the case of a private or dedicated network (e.g., Bell's CCSA voice network for a private corporation), a PSV may or may not exist. If it does exist, it is mainly used to provide access to off-net locations to the private users of the network.

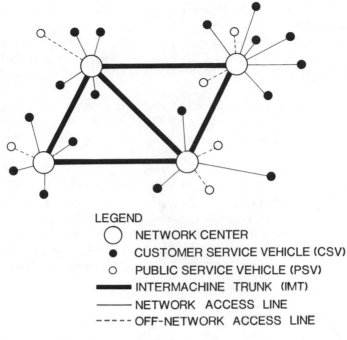

LEGEND
◯   NETWORK CENTER
●   CUSTOMER SERVICE VEHICLE (CSV)
○   PUBLIC SERVICE VEHICLE (PSV)
▬▬▬ INTERMACHINE TRUNK (IMT)
───── NETWORK ACCESS LINE
----- OFF-NETWORK ACCESS LINE

Fig. 13.1. A generalized model of a two-level network.

The following EOSN data is required for network planning:

1. Location as specified by a coordinate system. In North America, the V and H coordinate system (Ref. 19) is usually employed. In other countries, the longitude-latitude system is employed (see 10.1).
2. Identification number, as defined by the access code in both the existing and the planned networks. Most users prefer to use the existing access codes in the new network, because it enables them to maintain the existing directories. The public telephone numbers are also necessary for all locations. This becomes especially important when some locations must be maintained as off-net nodes to minimize costs. See Section I for a description of the different types of identification numbers in the United States.
3. Type of service vehicle, as denoted by make/model, public or private, source or sink or both, voice or data, and capacity for subscriber and access lines.
4. Number of actual subscribers and access lines connected to the EOSN.
5. Service availability, as defined by the various common or specialized car-

riers that serve that location and the types of services available at the location.

6. Service classification, as denoted by the high- or low-density rate centers, international dial capabilities, international boundary points, dial pulse, or Touch-Tone facilities.

In practice, it may be very difficult, if not impossible, to obtain a complete and accurate list of characteristics for all EOSNs. Even the most experienced communication managers are surprised with the results when they try to get such data systematically.

If a network is already in operation, the task becomes easier through a detailed study of the traffic data. Each completed call leaves a good trace of the calling and the called parties. A comparison with the collected data results in many discrepancies that must be resolved.

When a large, nationwide corporation does not have an existing network and desires an optimum network, creation of an EOSN data base easily becomes the most time-consuming task of the entire network planning process.

13.1.2 Network Centers

Network centers provide the various capabilities required by the users. The functions of a network center may be concentration of traffic, multiplexing, switching, queuing of calls or messages or packets, routing of calls or messages or packets, and interfacing between different media or networks. Network centers are also called *network nodes* or *machines*.

Network centers invariably do not alter the total traffic load on the network. They simply direct and route the traffic. Most of the intelligent network centers provide functions that enable a more efficient use of links as a result of more traffic carried by network links.

The following data on network centers is necessary for network planning:

1. Primary functions and all the additional capabilities, such as PABX or tandem switching, alternate or dynamic routing, queuing, conferencing or multiaddressing, closed user groups, abbreviated dialing, hot line, and speech interpolation
2. Basic design features, such as fixed-wired or stored program control, analog or digital switching, attenuation through the switch, blocking or nonblocking switch, modularity, etc.
3. Cost data, as a function of number of terminations and life cycle (if applicable)
4. Gradings, in the form of allowable availabilities of each route

5. Nodal capacity, in terms of maximum number of access lines and trunks allowed by each machine

13.1.3 Links

The links provide connectivity among the nodes of the network system. The links that connect the EOSNs to network centers (or machines) are called *access lines*. In the limit, the access lines become subscriber lines. The links that connect the network centers among themselves are called the *intermachine trunks* (IMTs), or simply *trunks*.

A network system can be divided into: (1) a *backbone network* that consists of network centers and trunks, and (2) several *access subnetworks,* each consisting of a network center and all the access lines and EOSNs served by that network center. In a lower-level network system, each of the subnetworks will consist of a PABX-type node and all the subscriber lines/user terminals served by the PABX.

The network planning process will require the following data pertaining to links:

1. Modularity defined as a single channel, T_1 carrier, dedicated fiber-optic cable, etc.
2. Transmission properties, defined as two- or four-wire circuit, line attenuation, and line resistance
3. Resource sharing option, defined as independent channel, demand-assignment multiple access (DAMA), carrier-sense multiple access (CSMA), etc.
4. Applicable tariffs for the leased circuits from the various common or specialized carriers or construction costs for private links

13.2 NETWORK FLOWS

The network planning process requires meaningful data related to the nature of traffic, the traffic units employed for representing traffic flows, and the expected behavior of traffic in a network system.

13.2.1 Nature of Traffic

Although the basic network planning process is identical for all types of traffic, the choice of a particular switching technology will depend upon the nature of the traffic. Some types of traffic may demand circuit switching, some types of traffic may demand packet switching, and some types of requirements may demand message switching techniques.

When long holding times are involved with traffic, as is the case for voice or file transfer applications, the current technology favors circuit switching.

When the traffic is characterized by very short durations and demands fast response times in inquiry/response or interactive environments, packet switching is recommended.

When the application demands end-to-end assurance and a great deal of processing or future retrievals, message switching should be the answer.

In Chapter 7, many existing switching systems were modeled, and an application summary was stated for each model. One must be abreast of the technological changes, however, before choosing a switching technology best suited to handle a given type of traffic.

13.2.2 Units of Traffic Flows

The network flows are measured by a nondimensional quantity called *traffic intensity*. The basic unit of traffic intensity is the *erlang* (ERL), named after A. K. Erlang (1878 to 1929), the Danish scientist recognized as the father of teletraffic theory. The numerical value of the traffic intensity in erlangs gives the average number of transactions (calls, messages) simultaneously in progress, or the average number of busy circuits at a time. For a single circuit, the traffic intensity is equal to the utilization factor.

If A is the traffic intensity in erlangs, L is the call arrival rate (average number of call arrivals per unit of time), and H is the average call holding time (average duration of a call), then

$$A = L * H$$

A is thus the average number of calls arriving during the average holding time.

There are three traffic quantities of interest in the design of a network system:

1. demand traffic
2. offered traffic
3. carried traffic

Each one of the above quantities is expressed in erlangs.

Demand traffic is the traffic load as seen by an ideal network system with no obstruction in the path.

Offered traffic is the sum of both successful and unsuccessful attempts.

Carried traffic is the actual traffic handled by the network system. Traffic carried may or may not result in conversation.

Another traffic unit used in the United States is the CCS (cent call seconds), or hundred call seconds per hour. Then, 36 CCS is equivalent to 1 call hour per hour, or:

$$1 \text{ erlang} = 36 \text{ CCS}$$

13.2.3 Traffic Flow Behavior

The traffic varies in step with the activities in a community. Many criteria of traffic variations may be employed:

1. Variations during the day—In general, the traffic may peak two or three times during a normal business day (Fig. 13.2). Because traffic is usually lower on Saturdays, Sundays, and public holidays, these days are generally ignored in the analysis. The maximum traffic demand generally does not occur at the same time every day.

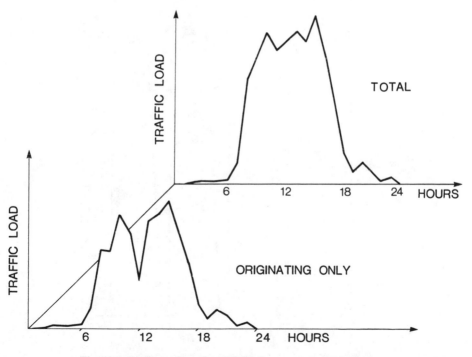

Fig. 13.2. Traffic profiles of an EOSN for an average business day.

2. Variations during the week—Certain business days may have systematically higher traffic loads than other business days in the week. Figure 13.3 depicts a typical variation of traffic through the month of September.
3. Variations during the year—Traffic loads follow seasonal variations and increase during certain periods, especially just before certain holidays, such as Christmas.
4. Unpredictable peaks—Extremely high traffic loads may be experienced during periods of calamities, such as an earthquake.
5. Growth trends—The traffic may show a consistent trend to increase. Sometimes, the traffic shows a close relationship with the economic state of the country or the corporation.

Traffic variations within a shorter interval, such as an hour, follow no regular patterns. These variations can therefore be considered purely random.

Traffic behavior examples are shown in Figs. 13.2 to 13.4. Figure 13.2 shows the originating and total traffic quantities for a customer service vehicle (CSV)

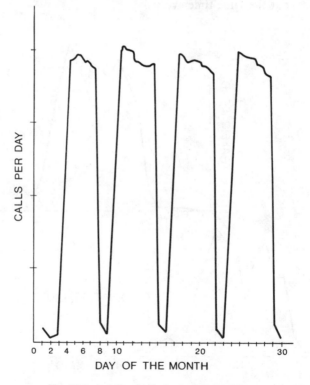

Fig. 13.3. A daily profile for a given month.

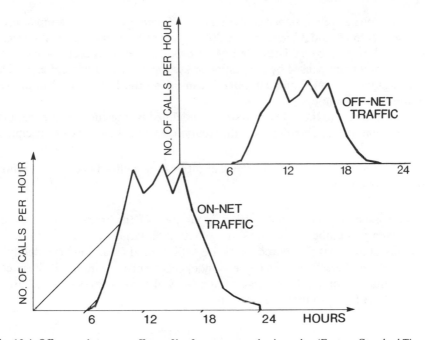

Fig. 13.4. Off-net and on-net traffic profiles for an average business day (Eastern Standard Time as Zulu Time).

for all hours in an average business day. Figure 13.4 illustrates the on-net and off-net traffic quantities in a network system for all hours for an average business day. Note that the traffic flows in Fig. 13.4 were normalized according to Eastern Standard Time used as Zulu Time. Although the above figures apply to voice networks, similar plots can be derived for other networks.

Traffic theory is generally based on the conditions observed during the busy hour. The *busy hour* is the 60-minute period during the day when the traffic is the highest in the long run (time-consistent busy hour). CCITT recommends measuring the 30 highest busy hours during the year and using the average for a busy hour model.

It should be apparent that the busy and the busiest hour may not coincide.

It should be instructive to study the behavior of the sources that generate traffic.

Assume subscriber *A* wants to talk to subscriber *B* in a voice-switched network. *A* may be successful in establishing a call at the first attempt. If unsuccessful, due to either (1) incorrect dialing, (2) congestion or technical faults in the network, (3) *B* is busy, or (4) *B* does not answer before *A* hangs up, *A* may retry the call or simply decide to either forget it all after a certain number of retries or delay another retry.

In a typical, well-designed system, about 70 percent of call attempts result in conversations, and 30 percent of call attempts result in no conversation (Ref. 6). The latter category is divided as follows: 5 percent caused by incorrect dialing, 5 percent caused by congestion or system faults, 10 percent caused by the engagement of *B*, and 10 percent caused by the failure of *B* to answer before *A* has hung up.

Traffic inputs to the network system are defined by the customer arrival rate distribution, the call holding time distribution, and the blocked calls discipline.

Arrival Rate Distribution.   The arrival rate can be defined according to three main distributions:

1. Poisson (random) input—This input models the traffic offered by an infinite number of sources (in practice, a large number of sources), assuming that the sources originate calls at random and independently of one another. The arrival rate is independent of the number of busy circuits (servers). The number of arrivals will form a Poisson distribution, whose first two moments are equal:

$$\text{mean } m = \text{variance } v$$

2. Bernoulli (smooth) input—This input models the traffic offered by a finite number of sources, assuming the calls originated at random and independently. The arrival rate decreases when the number of busy circuits increases, leading to a "smooth" distribution of call arrivals, where

$$\text{mean } m > \text{variance } v$$

3. Negative binomial (peaked) input—This input models overflow traffic. The arrival rate increases with the number of busy circuits, leading to a "peaked" distribution of call arrivals, where:

$$\text{mean } m < \text{variance } v$$

Holding Time (Service Time) Distribution.   The call holding time distribution is generally one of two: (1) the *negative exponential* type (e.g., in voice communication systems), and (2) the *constant* type, frequently encountered in data networks. See Ref. 1 for a detailed treatment of these and other distributions. The type of holding time distribution to be used has little influence on blocking probabilities, but it is crucial for delay probabilities.

Blocked Calls Discipline. The blocked customers' behavior, i.e., the behavior of customers who fail to find an idle server immediately, is generally modeled by one of three assumptions:

1. Blocked calls cleared (BCC)—An arriving customer (call) who finds all servers (circuits) busy disappears immediately and does not reappear as a subsequent attempt. This is the case of a pure loss system.
2. Blocked calls held (BCH)—Every arriving customer remains in the system for an exponentially distributed time, regardless of whether or when he receives service.
3. Blocked calls delayed (BCD)—Blocked customers are willing to wait indefinitely for an idle server.

Figure 13.5 indicates the traffic formulas to be used for several combinations of blocked call disciplines and arrival rate distributions, with the service times distributed exponentially. Figure 13.6 compares blocking probabilities for the three blocked calls assumptions, with random input and exponential holding times assumptions.

In all cases, a condition of statistical equilibrium, or stationarity, is assumed. According to this assumption, the traffic is neither rising nor falling, and the traffic process has been going on for so long that the initial condition is of no significance.

BLOCKED CALLS DISCIPLINE ⟶ ARRIVAL RATE ↓	BCC	BCH	BCD
SMOOTH	ENGSET	BERNOULLI	
RANDOM	ERLANG B	POISSON	ERLANG C
PEAKED	EQUIVALENT RANDOM THEORY		

Fig. 13.5. Traffic formulas or methods to be used for several input parameter combinations.

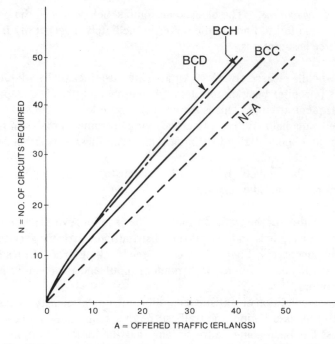

Fig. 13.6. Comparison of blocking formulas for a loss probability of 5 percent.

13.3 REQUIREMENTS

User requirements must be specified before they can be related to the design control parameters of the network system. The requirements are constraints to be met by the design results.

The user must supply the following data defining his requirements precisely. It is preferable to start with an extensive list. One can always decide to eliminate or relax a given requirement after discovering the price tag:

1. Cost constraints or other optimization criteria.
2. Traffic loads as derived from the user's perception of traffic demands in the existing and future environments. Depending upon the particular accounting procedures employed, most corporations choose either 7 or 10 years for the life cycle of the network system. Time-consistent busy hour traffic must be specified for the first year and all the subsequent years of the life cycle.
3. Throughput required during the average significant busy hours of every year. The units are calls per second, packets per second, or messages per second.

4. Quality of transmission in terms of voice noise levels or required bit error rate.
5. System reliability and availability required.
6. End-to-end blocking and distribution of connection times for CS systems and response time distribution for PS and MS systems.

It is not essential to know all the above requirements at every step of the network planning process.

The cost of the system is computed after the design is complete. The cost constraints are generally not known until all the competitive bids are compared by the customer. All the feedbacks from the customer are appraised, and only then can one make changes in the design to lower costs.

Quality of service, i.e., quality of voice, bit error rates, reliability, and availability, considerations are generally taken into account in the design of hardware and software modules that obey a given network architecture. A vendor with no consistent architecture should be prepared to spend a good deal of money on system integration and system tunings to achieve the quality of service requirements.

Most of the design processes begin with obtaining a topological organization, based on traffic loads and grade of service (GOS) requirements, while considering the following constraints:

1. tariff mixes
2. special nodal functions needed to be executed
3. constraints as to the location of network centers

Network systems are generally designed for each year of the life cycle. The transmission costs and the equipment costs are then derived for each month of the life cycle. Sometimes, the customer may demand the derivation of cost per transaction for each solution. Such data enables the customer to compare one solution, or vendor, with at least two other solutions.

Chapter 14
Topological Organization of the Network

Before beginning the actual network synthesis process, we must understand all the design parameters and alternatives that can affect the grade of service.

14.1 CONNECTIVITY

There are two aspects of connectivity that are considered for each synthesis job: (1) the manner in which EOSNs are connected to one or more network centers, and (2) the manner in which the network centers are connected to one another.

Assuming that the locations of all network nodes are known, an EOSN is generally connected to the closest network center. This approach generally tends to lower the cost of transmission to an acceptable level. A better solution will be to consider not only the distance, but also the traffic flow, to that network center in determining the connectivity. Another factor that can be considered, along with distance and traffic flow, is the transmission services available at the EOSN city.

In some highly survivable systems, an EOSN is connected to another network center or centers via a secondary access line group that is activated only when the primary network center or access line group fails.

Other networks use bypass access lines, one-way circuit groups from a network center to an EOSN, when the amount of traffic and the topology make them economically justifiable.

The manner in which the network centers are connected to one another is generally determined by such architectural considerations as nodal functions available and routing techniques employed.

14.2 NODAL FUNCTIONALITY

Hardware and software modules resident in each network node allow only a certain set of functions. Some of these functions deal with the nodal hierarchy and the signaling technique employed in the network system. Functions dealing with the manner in which grouping is achieved in the switch module and the manner in which the first available trunk is selected for the next path segment may influence the topological configuration.

14.2.1 Nodal Hierarchy

Some architectures allow one master node and all others as minor nodes. Such a design constraint permits only a star configuration, in which all minor nodes are connected to the master node directly. The architecture may apply to signaling only or to both transmission and signaling.

In the first case, each originating node passes the control information to the master node, which then determines the best route and directs the requesting node accordingly. Consequently, the network nodes may be connected to one another by two sets of trunks, one for handling signaling and another for handling traffic, according to a given routing philosophy. The backbone network for transmission may satisfy any topology, star or nonstar types.

In the second case, only a star configuration is permitted to handle both signaling and transmission. This topology is ideal where all users communicate with a central location (e.g., a headquarters). Such a topology is unsuitable for other traffic patterns.

When the number of nodes increases, as in a public network, one is forced to add levels to the backbone network hierarchy to achieve concentration and resource sharing. Each additional level is generally synthesized iteratively.

14.2.2 Functions of a Switch Module

Modern digital switch modules in CSSs are designed as nonblocking devices. Therefore, only the availability of access lines or trunks will determine the grade of service. Nonetheless, there are still many switch modules used in PABXs and network nodes that introduce a finite amount of congestion to incoming requests for service.

Depending upon the availability between inlets and outlets (see Fig. 7.5), a grouping arrangement can be specified as follows:

1. full availability group, in which every inlet has access to every outlet
2. grading, which allows an inlet to a limited number of outlets
3. link system, which defines the connection from the inlet to the outlet in the form of one or more link stages
4. graded link system, which is a combination of designs 2 and 3

See Refs. 2 and 3 for a detailed treatment of congestion in switching modules. Excessive blocking in network nodes will force a higher connectivity in the backbone network, thus permitting shorter paths between EOSNs.

14.2.3 Trunk Hunting Methods

There are two hunting methods commonly employed:

1. sequential method, where hunting for a free outlet always starts from the same position, and the first free outlet is seized
2. random method, where every outlet has the same probability of being seized

The method of hunting is practically of no significance for full availability groups. Because most engineers are used to seeing trunk usage reports that show ordered trunk utilizations, with the first trunk in the bundle depicting the highest use, some are bound to get confused. The blocking must be computed for a given hunting method used in a graded link system.

14.2.4 Handling of Unsuccessful Calls

When congestion is encountered, the network system may force the subscriber to make a new call attempt or may allow the subscriber to wait until served. The former situation results in a *loss* system and the latter in a *delay* system.

For a *loss* system, employed in a CS network node, one can assume: (1) no increase of call intensity from blocked calls, or (2) an increase of call intensity from call retrials.

For a *delay* system, one can assume the following: (1) unsuccessful calls wait until served, (2) waiting calls are abandoned by the subscriber with a given probability, or (3) waiting calls wait for a specified maximum time.

For each delay system, a queue discipline is defined for determining the order in which the waiting calls are served. Three disciplines are generally employed: (1) first-in-first-out (FIFO), (2) random service, and (3) priority service, in which each queued call carries a unique priority number.

If queuing is allowed at EOSNs only, there is no effect on the backbone network connectivity. When queuing is allowed in CS network nodes, the effect on the backbone network is difficult to analyze. Many other factors, such as off-hook or on-hook queuing, signaling technique, etc., must be taken into account.

14.3 ROUTING TECHNIQUES

The routing technique can influence the connectivity of the backbone network significantly.

The *deterministic* method allows a fixed primary route, and one or more alternate routes, between two network nodes. Wilkinson's approach (Refs. 4

and 5) is quite useful in designing economical CS networks with low blocking probabilities. The deterministic method is not commonly used in PS and MS networks.

Some of the new CS networks employ the *synoptic* method. The NMC node alters the deterministic routing tables when either a major node fails or a significant change in traffic pattern occurs. The NMC employs a superimposed network to receive diagnostic and traffic summary data.

Most of the new PS and MS networks employ the *adaptive* routing method. Despite the cost of additional trunks, this method allows orderly growth.

14.4 RESOURCE SHARING

Availabilities of satellite services and bandwidth sharing techniques can influence network connectivity and introduce savings.

Assuming network nodes to be ground stations and a pool of voice channels available from a satellite in the sky, all trunk bundles can be realized through a dynamic access method known as demand-assignment multiple access (DAMA). Such a pooling of resources results in significant savings.

In many cases, the EOSNs and network centers can be equipped with hardware modules to handle statistical concentration functions that yield substantial reductions in the number of circuits required. This approach is applicable for both voice and data networks. For voice, on the average $2*(n - 1)$ conversations can be concentrated into n circuits by filling the gaps in a ordinary conversation. Data communication has always used multiplexers/demultiplexers and statistical concentration for reducing costs of long-haul transmission. One caution is required when following this approach: the reduction in cost may be offset by the additional cost of concentration hardware and increased transmission costs resulting from the higher mileage rate applicable at a lower network mileage.

14.5 COMMON CHANNEL SIGNALING

Common channel signaling is sometimes preferred, for such facilities as network management, adaptive routing, conferencing, call-back queuing, etc., can be easily implemented. Common channel signaling requires a separate subnetwork used for signaling and network management. This technique is essential for a large public voice network. Its usefulness in a small corporate network is still debatable. Many future network services will tend to require common channel signaling. PS and MS networks do not employ this approach, for almost all network architectures employ in-band signaling.

Chapter 15
Design Methods

15.1. TRAFFIC DATA SYNTHESIS

Before the synthesis of a network is undertaken, the available traffic data has to be manipulated and transformed into useful input data for the synthesis process (Fig. 15.1).

Two types of traffic information may be available: single-hour traffic data and multihour traffic data.

15.1.1 Single-Hour Traffic Information

In the unlikely event that the peak hour coincides for all the end-of-service nodes, a single-hour traffic information would be appropriate, and then only if no measured types of services were to be considered.

Usually, single-hour data is used when better information is not available. An example is when the busy hour traffic is estimated on the basis of previous or related experience. Another example is when the call logs do not provide time-of-day information, and the busy hour traffic is given by an assumed percentage of the daily traffic. In this section, we will assume that the single-hour data does reflect an accurate busy hour traffic.

The busy hour is defined as an uninterrupted period of 60 minutes for which the traffic is at the maximum (Ref. 8).

The traffic recording machines will provide the carried traffic flow. The carried traffic is an acceptable approximation for the offered traffic, if the measured circuit group experiences a small congestion. As congestion increases, it becomes desirable to measure the number of call attempts, the duration of periods during which no circuits are available, and the number of call attempts experiencing congestion. The traffic offered is estimated by

$$A = \frac{C}{(1 - B)}$$

where C is the traffic carried, and B is the experienced loss factor. It should be noted, however, that it is very difficult to use anything but the carried traffic to dimension circuit groups.

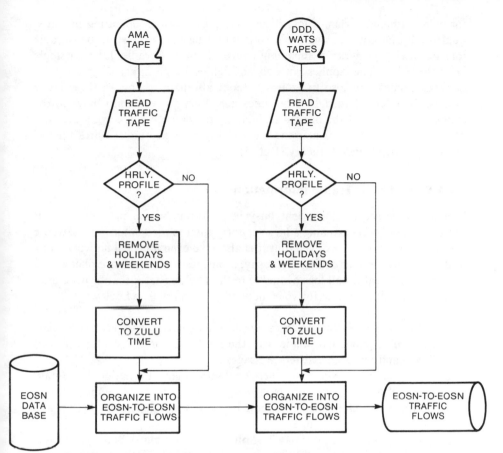

Fig. 15.1. Preparation of the traffic data for input to the network design.

Because the measuring period and the implementation date are always several months apart, a growth factor is usually introduced, requiring a traffic forecast. A forecast period is also necessary for planning the switching equipment, usually 5 to 10 years. Based on historical traffic data, curve-fitting for forecasting can be performed by using the least-squares method. A proper estimation requires a historical data period at least as long as the forecast period. Other factors enter in a forecast projection, such as tariff changes, stimulation factors associated with service improvement, discontinuities due to acquisitions and sales of subsidiaries, network structure changes, and other nondeterministic factors.

Once the appropriate traffic is estimated in a loss system, the number of circuits needed in a group will be determined based on the classical Erlang B formula. Although Erlang's loss theory assumes a system operating in statistical equilibrium over a long period of time, it has been shown to be suitable for engineering purposes in modeling conversation-type traffic during a single hour (Ref. 10). This applies not only to high-usage groups, i.e., groups with alternate routes, but also to groups without alternate routes. In these latter groups, the effect of retrials either does not affect or even contributes to the exponential nature of the offered traffic. As for the groups receiving overflow calls, the traffic offered is nonrandom, and their engineering requires the use of the equivalent random theory (Ref. 5).

15.1.2 Multihour Traffic Information

Usually, there are noncoincident busy hours throughout a network. This is obvious in a network spanning a large country such as the United States, where several time zones are involved, but it is also true even for local networks, due to different patterns of calling from, say, a business or a residence phone.

Some of the traffic call logs available in the United States that provide multihour traffic data suitable for voice network design are listed below:

1. Standard Bell System toll messages details—each record is a reproduced ticket of a phone call made over the DDD network. It contains direct-dialed and operator-assisted messages.
2. Other toll message details—these contain similar information to the standard Bell details, but appear in many different formats. Some are used by affiliated Bell Companies, some by GTE and independent Telcos, and some by Canadian companies.
3. WATS details—the format is similar to the standard Bell System format, but it shows WATS line numbers instead of DDD phone numbers.
4. 20 Percent AMA sampling—AMA (automatic message accounting) is a recording system that registers every fifth message appearing in a CCSA (common control switching arrangement) switching center. Each record in an AMA tape corresponds to a call originating in a customer vehicle of an existing CCSA network.
5. Tandem tie-trunk network recording—a recording system installed in a tandem PBX of a TTTN network that records messages flowing through and originating in the tandem PBX, but not the terminating messages. It does not distinguish between messages originating in different PBXs of the same tie-line group.
6. Station message detail recording—a recording system associated with the Western Electric dimension PABXs.
7. Rockwell-Collins digital tandem switch call logging—an example of a recording system for a private (noncommon-carrier-provided switching) network.

8. Enhanced private switching communication system—a recording system similar to the CCSA AMA sampling, but providing a 100 percent sample.

The format of some particular traffic data, usually supplied in the form of a magnetic tape, will be furnished by the telephone company providing that data.

15.1.3 Average-Hour Traffic

Traffic statistics for network planning should be collected, not only for all significant hours of each day, but also for a significant number of days in a year. CCITT recommends measuring carried traffic statistics for at least the 30 days (not necessarily consecutive) of the previous 12 months in which the mean busy hour traffic flow is the highest (Ref. 8). The recorded traffic flow statistics are then used to calculate the average traffic flow for the 30 and for the 5 busiest days during periods of one year.

A second-choice method recommended by CCITT when the first method is not possible, consists in a measuring period of 10 consecutive normal working days during the busiest season of the year.

In practice, statistics for a billing period are used. In North America, a billing period covers approximately one calendar month, and the busiest month of the year should be chosen. This traffic data is then processed through the following steps (Fig. 15.1):

1. Holidays and weekends are purged out of the data, as is any day with abnormally high or low traffic. This may include days immediately preceding or following holidays, vacation periods, election days. The data should thus be for a month with the least possible number of nonworking days.
2. Because traffic has a characteristic variation pattern during the week, the same number of days for each day of the week should be used if possible. In a move subject to controversy, the new Bell System planning tools discard Friday's data altogether (Ref. 7). Friday's traffic is usually the lightest in the work week.
3. If more than one time zone is involved, the connecting time information is all converted to a common reference time, the Zulu Time. Hours for daylight and nondaylight savings time are also converted.
4. Out of the remaining recording days, an average day is then constructed, where each significant hour is an average of the traffic registered in that hour for the recording period.
5. The traffic data is then associated with each end-of-service node where it originates and terminates, and a traffic flow file of EOSN-to-EOSN pairs records is constructed.

This averaging of traffic data introduces a new factor to be considered in the dimensioning of the circuit groups: the day-to-day traffic variation factor. This factor is caused by the mostly concave upward shape of the "loss factor versus offered traffic" curve (Fig. 15.2). The average loss over a period of time will exceed the loss estimated by using the average offered load (Fig. 15.2).

This effect is somehow compensated for by the fact that the measurement interval is finite (1 hour) and not infinite, as implicitly assumed in the Erlang theory (Ref. 11). The variance from the average-day load is made up of both the day-to-day load changes and the finite measurement interval bias. Tables and formulas are available with adjustment factors for the Erlang formula, that take these variations into account (Refs. 8 and 11). This adjustment process is, however, still an approximation and has recently been under attack (Ref. 12).

An easier way to get around this problem is to substitute the Molina traffic formula for the Erlang B formula whenever the offered traffic is averaged over a period of approximately 20 working days. It has been observed (Ref. 9) that for loss values from 0.005 to 0.03, the Molina formula gives a satisfactory estimate of the average loss using the average offered traffic to a full group. For engineering purposes, this conclusion can be extended to high-usage and final groups.

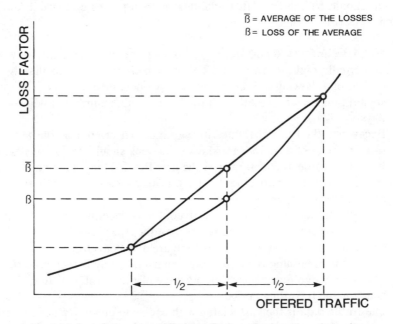

Fig. 15.2. Loss factor versus offered traffic for a fixed number of circuits.

If, however, only the five business days' traffic is used, the Erlang B formula should be adequate for circuit group dimensioning.

The design of data networks is based upon time delay constraints and not loss factors. Average utilizations during busy hours, computed using the above approach, yield average packet or message delays.

15.1.4 Shortcomings of Data Collection

The topological design of a network is an engineering, rather than a mathematical, process. Reasonable approximations that simplify the process are acceptable. The reason is that the traffic data upon which the process is based is never totally accurate. And it does not make sense to try to improve the network model accuracy by, say, 2 percent, if the traffic data used may be 10 percent off the real traffic upon implementation.

Several factors contribute to the difference between the predicted traffic and the actual traffic after cutover (Ref. 13):

1. Incompleteness of data collection—some recording equipment records only part of the calls, e.g., the AMA data for CCSA networks is a 20 percent sample. Recording equipment for billing purposes (AMA, SMDR, toll, and WATS tickets) records only the conversation time, not the call setup time. On the other hand, most of these systems register fractions of a minute as a whole minute.
2. Traffic carried versus traffic demand—only the carried traffic can be registered, the demand traffic can only be estimated. Most systems do not even record attempted but not completed calls. Abandoned and retrial calls are dependent on unpredictable human behavior. The difference between traffic carried and traffic offered is negligible for low-loss networks, but becomes significant with the deterioration of grade of service.
3. Recording errors—malfunction of the recording equipment and data handling errors are unavoidable. Experience with the AMA data for typical CCSA networks has shown that, on the average, 12 percent of the calls are incorrect. If the data is collected from several places, errors of this type are easily multiplied.
4. Corporate changes—changes of the population covered by the network will occur between the collection of data and the cutover period. In a public network, demographic shifts will be caused by migration patterns. In a corporate network, divisions may be acquired, others may be sold, new plants will open, some plants will be closed. The proportion of data versus voice traffic will increase. These changes are unpredictable, or at least their effect is unpredictable.
5. Stimulation factor—it has been observed that upon implementation of a

new network there is an upsurge of traffic. This is caused by the improved communications performance, availability of new applications, and psychological factors.

6. Controlling factor—if the old environment did not provide call detail control and the new network does, the abuse of calls will be discouraged, and the traffic will decrease.

The composite effect of all these factors is anybody's guess. It is not uncommon to see a difference of 20 percent between the predicted traffic and the actual traffic after implementation (Ref. 13). Stored-program-controlled switching has improved the collection of data dramatically, but, although the data has become more accurate and complete, some of the described factors will always be there, and the network planning process will remain a trade-off between desired accuracy and realistic assumptions.

15.1.5 Problems with Input Inventory

A little-publicized problem, but one that nevertheless causes big headaches, is the accuracy of the input inventory.

As a rule, more time is spent in building, correcting, and updating the end-of-service nodes data base than in the actual network synthesis process. This is due in part to the fact that the synthesis process is automated to a greater extent. But the main reason is the difficulty in obtaining an accurate image of the data base for the time period under study. Even if a data base has been compiled, e.g., a CCSA network is in operation, there will never be a perfect match between the data base and the traffic information. Weekly or daily changes occur, locations are always being added to or deleted from the network, and the interface with other networks (off-network traffic) has to be customized. If a data base does not exist, it has to be collected from several and diverse sources: different communication managers, different carriers, different operating companies. The process is very time consuming and of relative success.

15.2. NETWORK SYNTHESIS

15.2.1. Introduction

A network is made up of nodes and links. There are two levels of nodes: end-of-service nodes (EOSN), where calls originate and terminate; and network centers, which collect the calls from the EOSNs and send them to another network center or to the destination EOSN. The links among network centers are called *intermachine trunks* (IMT); the link between a network center and an EOSN is an *access line* (AL).

A general network model is a multilevel, hierarchical structure composed of subnetworks. The high level is an intercenter or junction subnetwork—the *backbone system*. The low level has several clusters of regional subnetworks, one for each network center—the *access system*.

In some networks there is no backbone system. In some networks the backbone system is itself composed of several levels. In still other networks, an EOSN may be in its own right a network center for a lower-level network. The structure described above is a general model, however, and any network design can be decomposed into designs of intermachine systems, access systems, or both.

The network cost C_N is the sum of several terms:

$$C_N = C_{AL} + C_{IMT} + C_{EOSN} + C_{NC} + C_O$$

where

$\quad C_{AL}$ = access lines cost

$\quad C_{IMT}$ = intermachine trunks cost

$\quad C_{EOSN}$ = costs associated with the end-of-service nodes. These costs are fixed and would be incurred even if the EOSN were not connected to the network, so they will not be considered in the network design

$\quad C_{NC}$ = cost of the network centers, including maintenance and support

$\quad C_O$ = off-network costs. These are the extra costs associated with interfacing to locations off the network, such as WATS lines charges and charges incurred by the use of other networks, e.g., DDD charges

The access lines cost is the largest and the most topology-sensitive of the cost components. The network topology has little influence on the off-network costs. As for the network centers, their proportion of the cost has been decreasing due to technological advances. The intermachine trunks are usually obtained through a bulk rate (specialized common carriers, satellite channels), and the access lines reach smaller towns where those services may not be available. The IMT's cost can further be decreased with alternate routing strategies, a capability not available to the access lines.

The synthesis problem can be formulated as follows:

Given:

1. location and weight of all EOSNs (network structure)
2. traffic between every pair of EOSNs (network flow)
3. grade of service required (network performance)
4. tariffs applicable
5. capacity of the network centers

Find:

1. the number of network centers (scale subproblem)
2. the location of the network centers (location subproblem)
3. the EOSNs homing, or assignment of every EOSN to a network center (allocation subproblem)
4. the path hierarchy to be followed by the traffic flows (junction subproblem and off-net routing)

such that:

the overall network cost is minimized

15.2.2. The Scale Subproblem

To find the optimum number of network centers that should be used in the network, the following induction-type process can be used:

Let N be the number of network centers and $N1$ be the value of N that gives the optimal solution. Starting with $N = 1$, a network is designed that minimizes the cost for successive values of N. When N increases, C_{AL} increases, and C_{NC} and C_{IMT} increase, yielding a concave function for the overall cost (Fig. 15.3). When no more savings are achieved by incrementing N, $N1$ has been found.

15.2.3. The Location Subproblem

Where to locate the $N1$ network centers is the most important and challenging of the subproblems. An exhaustive search process is impractical, but no other method can truly claim to reach the optimal solution. For engineering purposes, however, there are several methods quite satisfactory that reach a suboptimal, if not the optimal, solution in a few steps (Refs. 14 and 15). An algorithm that has been extensively applied (Ref. 16) will be described as an example:

1. Set number of network centers (N).
2. Set an initial guess for the location of the N network centers.
3. Connect each EOSN to one of the centers, such that the access line group cost is minimal (the term *cost* may mean just the mileage, or a monthly lease charge from one or more common carriers, or nonrecurring costs of a privately owned line, or any other quantifying measure). This step creates N clusters of access lines.
4. Add the cost of all the access lines in all the clusters. Let the sum be $P1$.

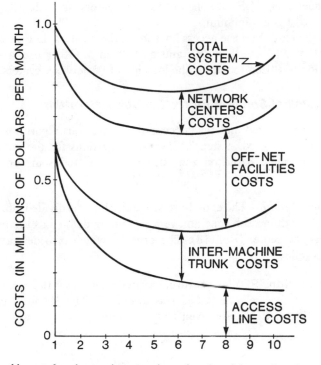

Fig. 15.3. Monthly costs for a large voice network as a function of the number of network centers.

5. Within each of the N clusters, relocate the corresponding network center, such that the sum of the costs for all the access lines of that cluster is minimal. To accomplish this, consider the EOSN locations in the cluster as candidates for the center site, and choose the one with the following criterion (this is called *median* in graph theory, Ref. 17):

$$\text{MED} = \min \left(\sum_j d_{ij} w_j \right) i$$

where

$$1 \leq i \leq M1$$
$$1 \leq j \leq M, \ M1 \leq M$$

M = total number of EOSNs in the cluster
$M1$ = number of EOSN sites that are acceptable as network centers
d_{ij} = distance (cost) from the ith EOSN to the jth EOSN and
w_j = weight of the jth EOSN (number of access lines in the group, traffic intensity, number of terminals, etc.)

6. Connect each EOSN to one of the new centers, such that its access line group cost is a minimum.
7. Add the cost of all the access lines in all the clusters. Let the sum be $P2$.
8. If $P2 < P1$, set $P1 = P2$, and go to step 5. Otherwise, a suboptimal solution has been found for the location of N network centers.

15.2.3.1. Initial Solution for the Location Algorithm

The convergence speed and the success of the previous algorithm depend on the initial solution used in step 2. Several suggestions for the initial solution are presented, some based on zone decomposition and some on the "add" technique.

Zone Decomposition. The end-of-service nodes locus is divided into N clusters or zones, and within each zone an average point is defined as the initial guess for the network center (Ref. 18). The process, which provides rapid convergence, is as follows:

1. Initially all the EOSNs constitute a single zone, and the *mean,* or center of gravity for the zone (COG_1), is evaluated. The V and H coordinates (Ref. 19) for COG_1 are given by the equations:

$$V(COG_1) = \frac{\left(\sum_{i=1}^{M} V_i w_i\right)}{\left(\sum_{i=1}^{M} w_i\right)}$$

$$H(COG_1) = \frac{\left(\sum_{i=1}^{M} H_i w_i\right)}{\left(\sum_{i=1}^{M} w_i\right)}$$

(15.1)

where V_i and H_i are the V and H coordinates, w_i is the weight of the ith EOSN, and M is the number of EOSNs in the zone.
2. All the EOSNs are decomposed into two zones, one that lies to the west of COG_1, and one that lies to the east of COG_1, all in terms of the V and H coordinates map (Ref. 18). For each one of the new zones a *mean* is now found, that is, COG_2 and COG_3 (Fig. 15.4).
3. The two zones are then decomposed into four zones: one north of COG_2, one south of COG_2, one north of COG_3, and one south of COG_3. Four new means $(COG_4, COG_5, COG_6,$ and $COG_7)$ are obtained for each one of the subzones.

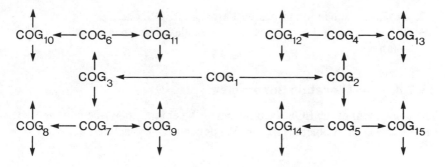

Fig. 15.4. A decomposition sequence.

4. After the above-mentioned steps have been repeated n times, the location of $2**n$ means can be obtained ($n\geq\ =0$).
5. The initial solution for the N network centers will be as follows:

N	Initial solution
1	COG_1
2	COG_2, COG_3
3	COG_1, COG_2, COG_3
4	$COG_4, COG_5, COG_6, COG_7$
5	$COG_1, COG_4, COG_5, COG_6, COG_7$
6	COG_2 to COG_7
7	COG_1 to COG_7
8	COG_8 to COG_{15}
etc.	

6. Instead of using the mean in step 5, we could use the median or the mode instead.

A variation of the process can be made by starting the decomposition north to south, rather than east to west.

Another variation is to use a least-squares approximation curve to divide the zones, instead of a vertical or horizontal straight line (Ref. 20).

Central Radiation. The central radiation approach is an "add" technique; it takes longer to converge than the zone decomposition technique, but it takes less time to initialize.

In this approach, the initial solution for N network centers consists of the N end-of-service nodes that are closest to the overall center of mass (COG_1).

Other "add" techniques can be described as follows:

1. Find the overall mode for all the EOS Nodes (or the median or the mean).

2. Delete the mode found in step 1 from the EOSN set.
3. Return to step 1 until you get N modes. Use them as the N initial solutions.

15.2.4. The Allocation Subproblem

The assignment of the EOSNs to the network centers, known as *homing,* solves the allocation subproblem. The solution depends on the network topology type.

15.2.4.1. Star-Star Topology

In a star-star (or tree) network, the obvious solution is to connect each EOSN to the "closest" network center. The meaning of the word *close* is taken here as not necessarily referring to the shortest distance, but rather to the lowest cost. In fact, most of the existing tariffs are not a linear function of the distance. In this topology, the network center acts as a concentrator of traffic only.

15.2.4.2. Mesh-Stars Topology

In a distributed network, however, the homing of the EOS nodes has an effect on the cost of the intermachine trunks, and the "closest"-home approach may not yield the lowest overall cost.

As a first approximation, the "closest"-home approach will be used for the iterations that lead to the definition of the number and location of the network centers.

Once the network centers are known, a homing matrix can be built. The generic element of the homing matrix is a_{ij},

where:
$$1 \le i \le M$$
$$1 \le j \le N$$
M = number of EOSNs
N = number of network centers and
a_{ij} = traffic flowing between EOSN i and network center j

Perturbations on the network topology can be made as follows:
Let

$$d_{ik} = \min (d_{ij})_j$$

where d_{ij} = distance (cost) between EOSN i and network center j.

If there is a network center $h \neq k$, such that

$$d_{ih} - d_{ik} = x$$
$$a_{ih} - a_{ik} = y$$

where x is relatively small, and y is relatively large, then: rehome EOSN i from network center k to network center h. If savings were introduced into the overall network cost, make the perturbation permanent.

The process is repeated for each EOSN. A new network model has to be drawn after each perturbation.

This process takes time and money, and common sense should dictate whether and how much it is justified for each particular case.

Another way of considering the effect of homing on the IMTS is to use a traffic-weighted ratio instead of the distance when solving the Location Subproblem.

15.2.4.3. Multicenter-Multidrop Topology

Packet and message switching systems provide examples of multicenter-multidrop topologies. In such a system, an EOSN is a data terminal, and a network center is a data central. Each data terminal is connected to a data central via several multiplexed or data concentrator-type links (Fig. 15.5). The objective function is to minimize the line rental or construction cost. A line capacity constraint is that the weight (number of data terminals) of each link is $\leq w_{max}$.

Let $v_1, \ldots, v_n$ be n EOSNs to be connected to a network center v_0. Each EOSN geographical position is identified by its V-H coordinates. Associate with each EOSN v_i a weight (number of data terminals) w_i (Fig. 15.5). Without any loss of generality, assume that $w_i \leq w_{max}$ for all $i = 1, \ldots, n$.

Assume that the cost of sending k units of traffic between EOSNs v_i and v_j, c_{ij}, is given by:

$$c_{ij} = a_{ij} d_{ij} + b_{ij} k, \quad i,j = 0,1, \ldots ,n \qquad (15.2)$$

where a_{ij} is typically a piecewise continuous function of the distance between v_i and v_j (Fig. 15.6). In the case of renting communications facilities, b_{ij} is usually assumed to be zero.

The problem of establishing a minimum-cost network may be posed as a max-flow-min-cut program (Refs. 21 and 22). At each node v_i, $i = 1, \ldots ,n$, assume that there are w_i units of flow available. The mathematical program is given by:

$$\text{Minimize} \sum_{i,j=0}^{n} a_{ij} d_{ij} g_{ij} + b_{ij} f(i,j)$$

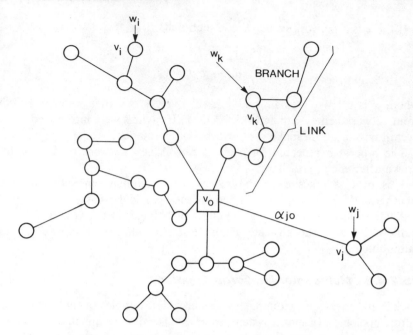

Fig. 15.5. A representation of a multidrop topology for design.

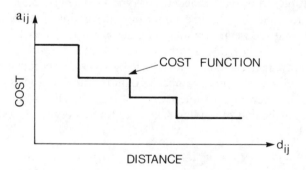

Fig. 15.6. A representation of the cost versus distance relationship.

subject to:

$$\sum_{j=1}^{n} f(j,0) = \sum_{i=1}^{n} w_i$$
$$f(i,j) \leq w_{\max}$$
$$f(i,j) \geq 0$$
$$g_{ij} = 1 \text{ if } f(i,j) > 0;$$
$$= 0 \text{ otherwise}$$
$$i,j = 0,\ldots,n \tag{15.3}$$

The mathematical program stated above can be very large if the number of EOSNs to be connected is greater than 20. Several practical algorithms exist, however, that provide results very close to the optimal solution. A design process for a multidrop network with proven results (Ref. 23) will be described here.

The multidrop network is designed in two stages:

1. obtain an approximate solution using a *feasibility algorithm;*
2. obtain a suboptimal solution using an *exchange algorithm;*

where an approximate solution satisfies the constraints (15.3), and b_{ij} is assumed to be zero.

Feasibility Algorithm. This algorithm uses the inherent data represented by the geographical distribution of the EOSNs for its search. The EOSNs are ordered in a decreasing sequence according to their distance from the center.

Let the EOSNs v_i, $i = 1, \ldots, n$ be at a distance $d(i,0)$, $i = 1, \ldots, n$ from the network center. Let the distances be $d(j1,0) \geq d(j2,0) \geq \ldots \geq d(jn,0)$. The distance $d(i,0)$ is proportional to the cost that may be incurred if the EOSN v_i is to be connected to the network center via a direct branch. Thus, if the highest ranking EOSN $j1$ is to be connected to the center directly, the cost incurred is highest. The algorithm takes advantage of this fact, and the highest ranking EOSN is chosen to be part of the first link. The closest feasible EOSN to it (high ranking in its neighborhood) is chosen to be the second node on the link. Other EOSNs are added, according to their proximity, to this link if the weight constraint is not violated. If no EOSN can be connected without violating the link weight constraint, a new link is started. The unconnected EOSNs are ranked again, and the procedure is repeated until all EOSNs are connected.

This algorithm can be defined as follows:

1. Let $X = (v_1, \ldots, v_n)$.
2. $i = 0$.
3. If $X = (0)$, STOP.
4. Order EOSNs in X according to their decreasing distance from the network center v_0. Let v_h be the highest ranking EOSN in X.
5. $i = i + 1$.
6. Let $Li = (v_h)$.
   Let $X = X - (v_h)$.
7. Let $v_m \in X$ such that

$$d(Li, v_m) = [\min_{vk \in X} d(Li, v_k) / w(Li) + w(v_k) \leq w_{max}]$$

where

$$d(Li,v_k) \equiv \min_{v_j \in Li} d(v_j,v_k)$$

and

$$w(Li) \equiv \sum_{v_j \in Li} w(v_j).$$

If no v_m exists, Go to 10.
8. $Li = Li + (v_m)$.
   $X = X - (v_m)$.
9. If $w(Li) < w_{max}$, Go to 7.
10. $Li = Li + (v_0)$.
    Connect EOSNs in Li, using a shortest tree algorithm (Ref. 24). Go to 3.

Exchange Algorithm. A feasible solution can be improved by exchanging EOSNs on different links. The number of iterations involved is reduced by examining the EOSNs of each feasible solution link in their order.

The algorithm starts by considering the farthest EOSN from the network center on the first link $L1$ (v_s). The closest EOSN on a different link Lj (v_c) is added to the first link if the total cost is reduced and the exchange is feasible (i.e., it does not violate the weight constraint). If the exchange is not feasible, the first combination of EOSNs closest to the center (in $L1$) with weights equal to the weight of the added EOSN (v_c) is moved to link Lj in exchange for v_c. If the total cost is reduced, this part of link $L1$ is excluded from further consideration.

The next farthest EOSN from the center on $L1$ is considered according to the same procedure. When all EOSNs on $L1$ have been considered, $L1$ is excluded. The procedure is repeated for all the links. This approach results in suboptimality, but guarantees that the algorithm will not cycle.

The feasible solution links are numbered cyclically $L1, L2, \ldots, Lk,$

$$k \geq \left\{ \left(\sum_{i=1}^{n} w_i \right) \Big/ w_{max} \right\}$$

1. Let $i = 0$.
2. $i = i + 1$
   $Li''' = Li$
   If $i = k + 1$, STOP.

3. Let $v_s \in Li$, such that

$$d(v_s, v_0) = \max_{vj \in Li} d(v_j, v_0)$$

Let $X = (v_1, \ldots, v_n) - Li$
4. Let $v_c \in X$, such that

$$d(v_c, v_s) = \min_{vj \in X} d(v_j, v_s)$$

$v_c \in Lj$.
5. $Li' = Li + (v_c)$
$Lj' = Lj - (v_c)$
If $w(Li') \leq w_{max}$, GO TO 7.
6. $w(Li') > w_{max}$.
Let $Y = (v_{i1}, \ldots, v_{ir})$
such that

$$\sum_{m=1}^{r} d(v_{im}, v_o) = \min_{v_{ip} \in Li} \sum_{p} d(v_{ip}, v_0) \bigg/ \sum_{p} w(v_{ip}) = w(v_c)$$

If no Y exists, $Li' = Li$, $Lj' = Lj$. GO TO 7.
Otherwise,

$$Li' = Li' - (v_{i1}, \ldots, v_{ir})$$
$$Lj' = Lj' + (v_{i1}, \ldots, v_{ir}).$$

7. $Li'' = Li - (v_s)$
$Lj'' = Lj + (v_s)$
If $w(Lj'') \leq w_{max}$, GO TO 9.
8. $w(Lj'') > w_{max}$.
Let $Z = (v_{j1}, \ldots, v_{jt})$
such that

$$\sum_{m=1}^{t} d(v_{jm}, v_0) = \min_{v_{jp} \in Lj} \sum_{p} d(v_{jp}, v_0) \bigg/ \sum_{p} w(v_{jp}) = w(v_s)$$

If no Z exists, $Li'' = Li$, $Lj'' = Lj$. GO TO 9.
Otherwise,

$$Li'' = Li'' + (v_{j1}, \ldots, v_{jt})$$
$$Lj'' = Lj'' - (v_{j1}, \ldots, v_{jt}).$$

9. Using the shortest tree algorithm on L (including $v0$), find link costs:

$$C = \text{COST}(Li) + \text{COST}(Lj)$$
$$C' = \text{COST}(Li') + \text{COST}(Lj')$$
$$C'' = \text{COST}(Li'') + \text{COST}(Lj'')$$

Let $C_{min} = \min(C', C'')$.
If $C_{min} = C' < C$, go to 10.
If $C_{min} = C'' < C$, go to 11.
If $C_{min} \geq C$, go to 12.

10. $C' = C_{min} < C$
$Lj = Lj'$
$Li = Li'$
$X = (v_1, \ldots, v_n) - Li'$.
go to 12.

11. $C'' = C_{min} < C$
$Li = Li''$
$Lj = Lj''$
$X = (v_1, \ldots, v_n) - Li''$.

12. $Li''' = Li''' - (v_s)$
Let $v_s \in Li'''$, such that

$$d(v_s, v_0) = \max_{v_j \in Li'''} d(v_j, v_0)$$

If no v_s exists, go to 2.
Otherwise, go to 4.

Examples   Figures 15.7 and 15.8 show two networks that have been designed using the described techniques. The network of Fig. 15.7 has 58 end-of-service nodes and a network center in Atlanta. The network of Fig. 15.8 has 40 end-of-service nodes and a center in Kansas City. The design constraint for both networks is $w_{max} \leq 13$.

15.2.5. The Junction Problem

The network centers and the links between them form a network of their own—the intermachine system. Whereas the end-of-service nodes were dumb nodes that needed a network center to do the concentration, switching, and routing for them, the network centers have the capability themselves. The

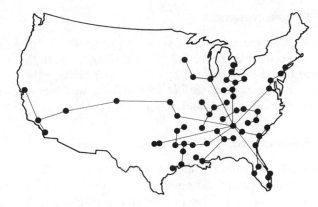

Fig. 15.7. Multidrop network homing—example 1.

Fig. 15.8. Multidrop network homing—example 2.

design of the intermachine system has thus more options. Three basic types of network topology can be used for the intermachine system:

1. Simple Network. In this network, the traffic flowing between two nodes has only the direct route available to it. Alternate routing is not provided, and all trunk groups are full groups.
2. Hierarchical Network. In this network, there are two levels of nodes. The links between pairs of lower-level nodes (high-usage links) can overflow their traffic to links connected to upper-level nodes (final links).
3. Symmetrical Network. This network allows alternate routing, but there is only one level of nodes. All the links have the same right of overflowing, or all the links are high-usage links.

15.2.5.1. Simple Networks

The design of this type of network is straightforward: all trunk groups are dimensioned to accommodate the full traffic flowing between the two nodes of the link. Some of the links may be canceled, either because there is no traffic through them or because they are not economically justified. In a simple network, there may be direct and tandem routes (Fig. 15.11).

15.2.5.2. Hierarchical Networks

A simple network is usually not an economical solution. The first alternative that comes to mind is a multistar-multicenter network, similar to the one used for the EOSN network. A set of upper-level nodes is selected, using techniques described in 15.2.1 to 15.2.3. The other nodes (lower-level nodes) communicate only through the upper-level nodes (Fig. 15.9). All the routes are tandem routes. This network is usually not any cheaper than the simple network. Furthermore, it complicates the traffic management, because it requires routing decisions. It also presents weaker transmission qualities, because most of the traffic follows a multihop path.

A compromise between the simple and the multistar networks is the hierarchical network, used in practically all public networks. Figure 15.10 is an example of a hierarchical network. A direct route is provided between lower-level nodes, but an alternate route is also provided through the upper-level nodes. Trunk groups that can overflow to other groups are called *high-usage groups*. They are dimensioned on an economic basis: circuits are provided only for traffic that flows more efficiently through a direct route. Trunk groups that do not have an overflow route, but receive overflow traffic from high-usage

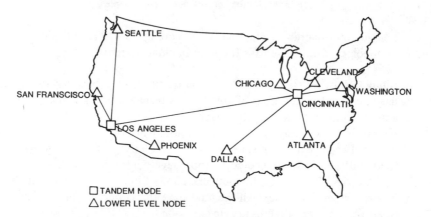

Fig. 15.9. A tandem-routing-only (multistar) network.

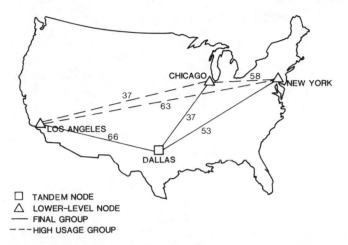

Fig. 15.10. A hierarchical routing network. The numbers represent the size of trunk groups.

groups, are called *final groups*. They are dimensioned according to the desired grade of service.

Dimensioning of High-Usage Groups. To understand how the high-usage groups are dimensioned, we will use the very simple network of Fig. 15.11(c). Let *AB* be the high-usage or direct route between *A* and *B*, and let *a* be the busy hour erlangs from *A* to *B*. *AT* and *TB* form the alternate route where the excess *AB* traffic overflows, *N* is the number of circuits to be found (size of the high-usage group). *N* can go from the extreme of zero, when all traffic is carried through the upper-level node (star network), to the extreme of *Nd* where *Nd* is the number of circuits necessary to provide the required grade of service to *a* without alternate routing (simple network).

The effect of *N* over the cost of the network is shown by the curve of Fig. 15.12. The objective is to find the minimum of this curve.

Let MUF be the *marginal utilization factor* for the final route *ATB*. MUF is the utilization of an additional circuit in the final route, or how many extra erlangs could be carried by the final route if one circuit were added to it.

Let *Q* be the cost ratio between the alternate and the direct route:

$$Q = \frac{C(ATB)}{C(AB)}$$

where $C(ATB)$ is the cost of one additional circuit in the alternate route ($=$ *AT* link cost $+$ termination cost in T $+$ *TB* link cost), and $C(AB)$ is the cost of one additional circuit in the direct route.

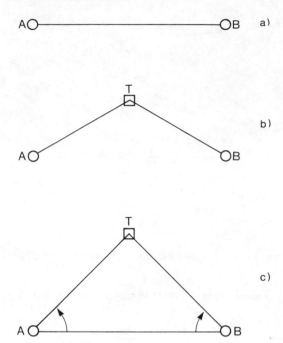

Fig. 15.11. Routing methods: (a) direct route, (b) tandem route, (c) alternate route.

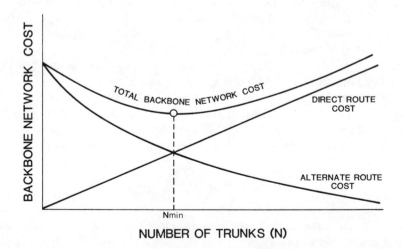

Fig. 15.12. Cost as a function of number of high-usage trunks.

Let $B(N,a)$ be the loss factor for a erlangs if N circuits are provided. Then $a \cdot B(N,a)$ is the traffic overflowing to ATB if N is the size of the high-usage group. The number of additional circuits in the final route necessary to carry this overflow traffic is given by:

$$\frac{a \cdot B(N,a)}{\text{MUF}}$$

and the cost of handling the $A - B$ traffic is given by:

$$K = \frac{a\,B(N,a)}{\text{MUF}} * C(ATB) + N*C(AB)$$

The minimum of this cost is achieved for $N = Nhu$, such that

$$\left[\frac{dK}{dN} \right]_{N=Nhu} = 0$$

or, assuming that MUF and the marginal costs are independent of N,

$$a \left[\frac{dB}{dN} \right]_{N=Nhu} = - \frac{\text{MUF}}{Q}$$

The left member of this equation is the load on the last trunk or marginal occupancy of the high-usage route. The ratio (MUF/Q) indicates the economic value for the load and is called economic erlangs, or EERL. As N is an integer, it is:

$$a[B(Nhu,a) - B(Nhu + 1, a)] = \text{EERL}$$

Let E be the required grade of service in terms of loss factor and Nf given by:

$$B(Nf,a) = E$$

Then,

1. If $B(Nhu,a) > E$, Nhu is the size of the high-usage group.
2. If $B(Nhu,a) \le E$, Nf is the size of the group. No traffic is allowed to overflow, and the group is called a *full group* (see Fig. 15.13).

Dimensioning of Final Groups.   The final trunk groups have two types of traffic flowing through them: first-offered traffic, of random nature, and over-

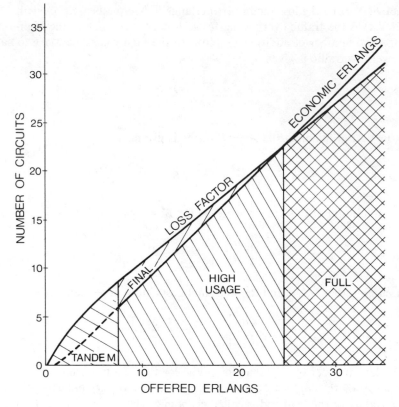

Fig. 15.13. Allocation of circuits among high-usage, final, and full groups, as a function of offered traffic and required grade of service.

flow traffic, of "peaked" behavior. Assuming that the traffic can be characterized by its first two moments (the mean and the variance), the final trunk groups are dimensioned using the equivalent random theory (Ref. 5).

Let

$$m_i, v_i, i = 1, \ldots, s$$

be the mean and variance of each one of the traffic parcels that flow through a given final group (first-offered traffic plus overflow traffic from several high-usage groups). If a_i is the original offered traffic in high-usage group i, m_i and v_i are given by: (Ref. 5)

$$m_i = a_i * B(n_i, a_i)$$
$$v_i = m_i [1 - m_i + a_i/(n_i + 1 + m_i - a_i)]$$

where n_i is the number of circuits in the high-usage group i. For the first-offered traffic, it is:

$$m_i = v_i = a_i$$

The total traffic will be characterized by its mean M and variance V,

$$M = \sum_{i=1}^{s} m_i$$

$$V = \sum_{i=1}^{s} v_i$$

An "equivalent random load" AE, which would produce an overflow traffic (M,V) when flowing through an "equivalent random group" of NE circuits, is evaluated. AE and NE can be estimated by the following equations (Ref. 27):

$$AE = V + 3P(P - 1)$$
$$NE = AE * F - M - 1$$

where

$$P = \frac{V}{M}$$

$$F = \frac{(M + P)}{(M + P + 1)}$$

The number of circuits in the final group N is determined such that the traffic lost from the system,

$$L = AE * B(NE + N,A)$$

satisfies the desired grade of service. Several loss factors can be defined:

1. the overall average loss

$$Ea = \frac{L}{\sum_{i=1}^{s} a_i}$$

2. the average loss for the traffic flowing through the final group

$$Et = \frac{L}{M}$$

3. the loss for first-offered, random traffic Er. Given that Er is not easily calculated, and because

$$Et > Er \text{ and } Et > Ea,$$

Et is usually forced to satisfy the desired grade of service. This leads to a safe-side, overdimensioned, final group, and recent investigations have tried to reach a better estimate [28].

15.2.5.3. Symmetrical Networks

Symmetrical networks have an unrestricted routing pattern. All the nodes are at the same level, and all the trunk groups are high-usage groups.

Military networks, where reliability is crucial, are usually of this type. If any node fails, rerouting of messages is facilitated with a symmetrical network. It has also been found (Ref. 29) that for small networks (six or fewer nodes) with low traffic densities, a symmetrical network is superior to a hierarchical one, in terms of economy and reaction to overloads.

Controls have to be imposed in symmetrical network routing options, to prevent "law and order" breakdowns such as:

1. Loops. A route should not pass more than once through the same node.
2. Excessive hops. There is a maximum number of links (hops) that a route can contain to avoid unacceptable degradation of transmission quality.
3. Mirrors. A ridiculous situation would be to have a call from link A alternating through link B, and at the same time a call from link B alternating to link A.

Symmetrical networks also have a tendency to deteriorate rapidly when the load exceeds the load for which the network was designed. To counteract this, symmetrical networks should always use a *trunk reservation* technique (Ref. 29). Under the trunk reservation technique, a small number of circuits in a link are only allowed to carry first-offered traffic. The remaining circuits in the link can carry either first-offered or overflow traffic. Trunk reservation has also been proven helpful for hierarchical networks.

Several attempts have been made to come out with a design strategy for symmetrical networks (several papers on the subject can be found in editions of the International Teletraffic Congress), but no general method for engineering an optimal or suboptimal symmetrical network has come forward or been accepted.

The choice of an alternate route in a symmetrical network follows the guidelines described in 14.3.

15.2.6 Design of Off-Net Facilities

In case off-net traffic forms a sizeable portion of total traffic handled by a backbone network, one must have the capability to compute the total network cost as a function of several off-net traffic routing arrangements such as:

1. Head End Hop Off (HEHO): According to this technique, all off-net traffic originating from a switching node is routed to the destination via off-net Access Lines (ONALS) such as Wide Area Telecommunication Service (WATS) Lines, Foreign Exchange (FX) Lines, Local ONALS (LONALS), etc.
2. Tail End Hop Off (TEHO): According to this technique, all off-net traffic is first routed to a network center closest to the destination and then routed to the destination via the most economical ONALS.
3. A mixed technique arbitrarily called WHOT (Ref. 30) according to

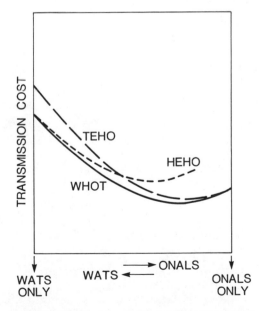

Fig. 15.14. Comparison of off-net call routing strategies.

which some off-net traffic is routed to the destination via WATS or similar type of lines using the HEHO routing approach, and some off-net traffic is routed to the destination via FX and LONALS using TEHO.

Figure 15.14 shows some curves showing the relationship between transmission costs, number of WATS and FX-type ONALS employed, and the type of routing technique employed. Our experience shows that the amount of OFF-NET traffic and the actual traffic flows greatly influence the optimum routing technique that must be employed to save millions of dollars per year in managing a typical corporate voice network.

Similar considerations will also apply for a corporate data communication network.

Chapter 16
Implementation and Postimplementation Issues

A successful completion of the network design process does not imply the end of the network planning process. Additional tasks dealing with cutover, transmission loss planning, sensitivity analyses, and on-line management and control must be executed.

16.1 CUTOVER PLANNING

Large common carriers generally employ flash cutover from the existing network to the new network. This requires a good deal of planning. Contingency plans for falling back on the old network must always be ready, in case the new network does not function.

To make the task a little more controllable and predictable, most vendors employ a phased cutover plan that lasts 3 to 4 weeks. Each step is planned in detail, additional links are ordered ahead of time, and phased integration is achieved. The following steps are executed in sequence:

1. Install the nodal hardware at each location, and perform all tests.
2. Interconnect the nodes with a minimal backbone network, and test the system with test messages.
3. Divert some of the existing access lines to the new network centers, so as to allow a desired fraction of the entire traffic to flow to the new switch. It is here that the original CSV data base becomes extremely useful.
4. Divert the first increment of traffic to the new network, and test the new network (see Fig. 16.1) with live traffic.
5. Divert the second increment of access lines from the old network to the new network, and increase the trunks accordingly.
6. Divert the second increment of traffic, and again test the new network with live traffic
7. Repeat steps 5 and 6 to complete the cutover.

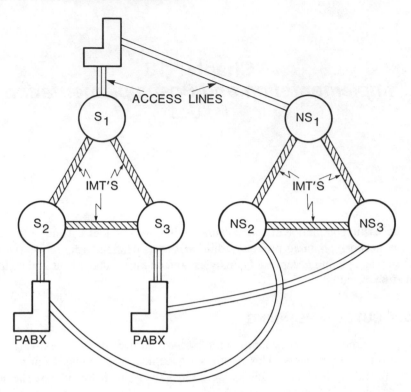

Fig. 16.1. Basic cutover philosophy.

At steps 3 and 5, some off-net access lines, e.g., WATS lines, are added at each new switch to permit the new network to handle certain traffic for which there are no on-net routes. All the small access line bundles are generally flash-cut.

The additional costs associated with migration result from the circuits needed during cutover and planning. Such costs are well spent for preventing surprises.

16.2 TRANSMISSION QUALITY PLANNING

It is extremely important to provide a good quality of transmission for end-to-end communication. In voice networks, this translates to an intelligent conversation, and in data networks it translates to no bit errors.

For CS voice networks, 12 to 15 dB of path loss is excellent, 15 to 18 dB of loss is good, 18 to 21 dB of loss is poor, 21 to 23 dB of loss is very poor, and path loss exceeding 23 dB is unsatisfactory.

Transmission path loss in a voice network may consist of the following items:

1. PTS transmission losses, as shown in Fig. 7.9 of Chapter 7
2. telephone-PABX path loss is less than or equal to 1 dB. Telephone-#1ESS Centrex varies from 3.5 to 6 dB
3. PABX-network switch path loss is 0 dB, if both are four-wire switches, and 2.5 to 5 dB if PABX is a two-wire switch and the network switch is a four-wire type
4. network node-network node path loss is the *VNL*, as defined in Chapter 7
5. four-wire network node-PTS Class 5 CO path loss is 3.5 to 5 dB

Based on the above figures, a typical on-net call in a corporate network may experience 10 to 27 dB of loss (from excellent to unsatisfactory), depending on the types of CVs used. An off-net call in a private network using #1ESS Centrex and the head-end-hop-off (HEHO) approach may experience a path loss of 18 to 34 dB (from poor to unsatisfactory). The same network using the tail-end-hop-off (TEHO) approach for routing off-net calls may experience 21 to 37 dB (from very poor to unsatisfactory). If very poor to unsatisfactory conditions are expected in any path, a common solution is to add an amplifier pad at the network center. Of course, this requires much care, for interfaces with the public telephone service may be involved.

A similar approach can be applied for planning transmission quality in a PS or MS network. There is one difference. Error control procedures are automatically employed in several PS network architectures to achieve an acceptable bit error rate.

16.3 SENSITIVITY ANALYSES

When the results of network synthesis (one for each year of the life cycle), cutover planning, and transmission quality planning are presented to the customer, the result is always requests for more analyses.

Frequently, the customer will want to compare the solutions with those involving one or more common carriers who charge for their switching hardware according to well-known tariffs. In such cases, monthly hardware costs are normalized and added to the non-recurring transmission costs for each solution. In general, a comparison between solutions of hardware vendors is difficult, if not impossible. Only the customer has the privilege of comparing the solutions from different hardware vendors. Even in that case, all vendors make different assumptions in reaching their conclusions, and these assumptions are never written down completely.

Experience shows that most solutions for corporate networks are heavily dependent on transmission costs and not much on hardware costs. This observation suggests that a greater emphasis be placed on network synthesis than on any other task. A few thousands of dollars spent on network design may save millions of dollars during the life cycle.

The customer may desire to vary some grade of service (GOS) parameters and see the effect on network cost before making any decision. In some instances, the customer may redefine the GOS. For example, he may specify a blocking factor or delay for each leg of the path.

In some cases, the customer may ask to relocate the network centers, because the corporation may have an excess of space in certain cities. This will increase the transmission cost during the life cycle. The customer must realize the penalty before making a final decision.

The customer may also desire an analysis showing the effects of connecting certain customer vehicle locations to the network. Such locations might have already been determined as uneconomical for direct access.

There are times when a customer desires to employ private microwave facilities in a region with many large customer vehicles. A feasibility study involving analyses of the frequency spectrum in the region and life cycle costs will be required.

The cost impact of several cutover plans proposed by the customer must be analyzed and compared to that proposed by the vendor.

Above, we cited some of the many types of analyses that need to be performed to satisfy the needs and desires of the customer. The network synthesis tools must be general enough to handle these unique situations.

16.4 ON-LINE MANAGEMENT AND CONTROL

After the network system is operational, it is necessary to continuously monitor the system performance and keep the system tuned to provide the desired service at the lowest possible cost.

Modern network nodes are generally equipped to provide 100 percent logs of all transactions. During the first few months, this capability should be used to capture the actual offered traffic and compare it with the models employed for network planning.

Some of the new network nodes also record detailed traffic statistics on each access line and trunk bundle for each hour. Some nodes even provide reports summarizing the traffic loads handled and the observed congestion during the peak hour for each bundle. Some nodes provide real-time alarms signifying trunk failure. Such data describes the traffic flows within the functioning network. Again, these flows can be compared with those anticipated during the synthesis process.

The 100 percent traffic logs can also be analyzed for EOSN-to-EOSN traffic flows and compared with the original communities of interest assumed.

If many discrepancies are discovered, it may become necessary to repeat the network synthesis process to obtain desired performance at a minimum cost.

The network synthesis process should be repeated whenever the system reports show either a substantially lower or a markedly higher grade of service than desired. That could be caused by significant changes in traffic volumes or traffic distribution, or it could be due to the inaccuracy of the initially available data, or even to a noncareful design.

A need also exists to continuously monitor the traffic flows to certain populous areas. When the off-net traffic handled exceeds a certain threshold, implementation of foreign exchange lines may become cheaper than the WATS lines approach. Of course, the applicable measured time costs must be included in the trade-off. Some communication managers may consider this task a part of the periodic network synthesis process. Another important service provided by the communication department is the distribution of a monthly cost allocation report to all the departments of the corporation. In other words, the monthly operating costs are distributed among all the users within the corporation according to usage. To accomplish this goal, one needs to maintain a data base for all network facilities, corresponding costs, and, of course, the monthly traffic log. A utility program must be employed each month to prepare such timely reports. Nevertheless, the task may not be easy.

One difficulty may result from the inadequacy of 100 percent transaction logs. Each log of the completed transaction may list only the three-digit CSV number and not the calling party's extension. This information may be inadequate when several departments share the same CSV. To correct this, some PABXs also transmit the four-digit extension number for recording at the network center, and some networks require dialing of special access codes that identify the calling party.

Another difficulty lies in the area of finding a judicious way to compute usage costs. A completed transaction may involve both on-net and off-net communication facilities. Some completed transactions may involve only access lines and no trunks. Some may use the network during busy hours and others may use it during nonbusy hours. Some generate transactions that are much shorter than others, but their frequency is relatively very high. An approach acceptable to all may be hard to find.

The communication manager must also develop a methodology for ordering new circuits or discontinuing some old ones. Several common and specialized carriers have to be contacted ahead of time to orchestrate this process. A similar interface must be developed to get the failed circuits repaired. Experience has shown that at least 10 percent of the circuits in older, less intelligent network systems were always malfunctioning at any given time. With the new network nodes, real-time fault reporting is possible. This translates into significant savings to the corporation.

An intelligent network system should be considered not as a headache, but as a tool for increasing the productivity of each worker. A network design is never finished, however, and continuing improvement of the network is an integral part of communications management. Integration of the several voice and data applications into an integrated system has to be contemplated. Such concepts as electronic mail, office-of-the-future, and digital transmission will introduce new parameters into the network design.

REFERENCES

1. Syski, R. (1960) *Congestion Theory in Telephone Systems*. Edinburgh: Oliver and Boyd.
2. Clos, C. A study of non-blocking switching networks. *Bell Syst. Tech. J.* Vol. 32, 1953, 406–424.
3. Lee, C. Y. Analysis of switching networks. *Bell Syst. Tech. J.* Vol. 34, 1955, 1287–1315.
4. Wilkinson, R. I. Working curves for delayed exponential calls served in random order. *Bell Syst. Tech. J.* Vol. 32, 1953, 360–383.
5. Wilkinson, R. I. Theories for toll traffic engineering in the U.S.A. *Bell Syst. Tech. J.* Vol. 35, 1956, 421–514.
6. Elldin, A. H. Basic traffic theory. *Seminar on Traffic Engineering and Network Planning*. Organized by the International Telecommunication Union in New Delhi, November 24 to December 5, 1975, pp. 11–133.
7. Katz, S. S. (1979) Improved traffic network administration process utilizing end-to-end service considerations. *Ninth International Teletraffic Congress*. Madrid: CTNE.
8. CCITT International Telegraph and Telephone Consultative Committee. (1979) *Orange Book, Vol. II.2, Telephone Operation: Quality of Service and Tariffs*. Geneva: International Telecommunications Union.
9. Wilkinson, R. I. Some comparisons of load and loss data with current teletraffic theory. *Bell Syst. Tech. J.* Vol. 50, 1971, 2807–2834.
10. Bell Laboratories Staff. (1977) *Engineering and Operations in the Bell System*. Bell Telephone Laboratories, Inc.
11. Hill, D. W., and S. R. Neal. Traffic capacity of a probability-engineered trunk group. *Bell Syst. Tech. J.* Vol. 55, 1976, 831–842.
12. Mina, R. R., and J. M. Kraushaar. (1979) The role of traffic engineering in the environment of a regulated monopoly telephone service. *Ninth International Teletraffic Congress*. Torremolinos, Spain.
13. Bridges, J. W., and D. E. White. The design process for private voice networks. *Business Communications Review*. Vol. 9, 1979, 17–26.

14. Boorstyn, R. R., and H. Frank. Large-scale network topological organization. *IEEE Trans. Commun.* COM25, 1977, 29–47.
15. Chou, W., F. Ferrante, and M. Balagangadhar. Integrated optimization for distributed processing networks. 1978 National Computer Conference. *AFIPS Conference Proceedings* Vol. 47, 1978, 795–811.
16. de Sousa, P. T. Design of multi-center/multi-star networks. *MIDCON Conference Record,* Dallas, Texas, 1978.
17. Harari, F. (1969) *Graph Theory.* Reading, Mass.: Addison-Wesley.
18. Sharma, R. L. Network topologies and their synthesis. *Proceedings of the Symposium on Tri-Tac Communications.* Arlington, Virginia, April 13–14, 1976, pp. 278–294.
19. McIntyre, H. B. What is this new V-H system? *New England Telephone and Telegraph Company, Background for Management* Vol. 33, December 1959.
20. Dirilten, H., and R. W. Donaldson. Topological design of teleprocessing networks using linear regression clustering. *IEEE Trans. Commun.* COM24, 1976, 1152–1159.
21. Ford, L. R., and D. R. Fulkerson. (1962) *Flows in Networks.* Princeton: Princeton University Press.
22. Hadley, G. (1964) *Nonlinear and Dynamic Programming.* Reading, Mass.: Addison-Wesley.
23. Sharma, R. L., and M. T. El-Bardai. Suboptimal communications network synthesis. *Proceedings of the International Conference on Communications,* 1970. San Francisco, pp. 19–11/16.
24. Prim, R. C. Shortest connection networks and some generalizations. *Bell Syst. Tech. J.* Vol. 36, 1957, 1389–1401.
25. Fried, T. Network planning. *Seminar on Traffic Engineering and Network Planning.* Organized by the International Telecommunication Union in New Delhi, November 24 to December 5, 1975, pp. 289–363.
26. Flood, J. E. (ed.). (1975) *Telecommunication Networks.* Stevenage, Herts., England: Peter Peregrinus Ltd.
27. Rapp, Y. Planning of junction networks in a multi-exchange area. *Ericsson Tech.* Vol. 1, 1964, 79–130.
28. Rao, R. N. (1979) Improved trunk engineering algorithm for high-blocking hierarchical networks. *Ninth International Teletraffic Congress,* Torremolinos, Spain.
29. Weber, J. H. A simulation study of routing and control in communications networks. *Bell Syst. Tech. J.* Vol. 43, 1964, 2639–2676.
30. de Sousa, P. T., and R. L. Sharma. Off-network routing arrangements in corporate networks. *INTELCOM Conference Proceedings,* Los Angeles, California, 1980.

Appendix
Evolving Standards for Information Exchange

A1. INTRODUCTORY REMARKS

Today, about 100 years after the invention of the telephone, any telephone user in most developed countries of North America and Europe can directly dial any subscriber in over 40 countries and complete a conversation with satisfaction. This did not happen at random. Credit must go to the various international organizations that set out a long time ago to develop reasonable standards for telecommunications over CS systems.

A clear choice again exists in the area of public data networks (PDNs). Either we let each of the vendors develop his own standard and create a great chaos, or we develop reasonable international standards for PDNs that will facilitate unfettered flow of data among people and nations.

People all over the world have a latent hunger for rapid information exchange with other people or groups at costs below what is possible today. Electronic mail, electronic fund transfer (EFT), point of sale (POS), travel/ hotel reservations, data base accessing, active political involvement, and home learning are some of many services that could make human life quite fulfilling. We believe that only through international standards for PDNs can we achieve that goal.

A2. INTERNATIONAL ORGANIZATIONS ENGAGED IN DEVELOPING STANDARDS FOR PDNs

The following organizations have responsibility for developing standards for PDNs:

1. CCITT (International Telegraph and Telephone Consultative Committee), which is a division of ITU (International Telecommunications Union)
2. ISO (International Standards Organization), which represents computer and terminal manufacturers
3. EIA (Electronic Industries Association)
4. ANSI (American National Standards Institute)

Although each group seems to develop its own standards, there is a good deal of cooperation among them. At all important meetings, representatives from all other groups are present, and their views are heard. An entire textbook would be needed to explain the detailed workings of each group and its output. For this reason, we will concentrate only on CCITT. Some references will be made to other groups' standards that are related to CCITT standards.

CCITT is divided into 17 study groups (SGs): SGI and SGII for telephone operations and tariffs, SGIII for general tariff principles, SGIV for transmission maintenance of international circuits and chains of circuits, SGV for protection against dangers and disturbances of electromagnetic origin, SGVI for protection and specification of cable sheaths and poles, SGVII for new networks for data transmission (both circuit-switched and packet-switched types), SGVIII for telegraph and data terminal equipment (DTE), SGIX for telegraph transmission quality, SGX for telegraph switching, SGXI for telephone switching and signaling, SGXII for telephone transmission performance, SGXIII for automatic and semiautomatic telephone networks, SGXIV for facsimile telegraph transmission and equipment, SGXV for transmission systems, SGXVI for telephone circuits, and SGXVII for data transmission over telephone and Telex networks.

Of these seventeen SGs, the standards developed by SGVII are of particular importance to modeling, analysis, and design of network systems. Of course, the standards developed by SGXI, SGXII, SGXIII, SGXV, and SGXVII are also important, for they deal with the existing CS systems that provide the majority of the analog facilities for data transmission. In the remaining pages of this appendix, we will focus mainly on the standards related to PDNs.

CCITT standards are really recommendations that are unanimously signed by the PTTs of all countries at the plenary session held once every three years. Two types of recommendations are of interest to those concerned with PDNs. The V. and X. recommendations deal with analog and digital transmission facilities and networks, respectively.

Some of the most useful V. recommendations are as follows: V.3 for international alphabet No. 5 for information interchange, V.15 for acoustic coupling for data transmission, V.19 for modems for parallel transmission using PTS signaling frequencies, V.20 for parallel data transmission modems for universal use in PTS networks, V.21 for 200-BPS modems standarized for use in PTS network, V.23 for 600/1200-BPS modems standarized for use in PTS network, V.24 for a list of definitions for interchange circuits between DTE and DCE (data circuit-termination equipment on the network side), V.26 for 2400/1200-BPS modems standardized for use on four-wire leased circuits, V.26bis for 2400/1200-BPS modems standarized for use in PTS network, V.27 for 4800-BPS modems for use on leased circuits, V.27bis for 4800-BPS modems with equalizer, standarized for use in PTS network, V.27ter for 4800/

2400-BPS modems standarized for use in PTS network, V.29 for 9600-BPS modems for use on leased circuits, V.35 for data transmission at 48-KBPS using 60 to 108 kHz group-BPS circuits, and V.36 for modems for synchronous data transmission using 60 to 108 kHz group-BPS circuits.

The various X. recommendations of interest to PDN designers are as follows: X.1 for international user classes of service, X.2 for international user facilities in PDN, X.3 for packet assembly/disassembly (PAD) facility in PDN, X.4 for general structure of signals of international alphabet No. 5 code for data transmission over PDN, X.20 for interface between DTE and DCE for start-stop transmission on PDN, X.20bis, which is compatible with V.21, X.21 for a general purpose interface between DTE and DCE for synchronous operation of PDN, X.21bis for use on PDN of DTEs designed for interfacing to synchronous V-series modems, X.24 for a list of definitions of interchange circuits between DTE and DCE on PDN, X.25 for interface between DTE and DCE for terminals operating in the packet mode on PDN, X.26 for electrical characteristics of unbalanced double-current interchange circuits for general use with integrated circuit equipment in the field of data communication (it is identical to V.10), X.27 for electrical characteristics for balanced double-current interchange circuits for general use with integrated circuit equipment in the field of data communication (it is identical to V.11), X.28 for DTE-DCE interface for start-stop mode DTE accessing the PAD facility on a PDN situated in the same country, X.29 for the procedure for exchange of control information and user data between a start-stop mode DTE and PAD facility, X.60 for common channel signaling for synchronous data application, X.70 for terminal and transit control signaling system for start-stop service on international circuits between asynchronous data networks, X.71 for decentralized terminal and transit control signaling system on international circuits between synchronous data networks, X.75 for data interchange on international trunk (single or multichannel) connecting gateway nodes, X.95 for network parameters in PDN, X.96 for call progress signals, and X.121 for an international numbering plan for PDNs.

Figure A.1 illustrates some important CCITT standard interfaces.

Several EIA standards are related to CCITT standards. To illustrate, the best known EIA standard, RS-232-C, is equivalent to a combination of V.24 and V.28 (an older version of V.10). The modern EIA standard RS-423 is a combination of V.26 and V.10. The proposed EIA standards RS-XYZ and RS-ABC are combinations of V.24 and V.10, and V.24, V.10, and V.11, respectively.

ISO standards also have equivalences to other standards. To illustrate, ISO standards DP2110 and DP4902 are equivalent to EIA standards RS-232- and RS-XYZ/ABC, respectively.

To get a deeper understanding of CCITT standards, one needs to further

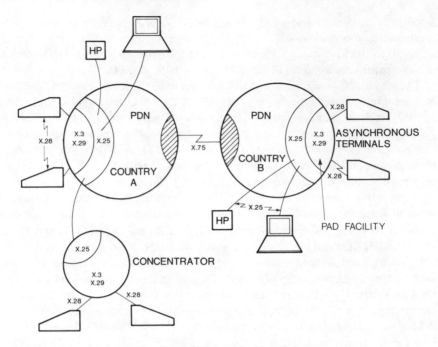

Fig. A.1. CCITT standard interfaces.

study the X.1 and X.25 recommendations. X.1 recommendations deal with the following classes of service:

Asynchronous circuit-switched system
   300-baud, 11-unit code, start-stop
   50 to 200-baud, 7.5 to 11-unit, start-stop
Synchronous circuit-switched system
   600-BPS terminals
   2400-BPS terminals
   4800-BPS terminals
   9600-BPS terminals
   48,000-BPS terminals
Packet-switched system
   2400-BPS terminals
   4800-BPS terminals
   9600-BPS terminals
   48,000-BPS terminals

CCITT recommendation X.25 defines the DTE-DCE protocols for PS classes of service, and recommendations X.3, X.28, and X.29 define the pad facility, DTE-DCE interface for start-stop terminals, and the procedure for exchange of control information between start-stop terminal and pad facility, respectively. X.25 is based on the virtual circuit concept, as employed in Telenet, Transpac, and other PDNs, and not on the datagram concept, as employed in Arpanet and Cyclades. Although X.25 was created to reduce the software modifications required on hosts or intelligent terminals, hardly any vendor offered the minimal software modules required. The situation will improve shortly, for PSSs are now everywhere. As the world was full of start-stop asynchronous terminals, and there was an urgent need for them to be used in a timesharing (TS) or transaction processing mode, this environment created the PAD and associated protocols.

Concurrently with the above developments, a great deal of progress is being made in large-scale integrated (LSI) circuit technology. It is now possible for an LSI chip to handle several of the X.25 functions. See Ref. 30 for a description of such a chip soon to be marketed.

CCITT's X.25 and other PSS-related recommendations are still not understood properly. We will now attempt to describe X.25 in a manner different from that employed in CCITT publications.

A.3 THE X.25 RECOMMENDATION

X.25 provides a multilayered access protocol that enables a packet mode DTE to communicate with a PS node of a PDN . In no way does X.25 define all the protocols required for implementing an entire PS network. Nonetheless, X.25 is an important aspect of a multilevel network architecture.

X.25 defines and standardizes only the first three levels of as many as seven layers that may be required to accomplish not only data communication, but also process control (e.g., DP).

Level 1 is related to the physical/electrical interfaces between the DTE and DCE. Level 2 is related to the link control or control of data flow between the DTE and DCE in a bit synchronous fashion. Level 3 is related to the so-called network control, or procedures for setting up or disconnecting the virtual circuit and controlling the flow of packets in the network.

In a PDN, each packet-mode DTE has a unique address assigned according to the X.121 recommendation. At the start of a call, the PS node receives a call request packet from a DTE. This packet contains the addresses of both the calling and called DTEs. According to X.25, the virtual circuits can be set up only on the access links connecting the calling DTE to the originating PS node or the called DTE to the destination PS node. Additional protocols are needed to define the way the packets will flow within between the network nodes.

If the DTE is a host, several virtual circuits (VCs) can be set up. At present,

12 bits in the packet format (see Fig. A.2) allow up to 4096 concurrent VCs. Each packet is embedded in a frame, which is a block of serial data exchanged between a DTE and a PS node.

Each station, be it a DTE or PS node, has two logical functions needed for addressing and signaling. The two functions are called *primary* and *secondary* functions, as illustrated in Fig. A.3. The primary function transmits commands and receives responses. The secondary function transmits responses and receives commands.

The structure of frames used for DTE-DCE communication is common to all bit-oriented protocols (BOPs), such as high-level data link (HDLC) and synchronous data link (SDLC). This link control forms the basis for the Level

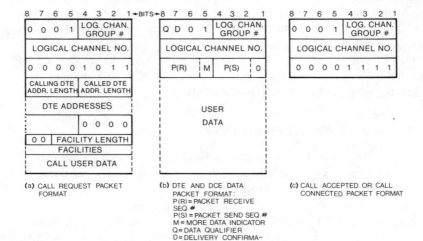

Fig. A.2. Some typical packet formats for X.25.

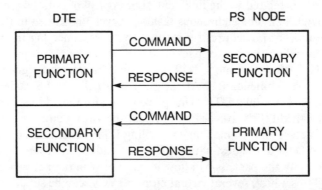

Fig. A.3. Addressable functions within a DTE or PS node for CCITT X.25.

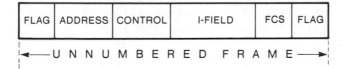

Fig. A.4. Standard frame formats for CCITT X.25.

2 protocol of X.25, which employs an outgrowth of HDLC, as defined originally by ISO.

A frame consists of a flag field, an address field (or A field), a control field
(or a C field), an information field (or an I field), a frame check sequence
(FCS), and another flag field. A frame may or may not consist of the I field,
depending upon the type of field. See Fig. A.4, which also depicts three types
of frames:

1. supervisory frame (or S frame), which is used to perform supervisory
   control of a link, such as acknowledging packets, requesting retransmission of packets, and requesting temporary suspension of transmission
2. unnumbered frame (or U frame), which is employed to set up, disconnect,
   and reset virtual circuits or links
3. information frame (or I frame), which is used to send data through the
   PDN

There is a flag at each end of the frame. Its purpose is to designate the start or the end of a frame. The X.25 flag is a bit pattern 01111110. To provide data transparency within the frame, each transmitting station must insert a 0 after each sequence of five contiguous 1's within the frame. This will prevent an inadvertent reading of a flag within the frame. Each receiving station must have the capability to automatically delete the inserted 0's.

The 16-bit frame check sequence is produced by a computation that checks all bits between the opening flag and the first bit of FCS. The 0's inserted for data transparency are not checked.

Level 2 link control does not involve itself with the data within the *I* field of an *I* frame. The packet data, as enclosed within an HDLC frame, moves from one PS node to another until another X.25-based link control delivers the user data to a destination DTE.

The Level 2 protocol may take one of these two forms:

1. link access procedure (LAP), which was part of the original X.25
2. link access procedure, balanced (LAPB), which is in the latest X.25.

The two procedures differ only in the way links are set up, disconnected, or reset.

There are four types of network parameters specified by X.25 Level 2 protocol: $T1$, $N1$, $N2$, and k. $T1$ is the timeout set for the primary timer; if $T1$ is expired and a response to a command is not received, the command may be retransmitted. $N1$ is the maximum number of bits that can be sent in a packet. $N2$ is the maximum number of command retransmissions allowable as a result of $T1$ timeouts. Parameter k is the maximum number of outstanding (transmitted but unacknowledged) packets that a station may have at any given time. According to X.25, k cannot exceed 7.

The Level 2 protocol was described above; Level 3 (packet or network transport level) can be described as follows.

Up to 15 groups of 255 logical channels can be concurrently active at any time. There is one-to-one correspondence between the DTE and DCE channel numbers. Permanent virtual circuits and temporary virtual calls are two facilities avaiable with X.25. Permanent VC does not require a call set up procedure (see Fig. A.5). The virtual call requires a call setup procedure. X.25 specifies 3 different types of frames, as discussed above, and 14 different types of packet formats. Most of these formats deal with supervisory control packets that do not contain data and are only a few bytes (or octets) long. Bits within an octet are numbered 1 to 8. Bit 1 is the low-order bit and is transmitted first. See Fig. A.2.

During the call setup period, all the facilities desired are specified in the call

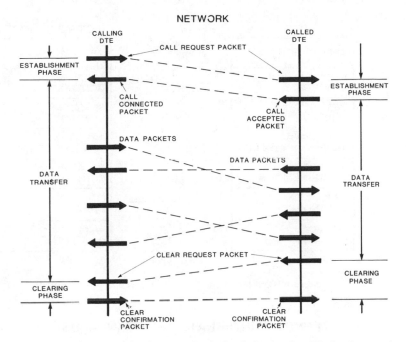

Fig. A.5. Call establishment, data transfer, and call clearing for virtual call protocol.

setup packet. The called DTE may accept or reject the call by means of an appropriate packet.

Data packets can be sent at any time using permanent VCs or after a virtual call has been established. Data packets are identified by setting the qualifier to 0 (bit 1 of the third octet). The data field of the packet starts from the fourth octet and can contain bits equal to a number that is power of 2 and in the range of 16 to 1024. The subfields $P(R)$, $P(S)$, and M of the third octet of a data packet are used for data transfers and flow control, as described previously.

The capability also exists for reset and restart. Reset procedure is used to reinitialize a virtual call in data phase or a permanent VC. It removes in each direction all data or interrupt packets that may be in the network. The reset procedure can be initiated by either end. The restart procedure is used to reset all virtual calls and permanent VCs.

The X.2 recommendation defines several user facilities. Further work is still going on in this respect. Facilities, such as closed user group, reverse charging, reverse charge acceptance, flow control parameter selection, and one-way logical channel, are some of the many that will become available to PDN users.

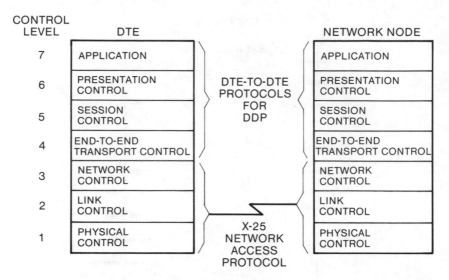

Fig. A.6. X.25 and its relationship to the ISO's seven-level open system architecture.

A.4 FUTURE TRENDS IN INTERNATIONAL STANDARDS

To accomplish information processing tasks within a network system, a user requires additional layers in the network architecture. X.25 concerns itself with only the lower three levels, namely, physical/electrical, link control, and packet/network control. International standards organizations are already busy recommending higher levels for new network architectures. This effort is expected to continue during the next decade.

A promising seven-level network architecture for *open-system* interconnections has recently been proposed by ISO. See Fig. A.6 for a relationship between X.25 and ISO's seven-level open system architecture.

Level 4 (end-to-end transport control layer) provides control from user node to user node across the network. Included on a user-to-user basis are addressing, data assurance, and flow control at the message level.

Level 5 (session control layer) sets up, maintains, and disconnects the logical connections for transfer of data among end users.

Level 6 (presentation control layer) provides data formats and data transformation formats.

Level 7 (application layer) controls the actual DDP tasks.

The emerging international standards will eventually provide intersystem compatibility to users. Users must remain involved to hasten that day.

Glossary of Acronyms

ACD	automatic call distributor
ACF	advanced communication function
ACK	acknowledgment
ACS	advanced communication service
AL	access line
ALU	arithmetic logic unit
AM	amplitude modulation
AMA	automatic message accounting
AMLC	asynchronous multiline controller
ANSI	American National Standards Institute
ARPA	Advanced Project Research Agency
ASCON	automatic switched communication network
ASK	amplitude shift keying
AT&T	American Telephone & Telegraph Co.
ATA	American Transportation Association
ATDM	asynchronous time division multiplexing
ATDMA	asynchronous time division multiple access
BBN	Bolt, Beranek and Newman
BCC	blocked call cleared
BCD	blocked call delayed
BCH	blocked call held
BER	bit error rate
BINS	Barclay's integrated network system
BLU	basic link unit
BNR	Bell Northern Research
BOP	bit-oriented protocol
BPS	bits per second
BSC	binary synchronous communication
CATV	cable television
CCIS	common channel interoffice signaling
CCITT	International Telegraph and Telephone Consultative Committee
CCP	communication and control processor
CCS	hundred call seconds
CCSA	common control switching arrangement
CCSE	corporate communication switching equipment
CCU	communication control unit
CDC	Control Data Corp.

CDMA	code division multiple access
CEC	Commission for European Communities
CNCP	Canadian National Canadian Pacific
CNS	communication network systems
CO	central office
COG	center of gravity
COS	communications operating system
CP	communications processing
CPU	central processing unit
CS	circuit switching
CSMA	carrier-sense-multiaccess
CSU	channel service unit
CSV	customer service vehicle
CV	customer vehicle
DAMA	demand-assignment multiple access
DAP	device access protocol
DARPA	Defense Advanced Research Project Agency
DB	decibel
DBA	data base access
DBM	data-base-management
DCA	distributed communications architecture
DCE	data circuit-termination equipment
DCP	distributed communications processor
DCPSK	differentially coherent phase shift keying
DCS	distributed computing system
DDBM	distributed-data-base-management
DDCMP	digital data communication message protocol
DDD	direct distance dialing
DDP	distributed data processing
DDS	Dataphone digital system
DEC	Digital Equipment Corp.
DF	disk file
DLA	delayed acknowledgment
DM	delta modulation
DMA	direct memory access
DNA	distributed network architecture of NCR and digital network architecture of Digital Equipment Corp.
DNIC	data network identification code
DP	data processing
DSA	digital service area
DSDDS	Dataphone switched digital data system
DSU	data service unit
DTE	data terminal equipment
DTMF	dual-tone multifrequency
DTN	data transporting network
DTS	digital tandem switching

DUC	data unit control
DUV	data under voice
EDS	electronic data systems
EEC	European Economic Community
EFT	electronic fund transfer
EIN	European Informatic Network
EM	electromagnetic
EO	end office
EOSN	end-of-service node
EPSS	experimental packet switching service
ESRA	en route station routing approach
ESS	electronic switching system
FAX-PAK	facsimile-packet switching system
FCC	Federal Communications Commission
FDM	frequency division multiplexing
FDMA	frequency division multiple access
FDX	full duplex
FE	front end
FIFO	first-in-first-out
FM	frequency modulation
FSK	frequency shift keying
FTP	file transfer protocol
FX	foreign exchange
GOS	grade of service
GTE	General Telephone and Electronics Corp.
HDLC	high-level data link control
HDX	half duplex
HEHO	head-end-hop-off
HF	high-frequency
HLC	high-level center
HP	host processor
HU	high usage
IATA	International Airline Transportation Association
IBM	International Business Machines Corp.
ICS	Infocall Service
IED	Information exchange distribution
IES	Infoexchange Service
IGS	Infogram Service
IMA	input message acknowledgment
IMP	interface message processor
IMT	intermachine trunks
INAP	Infogram network access protocol
IPL	initial program load
IPSS	international packet switching service
IR	inquiry response
IRC	international record carriers

ISO	International Standards Organization
ITU	International Telecommunication Union
LAP	link access procedure
LAPB	link access procedure, balanced
LCM	line concentrator module
LD	long distance
LIFO	last-in-first-out
LL	local loop
LNA	local network architecture
LSI	large-scale integration
LSO	local service office
LTU	line termination unit
LU	logical unit
MA	multiple access
MATDM	message-asynchronous time division multiplexing
MCI	Microwave Communications, Inc.
MCMD	multicenter, multidrop
MCMS	multi-center, multi-star
MF	multifrequency
MIPS	million instructions per second
MIS	management information system
MJU	multipoint junction unit
MMOS	message multiplex operating system
MPL	multipoint private line
MS	message switching
MSK	minimum shift keying
MST	minimal spanning tree
MSU	multiplex service unit
MT	magnetic tape
MTBCF	mean time between catastrophic failures
MTBEB	mean-time-between-error bursts
MTBF	mean time between failures
MTBMF	mean time between major failures
MTBNF	mean time between nodal failures
MTBSF	mean time between subsystem failures
MTS	message telecommunications service
MW MULDEM	microwave multiplexer-demultiplexer
N-SMLC	network synchronous multiline controller
NAK	no acknowledgment
NAU	network addressable unit
NBS	National Bureau of Standards
NCC	network control center
NIM	network interface machine
NMC	network management center
NNX	network numbering exchange
NPA	numbering plan area

NPL	National Physical Laboratories, U.K.
NSC	Network Systems Corp.
NSP	network service protocol
OS	operating system
OSRA	originating station routing approach
PABX	private automatic branch exchange
PAD	packet assembly/disassembly
PAM	phase amplitude modulation
PATDM	packet-asynchronous time division multiplexing
PC	primary center
PCM	pulse code modulation
PCTG	Programmable Channel Termination Group
PDM	pulse duration modulation
PDN	public data network
PLU	primary logical unit
PM	phase modulation
PMT	packet-mode terminal
POS	point of sale
PPL	Pluribus private line
PPM	pulse position modulation
PPS	private packet service
PPX	private packet exchange
PS	packet switching
PSE	packet switching exchange
PSI	Pluribus satellite interface message processor
PSK	phase shift keying
PSV	public service vehicle
PTS	public telephone system
PTT	Postal, Telephone, and Telegraph
QOS	quality of service
RAM	random access memory
RC	regional center
RCA	Radio Corp. of America
RCP	Royal Canadian Police
RFP	request for proposal
RHO	regional hub office
RJE	remote job entry
RJEP	remote-job-entry protocol
ROE	remote order entry
ROI	return-on-investment
ROM	read-only memory
RTIU	remote terminal interface unit
RU	request unit
SBS	Satellite Business Systems
SC	sectional center
SCC	specialized common carrier

SCMD	single-center, multidrop
SCSS	single-center, single-star
SDLC	synchronous data link control
SDM	space division multiplexing
S/F	store and forward
SG	study group (CCITT)
SITA	Societe Internationale de Telecommunications Aeronautiques
SMDR	station message detail report
SMLC	synchronous multiline controller
SNA	system network architecture
SNAP	standard network access protocol
SOM	start of message
SOW	statement of work
SPC	stored program control
SPLS	shared private line service
SPNS	switched private network service
SSB	single-side band
SSCP	system service control point
STP	signal transfer point
SWIFT	Society for Worldwide Interbank Financial Telecommunications
TAC	Telenet access controller
TC	toll center
TCO	Telenet central office
TCTS	Trans-Canada Telephone System
TDM	time division multiplexing
TDMA	time division multiple access
TDX	time-division-exchange
TEHO	tail-end-hop-off
TELCO	telephone company
THI	terminal handler interface
TIH	terminal interface handler
TIP	terminal interface processor
TM	transaction module
TN	transport network
TP	Telenet processor
TS	timesharing
TST	time-space-time
TTTN	tandem tie-trunk network
VAN	value-added network
VC	virtual circuit
VG	voice-grade
VTP	virtual terminal protocol
WATS	Wide Area Telecommunications Service
WUI	Western Union International
XTEN	Xerox Telecommunication Network

Index